THE MARKETING SOURCEBOOK FOR SMALL BUSINESS

JEFFREY P. DAVIDSON

WILEY

JOHN WILEY & SONS

New York · Chichester · Brisbane · Toronto · Singapore

Library of Congress Cataloging in Publication Data:

Davidson, Jeffrey P.
　The marketing sourcebook for small business / by Jeffrey P. Davidson.
　　p.　cm.
　Bibliography: p.
　Includes index.
　ISBN 0-471-61512-9
　　1. Marketing—Handbooks, manuals, etc.　　2. Public relations—
Handbooks, manuals, etc.　　I. Title.

HF5415.D3475　　1989　　　　　　　　　　　88-31168
658.8—dc19　　　　　　　　　　　　　　　　CIP
ISBN 0-471-61512-9

Printed in the United States of America

10　9　8　7　6　5　4　3　2　1

This book is dedicated to

Shirley Davidson
who gave me the springboard for life

Pat McCallum
who helped me to find my position in it, and

Sue Millard
who makes it all worthwhile.

OTHER BOOKS BY JEFFREY P. DAVIDSON

Marketing on a Shoestring
Avoiding the Pitfalls of Starting Your Own Business
Getting New Clients
Blow Your Own Horn
Marketing Your Community
The Achievement Challenge
Marketing Your Consulting and Professional Services

Cassettes include:

Getting New Clients
Marketing Your Career
Blow Your Own Horn
Getting Published

FOREWORD

J.B. Say, the French economist, laid down the rule for bottom-line management in the industrial age: "Lower costs in order to raise profit." This was reasonable advice when industries, markets, and products were stable. It is questionable advice in a business environment of exploding change and rampant complexity—the business environment of the 1990s. In the information age, sales—the top line—is upstaging the bottom line.

If your focus in the quest for profit and cash flow is to reduce costs, sooner or later you will run out of steam. No amount of imagination and creativity can cut costs below a certain irreducible limit. On the other hand, if you shift your imagination and creativity to generating revenue, there is no limit to what you can do. Marketing in the information age is a whole new world, abounding with opportunities to expand sales. Enter Jeff Davidson and his *Marketing Sourcebook for Small Business*.

The Marketing Sourcebook is a treasure chest of tools you can use *right now* to expand your sales. Jeff Davidson hands you a quick justification for gearing for change in the marketplace . . . just in case you need it. Then he launches into a series of no-nonsense chapters bursting with vital information sources for businesses seeking new niches. For example, in Chapter 4, Precision Targeting, Jeff cites dozens of publications, databases, and software packages: *Investext*, which contains the full text of industry and company research reports produced by financial analysts of leading investment firms; *Metro Insights*, which provides a wealth of information on 100 key U.S. metropolitan markets, including demographic and labor force profiles, consumer spending, and income statistics; and *Marketing News*, which provides one large alphabetical list of software supporting marketing and marketing research.

The Marketing Sourcebook is a true sourcebook. Jeff gives you names, addresses, and phone numbers (toll-free when possible) and a concise blurb on what each source offers you. He compiles thorough lists of resources, and you distill from his smorgasbord the precise combination of tools you need to bolster your own observations and intuition.

In the 1990s, the application of these tools will make or break most companies. Why? The business environment of the 1990s is a maelstrom of moving targets.

We depart an age in which industrial-age companies muscled their way into defined markets, competing for market share, and almost every business plan assumed that the new company would move into a given industry with a known market and start chipping away at it in the name of competition. Today's proliferation of values, needs, and wants, born of the worldwide information explosion, means far fewer big stable markets to shoulder your way into. Information tools and new perspectives such as those Jeff provides help you make sense of the maelstrom, and thereby home in on the juicy niches as they emerge.

Once you've found a niche, potential customers in that niche have to find you. Having listed a myriad of tools to help you perceive niches, Jeff devotes a substantial portion of the *Marketing Sourcebook* to the nuts and bolts of positioning. He walks you step by step through advertising, PR, and promotion strategies.

Jeff illustrates his points on positioning with anecdotes: he reproduces, for example, an open letter in the *New York Times* that Harry Hoffman used to position Waldenbooks, and he dissects why this piece of advertising worked. You'll find yourself reading these little stories and gazing off into the distance considering how you can do it too, in your own way.

"If you get on the right track and stay there," observed Will Rogers, "you'll get run over." Your position must evolve with time and with your customers. In Part IV of *The Marketing Sourcebook*, Jeff outlines efforts the people inside your company can make to continually respond to customers. He explains, for instance, why aftermarketing is a crucial component of an overall marketing program.

I run a business, and I didn't want to give Jeff his manuscript back after writing this foreword. This is not a book you read once, but a compendium you'll refer to again and again. I think the 1990s will unfold more opportunity for entrepreneurs than any decade in history. It will be a fun time, a challenging time, to do business. May the *Sourcebook* be with you.

KATE McKEOWN
Author of *Beyond IBM: Leadership, Marketing
and Finance for the 1990s*

ACKNOWLEDGMENTS

In completing an observational and instructional book of several hundred pages, such as this one, there naturally are dozens of people to thank for information, ideas, concepts, quoted passages, exhibits, and so forth. I would like to thank Michael F. Baber, Bob Battenfield, Herb Baum, Gary Berman, Jonathan D. Blum, Thomas A. Bracken, Dr. Luther Brock, Juanell Teague, Regis McKenna, Martin I. Horn, Martha Farnsworth Riche, Louis Harris, Alvin Toffler, Edward Cornish, John Naisbitt, Gregg Cebrzynski, Richard A. Connor, Holland Cooke, Anthony M. Franco, Kevin Foley, Larry Kim Garvey, David Voracek, Dr. Christopher H. Lovelock, Charles B. Weinberg, James O'Toole, Robert L. Shook, Joe Spence, and Mary Walton.

Also Al Ries and Jack Trout, Jonathan Evetts, Allen Konopacki, John Pannullo, Murray Forseter, Mitchel A. Wald, George Haber, Marie-Jeanne Juilland, Steve Kichen, James Laabs, Jack Lorms, Andy Marken, Don Oldenburg, Dave Olson, Mona Piontkowski, Diana Schneidman, Joe Agnew, Harry Hoffman, Marily Mondejar, Ira Westreich, Anthony Casell, Herman Holtz, Ron Zemke, Don Bagin, Pal Asija, Ken Love, Robert S. Cunningham, Dr. Michael Reagan, and Katherine Reynolds.

Also, Robert Mueller, Edward McSweeney, Mark N. Kaplan, Carole Jackson, Cavett Robert, Carol Cherry, Victor Morris, Robert Cialdini, Steven Salerno, Donald Moine, David Yoho, Leonard M. Fuld, Arnold Sanow, William Hunter, Rudy Brokenleg, James Wilhoit, Guy Lupero, and Jerome McCarthy.

I would also like to thank the strong supporting cast at John Wiley & Sons, including my editor and friend John Mahaney, who helped me to formulate and develop the concept for this book, Tom Gilmartin, Mary Daniello, Richard Freese, Richard McCullough, Arlynn Greenbaum, Irene Majuk, and Steve Kippur.

Glenn Juman and Erin Austin provided timely research assistance. Jill Korroch, Pamela Persigehl, Brad Ulrich, and Michele McCausland provided high-quality editing assistance. Dawar Osman prepared the index. Ingeborg M. Stochmal deftly handled the copyediting. C. L. Hutson Co. expertly handled the page proofs. Finally, a special note of thanks goes to Judy Dubler who marvelously has handled all word processing on this book and seven previous books.

CONTENTS

APPENDICES

CHARTS AND EXHIBITS

CASES AND MINICASES

INTRODUCTION

This book is about examining your firm or company in a way that may be new to you. Our society is changing more rapidly than our ability to respond to the changes, much less understand them. This is a sourcebook of ideas, information, and techniques, which will help you to deal with the task facing most owners and managers of small businesses: effective positioning. We focus on what *can* be done to impact your market by positioning your business to occupy a special place in the minds of those you wish to serve. We also examine other areas, such as how to become a key vendor to large corporations, how to get information about your competitors, and how to *stay* in the forefront of your customers' minds.

The marketplace today is decreasingly receptive to traditional marketing strategies. A company must create a position in the prospect's mind. Too many products, too many companies, too many messages, and too many distractions command the attention of the customer—most of them forgotten.

Positioning is an organized system for finding a window in the mind, recognizing that the most effective communication occurs when optimally placed and timed. Being the "first" remains one of the quickest and easiest ways to gain a position in someone's mind. Who was the first

American woman in space? Without hesitation you can probably offer the name "Sally Ride." You are correct. Now name the second American woman in space. If you are like most people, you will have no idea. (The answer is Judy Resnik, who was a member of the unfortunate *Challenger* shuttle crew.)

The Marketing Sourcebook acknowledges that the rapid changes in society and the increasing information din pose a supreme challenge to small- to medium-sized businesses that seek to increase, or simply maintain, market share. *The Marketing Sourcebook* explores effective marketing using down-to-earth approaches, bolstered by a generous offering of examples and case histories.

In my work with over 250 small- to medium-sized businesses, I have learned that entrepreneurs are continually in need of three things:

More Time. As we shall see in Chapter 1, time has become a most valuable commodity in our society. There never seems to be enough time and there always seems to be too much to do.

Capital. "What I could do if I only had the money" is an all-too-familiar lament of today's entrepreneur. For many businesses, lack of capital will always be a sore spot.

Effective Marketing Strategies. Often even seasoned entrepreneurs rely on "desk analyses" rather than find out where customers and clients are heading and how to reach them effectively.

Effective positioning can assist businesses in all three problem areas. The company that is properly positioned saves time in the sense that the targets it is trying to reach obtain an adequate notion of what the company stands for, represents, and offers. Effective positioning, in the long run, can help further the company's progress toward desired revenues, even in the face of limited capital. With positioning, each ad, message, employee, every square inch of floor or office space contributes to the delivery of a consistent theme to the target market. Positioning helps alleviate the need to continuously devise entirely new marketing strategies. By securing a well-placed corner in the minds of those they wish to serve, businesses can reduce the need for new ad campaigns and promotions.

Positioning is a way of thinking rather than a fixed set of guidelines or principles. The position that your business develops in your market or industry often may be right only for you and for no other business. You may become the leader in an emerging industry, or a highly successful alternative to the leading company in a mature market. (Remember how Avis tried harder because it was only number two?) You may be the only store open for 24 hours or the most exclusive shop in town exhibiting wares by appointment only. Position marketing is not limited to a particular strategy.

Positioning can be enhanced through advertising, public relations, your company's location, and even in the way in which you are financed. Regardless of how it becomes established, the position you occupy in the minds of those you wish to serve contributes to the success or failure of the business. In the ultracompetitive, swiftly changing overinformation environment of the 1990s, position marketing will become an essential element of survival.

Part I: A New Ball Game

Chapter 1, *Positioning, Marketing, and the 1990s*, explores the concept of position marketing and highlights its growing importance for successful businesses operating in our time-pressed society. Chapter 2 discusses the implications of *The Age of Image* on businesses and advises that businesses *are what they project . . . and live up to*.

Chapter 3, *Redefining Your Business*, introduces the notion of defining the business and the marketing effort in terms of the benefits of the niche, and that of realigning corporate resources to support this redefinition. Chapter 4, *Precision Targeting*, conveys the basics of identifying, understanding, and monitoring the market. Considerable low-cost data are available today for developing an accurate, complete profile of any target group.

Part II: Positioning Approaches

Chapter 5, *Advertising for Position*, provides a brief overview of how some companies have used advertising to establish position. The remainder of the chapter, in cognizance of the volume of literature on effective advertising, lays out the groundwork for selecting an agency and working effectively with it to create an optimal position. Chapter 6, *Public Relations and Promotion for Positioning*, offers guidelines on what can be done and how to manage public relations in support of your positioning efforts.

Chapter 7, *Location and Positioning*, examines key components of retail, business services, manufacturing, and professional service locations. Chapter 8, *The Impact of Financial Image*, highlights the importance of the image of financial strength to investors, lenders, corporate buyers, and others when positioning your business as a winner. It offers steps for presenting finances in a favorable light.

Part III: Positioning withing Selected Industries

Chapter 9, *Building the Professional Service Firm*, examines critical elements of positioning within the services and offers numerous anecdotes. Chapter 10, *Becoming a Retail Institution—McDonald's and Other Tales*, details the factors that McDonald's employs to stay at the forefront of the fast-food industry while its competitors continue to miss the boat. The next part of the chapter examines a unique operations assessment service used by successful retailers. The last part of the chapter examines the "Staples" phenomenon—a winning concept in retail office supply. Chapter 11, *Attaining Key Vendor Status*, focuses on the key elements of positioning for vendors seeking long-term partnerships with major corporations.

Part IV: The Customer and Your Business

Chapter 12, *The Marketing Team*, highlights the movement and growing need to ensure that all staff members are productive, effective contributors to a firm's marketing efforts. Chapter 13, *Selling—The Newest Profession*, summarizes trends in professional selling. It explains how a new kind of sales training enables salespeople to respond better to the changing needs of consumers and to help establish company position. It emphasizes that today's marketer must serve as a consultant, not just a sales representative.

Chapter 14, *Staying in the Forefront*, offers an assortment of techniques for ensuring that your position remains secure. It introduces the notion of aftermarketing and how this should be incorporated as part of the overall marketing program. It also discusses positive stroking and how this technique enhances your position. Chapter 15, *Self-Assessment:*

Customers Won and Customers Lost, offers instruction on assessing the effectiveness of your marketing efforts in light of your position. Specifically, it addresses how to assess customers won and customers lost, and helps you to fine-tune your position.

Part V: Cases

Chapter 16 tells the story of *The Accounting Firm That Wanted to Be Exciting*. LMV tried to use an article on the company, which appeared in an airlines magazine, to make the company appear exciting. Instead, it appeared frightening. In Chapter 17 we will discuss *Custom Builders—A Position in Search of New Markets*. Custom Builders, Inc., with a little guidance, took a methodical, segmented approach to targets that were already favorable to a firm in its position.

Chapter 18, *A Small Shopping Center Competing with Giants*, offers a reprint of an actual consulting report summary. It tells how a funny-looking, out-of-the-way, too-small shopping center positioned itself among a strong field of competitors.

Appendix

A roster of new terms and concepts introduced in the book follows Chapter 18. Further reading, a bibliography, and a list of marketing associations are also provided in the Appendix.

PART ONE

A NEW BALL GAME

1

Positioning, Marketing, and the 1990s

As the quiet Fifties set up the
tumultuous Sixties, so the
unaddressed issues of the quiet
Eighties are setting us up for a very
noisy Nineties.

WILLIAM L. RENFRO

The coming years will be marked by a growing
form of uncertainty. We exist in an era where no one is sure whether
the economy is weak or strong, whether inflation is dead or ready to
resume, whether government has been harmful or helpful to business.
This book is a sourcebook of ideas to help your business flourish despite

the fluctuations in the business environment. The concept of *positioning* serves as the anchor to the suggestions presented.

In this chapter we will:

☐ Introduce and define position marketing

☐ Explore the impact of the rapid changes in the world and in our society

☐ Discuss the stress caused by increased choices and decreased time

☐ Summarize the growing impact of a large singles population

☐ Quickly take the pulse of what is new or different

☐ Explore trends and find ways to predict and track them

Positioning is the art of creating a place in the minds of prospects. The concept was developed as a response to the problems of communicating in an overcommunicated society; in this society it is essential for a company to create a position in the prospect's mind.

Positioning can take many forms. Introducing a new product line involves effective positioning. Standing out in a field of also-rans requires positioning. Reviving a product or service, establishing yourself as first, or even last, are all enhanced by positioning.

Al Ries and Jack Trout, partners in their own New York–based communications firm and prolific authors, offered a convincing argument for the dire need of positioning among businesses. They pointed out that the average person accounts for 94 pounds of newsprint per year. I would like to add that an additional 475 pounds of other printed information is consumed per person per year in our society.

They noted that the Sunday edition of a large metropolitan newspaper like *The New York Times* weighs 4½ pounds and contains some 5000 words. To read it all, they said, would take approximately 28 hours. Since 1981, however, *The New York Times* has added several more pages of advertising as well as a few more supplements; has more in-depth sports, financial, and scientific reporting; and, thus, is slightly heavier, contains more words, and in its entirety takes longer to read.

In 1981, 98 percent of all American homes had at least one television set. Today, most homes have two sets or more, and 55 percent of all homes have VCRs. In 1981, 96 percent of all television households could receive four or more stations, with one-third receiving ten or more. Today, 96 percent of all television households can receive seven or more stations and one-third can receive 42 to 115 or more. But, as we will see on page 13, the information din is just one of five elements that contribute to our time-pressed, clock-chasing society.

POSITIONING: KEY ELEMENT FOR EFFECTIVE MARKETING

"Today, few companies are positioned for profit. Position is difficult to establish," says Andy Marken of Marken Communications in Sunnyvale, California. "People often underestimate the time, money, and experience required. Once accomplished, and the compnay establishes its 'share of mind,' positioning will be translated into share of the market. Positioning involves risks. It requires a broad, long-range view of the company and its activities. Positioning is a form of return on investment." For example, in five years only 5 percent of today's new technology-based firms will still be in business, mostly due to the result of poor or nonexistent positioning, according to Marken.

Positioning provides a reason *for people to be receptive to advertising and sales messages*. "Positioning is not what you do to your product or service," says Marken, "but what you do to reach the mind of the prospect."[1]

"Strong, accurate positioning represents the most important decision management must undertake for the company and its marketing," he notes. Four key obstacles to maintaining position include the speed of innovation, shorter product life cycles, faster decisions, and a market structure that is constantly changing. People are being bombarded with thousands of messages a day. The volume of advertising increases, while the relative effectiveness is decreasing.

[1] Andy Marken, "Positioning: Key Element for Effective Marketing," *Marketing News*, Feb. 13, 1987.

Getting your message noticed has become a challenge. Positioning provides a preexisting reason for people to be receptive to a firm's promotional messages. Once developed, Marken says, "it should be consistently carried out in all of the firm's communications activities." Too many companies fail because the first approach for most people is to think in terms of writing advertising or promotional copy, he said.

Regis McKenna, a top marketing consultant with offices in the U.S., Europe, and Asia, says that "corporate positioning is based on many factors, including management strength, corporate history, and even the personalities of top executives." In high-technology industries, McKenna points to four key elements of positioning:

1. Using word of mouth, the most powerful form of communication in the business world
2. Cultivating the infrastructure, including financial analyst, venture capitalist, research house, business press, and industry movers and shakers
3. Forming strategic relationships with other companies where the benefits are mutual
4. Selling to the right customers who enhance your credibility

"The most important factor by far is financial success," McKenna says. "Without financial success everything else is meaningless. The minute profits decline, the market begins to worry. All else is called into question." As we shall see in Chapter 8, exhibiting a strong financial image, particularly in start-up situations, is a key element of positioning.

THE CHANGING WORLD

Understanding what is happening to our population and society in general will enable you to better position your business for long-term success.

More than ever before, effective marketers will also have to be futurists.

"Predictions, Projections, and Trends" that will impact society and business were presented by Martin I. Horn, associate director of marketing decision systems at DDB Needham Worldwide in Chicago, to the 25th Annual Conference of the National Association of Television Program Executives. These predictions are based on information gleaned from a variety of sources, including the Bureau of the Census, *American Demographics*, the Institute for Strategy Development, the Roper Organization, *The Futurist*, and the *DDB Needham Life-Style Study*.

In *ascending* order, here are highlights of what Horn believes will impact our culture.

The Youth Culture as We Know It Will Be Dead

Because of the maturation of baby boomers, the proportion of older Americans to younger Americans will rise dramatically in the next 25 years. One-fourth of the U.S. population, about 74 million people at the time, will be at least 55 years of age.

Even as we grow older, we will continue to think and act much younger than we really are. The *DDB Needham Life-Style Study* indicates that the majority of people 55 and over say they look, act, and feel *at least* 10 years younger than the calendar says they are. And, as baby boomers age, the gap between chronological age and psychological age will widen.

The Family Will Make a Comeback

Horn says: "Despite what we've heard about its demise, the American family is strong and will continue to be so. Divorce rates will stabilize and single-parent households will grow more slowly." Families will be smaller, but more tightly knit. Despite the increased likelihood that *both* mom and dad will be working, parenting will be taken more seriously. Traditional family values will survive.[2]

Note: For a diametric view, consider the prediction of *American Demographics* publisher Martha Farnsworth Riche, who says the three

---

[2] Martin I. Horn, DDB Needham Worldwide, "Predictions, Projections, and Trends," delivered to the 25th Annual Conference of the National Association of Television Program Executives, Houston, TX, February 27, 1988.

"Ds," delayed marriage, deferred childbirth, and divorce, *will diminish most remnants* of the traditional family.

One's Company—Two's a Crowd

The number of people who live alone, which nearly doubled between 1970 and 1985, will increase more slowly through the end of the century. Still, the total number of people living by themselves will grow by 50 percent. In 1985, there were over 20 million people who lived alone. By 2000, that number will jump to 32 million. (Could the impact of a growing single population dramatically change society? See page 17.)

The Melting Pot Will Continue to Bubble

Currently nearly one in five Americans is Black, Hispanic, or Asian. The Hispanic population is growing twice as fast as the Black population. The Black population is growing twice as fast as the White population. Immigration accounts for one-fourth of the U.S. population growth. By the end of the 1990s, it will account for one-third of the growth.

The "ZZZZ" Generation Will Continue to Doze

Most Americans are conservative. A majority see themselves as old-fashioned and as homebodies. Most people would rather spend a quiet evening at home than go out to a party. Although there may be occasional blips on the monitor, for the most part our life-style lifelines will remain steady.

The Sexes Will Converge and Diverge

This seemingly contradictory prediction reflects a complex web of behavior. The notions that "all sex roles will permanently converge," or that "all irreducible differences between the sexes will be forever irreducible," are both too simplistic. Horn believes that over the next 25 years:

- Women will become more like men
- Men will become more like women

- Sexes will converge
- Sexes will diverge
- Sexes will change together
- Sexes will remain different

We Are Placing a Growing Premium on Time

One of the major trends shaping the future of American business is the growing premium people are placing on their time. (See page 13 for an extended discussion.) They are seeking greater control over it. As the Roper organization asserted in a recent study, we can expect to see a "new determination among consumers to tailor daily schedules to their needs rather than having schedules imposed on them."

The Rise of Atomized and Component Life-Styles

Both concepts refer to a growing life-style fragmentation among Americans in which, the Roper organization reports, "people choose products and services that best express a growing sense of uniqueness. The trend is away from social conformity and toward the component life-style. New and surprising combinations of consumer interests, spending patterns, buying habits (and I'll add media habits) will be the rule. . . ." As a result, standard ways of segmenting markets will become outmoded as marketers "atomize" huge markets into smaller and smaller ones.

Atomization, fragmentation, and component life-styles will extend directly to business. There will always be a mass audience for certain types of programming, but television will more and more follow the patterns established by radio and magazines, in which specialization is the key.

In this new television viewing environment, some predict a competitive tug-of-war will take place. The spread of independently produced programs for syndication should divert a significant portion of future broadcast revenues away from the networks. But satellite broadcasts may strengthen the networks and eliminate local television stations. Cable channels will disrupt the independents and the networks (if both still exist) not only by offering alternative programming but by allowing two-way communication between the viewer and the program (which is already available) as well as two-way communication between subscribers.

The Dominating Social Trend That Will Stay Dominant

The public's response to this issue has traditionally been strong, and it is getting stronger. There is no telling where it will stop. In conclusion, Horn predicts that no matter what demographic shifts we experience, this trend will maintain its unwavering hold on the American public.

What is it that people will continue to agree with in the future as they have in the past?

> ## "TELEVISION IS
> ## MY PRIMARY FORM
> ## OF ENTERTAINMENT"

WHAT ELSE IS LIKELY FOR THE 1990s?

Here are 18 likely events based on emerging trends or other safely predictable phenomena.

People will be living to older ages. By 1995, our population may experience a 10-year across-the-board increase in life span. At the same time, rising numbers of elderly citizens will be unable to support themselves. *American Demographics* reports that by the mid-1990s, the over-65 age group will represent one-eighth of our population. The fastest growing age group in America today is the over-85 population. *Age Wave* by Dr. Ken Dychtwald describes how America must change as the median age of its population advances.

Growth in the service sector seems certain. The Bureau of Labor Statistics reports that in 1984 the service sector accounted for 72.2 percent of the labor force and that this number is predicted to rise to 74.4 percent by 1995. Before the end of the 1990s, more than 85 percent of the work force could be employed by the service sector. However, many service sector jobs are low paying compared to jobs lost in manufacturing, agriculture, transportation, and other areas of the economy.

The advice business will continue to flourish. The consulting industry saw a healthy growth of about 20 percent through the 1980s. New technology, the entrepreneurial boom, and further expansion of global markets should result in steady growth. More than 4000 how-to books are currently available in bookstores—an all-time high.

Middle managers will continue to be squeezed from corporate ranks. Domestic corporate downsizing will continue unabated. Ultraefficient computers and information management systems will diminish the need for middle managers. The inability of millions to rise further in their organizations will affect vast sectors of the population. Mass frustration may ensue—while there will be limited opportunities for advancement, the desire for economic or financial success will continue. Many people will opt to work second and third jobs or seek longer hours on their principal jobs. Vast numbers of others may simply drop out of mainstream economy. The Internal Revenue Service reports that larger numbers of our population are already reporting no income whatsoever.

Minorities will become the majority. By the early 1990s, minority children will be in the majority in our public school systems. Also, within 50 years, observes Senator Daniel Inouye, Blacks, Hispanics, Asians, and Middle-Eastern Americans will represent 51 percent of the U.S. population.

More minorities wil enter the work force. In 1975, Blacks comprised 9.9 percent of the civilian work force. In 1985, the figure rose to 10.7 percent. By some estimates, that figure will rise to as much as 12 percent by the mid-1990s. Hispanics comprised 6.7 percent of the work force in 1985. By the mid 1990s, this figure could grow by several percentage points.

Females will continue to enter the labor force in large numbers. The U.S. Department of Labor projects that women will represent nearly two-thirds of new entrants into the work force through the 1990s. By around 1995, women will comprise approximately 57 or 58 percent of the total work force. This influx will cause tremendous growth in child care and day care facilities, and in new work-at-home programs initiated by employers.

The entrepreneurial boom will continue. The Internal Revenue Service reports that there was a 20 percent increase in the growth of self-employed people from the mid-1970s to the mid-1980s. This growth is likely to continue as more than 12 million workers will be squeezed from the ranks of corporate America and more entrepreneurial role models are established. In the mid-1980s, as Dun & Bradstreet reports, more than 600,000 new businesses were started each year. By the mid-1990s this figure is likely to rise to 800,000 or more. More businesses will fail and more individuals will experience personal economic upheaval.

Problems with chemically dependent workers continue. While early progress in the war on cocaine might be achieved by the beginning of the 1990s, the problems of a work force prone to substance abuse— alcohol, drugs, pills—are likely to continue throughout the decade.

The fear of AIDS will alter social patterns. Unless a cure or prevention for AIDS is discovered, it is likely that the fear of AIDS will dominate social patterns throughout the 1990s. Some sociologists believe that the fear of AIDS may prompt a rise in the marriage rate and a decrease in the divorce rate. The incidence of AIDS is also likely to cause severe strains on our medical and health systems, and to foster confrontation and social power struggles.

The video revolution will continue. U.S. *News and World Report* observed that more than one billion videos were rented in 1986. More than 55 percent of all homes have VCRs at present, with this number expected to grow to over 75 percent by the mid-1990s. Though the home viewer may not like it, futurist Marvin Cetron believes we may soon see video cassettes that include advertising, because the payoffs to film and program producers would be so high.

The entertainment industry will continue to flourish. The U.S. population has been lulled into an entertainment stupor. The entertainment industry will enjoy unprecedented success. Jack Valenti, head of the Motion Picture Association, points out that at present the entertainment industry represents the nation's second largest export. Annual motion picture production has increased from an average of 175 in the mid-1970s to 550 in the mid-1980s, and will likely increase by several hundred more per year by the mid-1990s. Entertainment will also gain stronger footholds in business, education, politics, and religion. The importance of the image will grow unabated. (See Chapter 2.)

The star system will dominate our culture. It is Carl Sagan in astronomy, Dr. Denton Cooley in heart transplant surgery, and Dr. Ruth in sexual/ relationship advice. Increasingly a few subject-matter experts from each industry who have been embraced by the media lead or dominate information dissemination in their fields.

The rise of cocooning. Worldwide terrorism, the greenhouse effect, increasing travel costs, and the availability of high-tech home entertainment equipment will exacerbate the rise of cocooning. John Naisbitt, author of *Megatrends*, predicts that people will be increasingly inclined to invest in home entertainment devices and be perfectly satisfied and comfortable in doing so. Nevertheless, experimental vacations and creative travel will be sought by a distinct segment of the population.

The emergence of a computer literate society will, after years of overly optimistic predictions, be well on its way by the mid-1990s, as some futurists believe. In major cities, nearly the entire population will be familiar, and perhaps proficient, with the use of computers.

Desktop publishing will become more simplified and more widespread. Every personal computer owner will acquire the power to become a publisher. The cost will decline and the proliferation of printed material will increase. More books, many of low quality, will be published each year.

Accommodating the illiterate. As the microchip becomes more powerful, according to Alvin Toffler, author of *Future Shock* and *The Third Wave*, more products and appliances will provide oral instructions to the consumer. In addition, there will be an increase in idiot-proof cash registers, automated bank teller machines, transit fare collecting equipment, and other products and devices routinely encountered by the general public.

Dramatic impact of the greenhouse effect. During the last ice age, the mean average temperature of North America was only 4 degrees cooler than the average for this century. Now we are faced with the prospect of hotter than average temperatures for the next several decades. By the early 1990s, mass northern migrations may occur, making the South the rust belt, while the northern states become revitalized. Also look for higher food prices, a new sense of conservation, and environmentalist domination of political thought.

A TIME-PRESSED SOCIETY

Our population experiences increasing time pressure with each passing year. Human orientation to time has constantly changed throughout the ages, *but never so markedly* as in the last few decades—the Information

Age. Enhanced physical and informational mobility adds to our *expectations* regarding what can and should be accomplished in our lives. We all want *to do* more.

As I see it, five elements will continue to impact our time:

- Increasing population
- Too much information
- Media growth
- The paper trail culture
- An abundance of choices

1. Increasing population. An *absolute increase* in domestic and world population directly impacts our individual time consumption, even as the *rate of growth decreases* in the United States and many western nations. A bit of explanation is required. World population increases by 239,000 each day. More than half of all human beings ever born are alive today. As education and skill levels advance globally, more nations impact and directly compete with the economies of one another.

After World War II, the United States was the only industrialized nation with its factories intact. Our superior mass production and distribution facilities yielded some 25 years of unparalleled prosperity. Since the 1970s, foreign manufacturers have matched and often surpassed domestic capabilities in one industry after another.

Effective foreign production and distribution systems have added to the time pressure of vast segments of the U.S. economy and work force. Increasing pools of educated, skilled workers in Japan, Korea, and Taiwan have helped to dismantle U.S. supremacy in many industries.

The success of foreign competition in the United States and in world markets requires a concerted, diligent effort on the part of our domestic corporations and their employees to remain competitive. So not only do the Japanese, along with other relentless competitors, sell us cars and VCRs, they also cause our CEOs and top managers to endure sleepless nights thinking of new ways to generate greater productivity from an already time-pressed work force.

Independent of foreign economic pressure, the American society grows more complex as a function of its own increasing population. This complexity results in greater amounts of each person's time being consumed simply to ensure that basic necessities are secured. Has our growing population dispersed over the nation's millions of square miles? Not at all—97 percent of the U.S. population resides on 3 percent of its land mass; 50 percent of the population resides within 50 miles of the Atlantic or the Pacific Ocean.

This lack of dispersion contributes to massive traffic and urban congestion, a pattern that will linger far into the twenty-first century. There are *more cars per capita* now than ever before. More congestion results in more frequent delays. City planners report that there will be no clear solution for decades.

2. Too much information. As a free and educated population is served by commercial mass media, the volume and flow of new information can and does increase without limitation. The *actual explosion of information* spewing forth since the phrase was first coined dwarfs the original meaning. The explosion of information in all areas renders us overstimulated. Before you absorb and apply yesterday's intake, the explosion of new information floods your receptive capacity. Our sense of available time is strained. Keeping up seems impossible, yet we feel compelled to make the effort.

Spending more time tuned to electronic media, we are exposed to tens of thousands of messages and images. As each breakthrough in communication and entertainment technology is introduced, it is accompanied by predictions of doom for its predecessors. Television was supposed to have finished radio; VCRs were to have sunk movie theaters.

3. Media growth. Instead of replacing their forebearers, we have *added* each new technology to our lives. As more people, media outlets, products, information items, and choices compete for our time, we invariably perceive that we have less time.

A growing world population, electronically linked, ensures that the news and information explosion will continue unabated. Television news features grow shorter to match the *decreasing attention spans* of viewers.

4. The paper trail culture. Besides straight reading, we are deluged with *unceasing documentation requirements*—paperwork—to maintain our standing in society. Contemporary society is obsessed with documentation. Time spent battling the paper glut plagues most of us; don't take it personally. The profuse amount of paper in our lives is symptomatic of an epidemic misunderstanding of the nature of change.

Attempting to contain what seems unmanageable, organizations and institutions create paper accounting systems. These systems provide temporary relief and some sense of order. Usually they become ingrained and immovable, creating additional muddle. Personal paper trails encroach upon our time. We use paper for personal control, job security, covering our tracks, legal backup, and so forth.

5. *An abundance of choices.* As Alvin Toffler says in his 1969 book *Future Shock*, individuals will have more choices in the future (and today qualifies as the future). Toffler describes how more choices tend to inhibit action, which results in greater anxiety and the perception of less freedom and less time.

An overassortment of consumer options diminishes our time. You and I are bombarded by more products, information, and choices with which to contend. Next month there will be more. Having an abundance of choices would seem a blessing. However, the abundance quickly becomes "too many," a curse which confounds our ability to choose and which consumes more time.

Take a look at the supermarket glut:

Gorman's *New Product News* reports that in 1978 the typical supermarket carried 11,767 items. By 1987, that figure had risen to an astounding 24,531 items—more than double in nine years.

More than 700 microwave food products were introduced in 1987.

As more specialty foods, cuisines, dietary supplements, and nonfood items are introduced, the typical supermarket soon will carry 40,000 items. Will there be room? Yes. Each product line carried will occupy a lesser amount of shelf space.

Elsewhere in the supermarket, Hallmark Cards now offers cards for 105 familial relationships.

Every new product to which you are exposed pilfers a portion of your time, however meager, with a predictable, cumulative effect.

A SOCIETY DOMINATED BY SINGLES?

The number of singles in the United States is growing rapidly. In each decade since the 1960s, the numbers of unmarried males and unmarried females are growing at a faster rate than the population. In 1985, according to the U.S. Bureau of the Census, 59 percent of women in their early twenties were single; by contrast in 1970 the figure was 36 percent.

In 1985, women in their early thirties were twice as likely to be single as women of the same age in the 1970s. In a widely read and debated issue of *Newsweek* (3/11/86) it was reported that among single women age 30 and over, 80 percent will never marry. Among those age 35 and over, 95 percent will never marry.

Among men and women who do marry, today more than half become divorced. Of those who remarry, 33 percent will divorce a second time, of those who marry a third time, 60 percent will divorce again. The heavy divorce rate is a strong contributor to the single population.

Edward Cornish, president of the World Future Society, says, "Singles are changing the tone of economic, educational, and even religious events." People are marrying later or not at all, and the majority of those getting married get divorced. Many singles continuously search for new mates and friends. They join social, political, and religious groups. They enroll in continuing education classes and cultivate new leisure-time activities.

Some studies indicate that the more educated a person becomes, the less likely he or she is to marry, and the fewer children he or she has if married. The typical single will be better educated and compensated than his or her married counterpart. The home as cocoon or fortress could become enticing to the well-compensated single who is disenchanted by the endless search for a fulfilling relationship.

Many singles will end up spending most of the time in their homes, alone, equipped with electronic gadgets and toys, amusements and pleasures that consume their leisure hours. This will further prompt the growth of more industries, including book publishing, wide-screen televisions, VCRs, kitchen appliances, home furnishings, hot tubs, saunas, computers, and other items that can be enjoyed by one.

More singles lead to greater prosperity for industries such as entertainment, amusement, travel, gourmet foods, and surrogate companionship. Other industries could decline, including children's clothing, toys, pediatricians, maternity wards, schools, and educational tools.

Singles will have competitive advantages over their married counterparts, particularly in terms of career advancement. This will become more pronounced with the widespread introduction of domestic service businesses, including grocery delivery services and maid services. As more and more singles rise within the ranks of business and industry, the standard to which all other career professionals aspire will increase. Those raising children will be at a distinct disadvantage in terms of available time and energy that can be expended on a career. As more singles enter politics or rise to other positions of influence and power, more legislation favorable to singles will be enacted.

BECOMING YOUR OWN FUTURIST

As mentioned, the effective marketer of the 1990s will become his or her own futurist—the changes are simply coming too fast to do otherwise. Juanell Teague, based in Dallas, is best known as the Business Coach of the Future. She teaches how to custom design your life or business through strategies that transform your professional career and personal life beyond expectation.

Teague says, "Anyone can chart his/her professional course to take advantage of current and forthcoming trends. Foreknowledge of important business and social trends provides a competitive edge in any field." She believes that by becoming your own futurist, you can free yourself from the many uncertainties of tomorrow by being several steps ahead today.

"Experts say the world has changed more in the last 45 years than it did in the preceding 4500," observes Teague. The first half of the 1990s will bring more change than all of the preceding 4545 years. Reaction time is now reduced to nothing—predicting the future is often a matter of survival. This is especially true for entrepreneurs because customers expect them to know more than they do, to be way out ahead, mapping the terrain.

Ignoring trends is risky. Many businesses begin to decline because all energy is spent solving immediate problems with no time left over to calculate and plan for the future. When the world changes, a successful business must change with it.

Developing Skills for Predicting Future Trends

Teague advises reading the right books. She believes that John Naisbitt's *Megatrends* is the classic in the field. "Read it thoughtfully and decide where he hit the mark, where he missed the mark and how you have been affected by the changes he discusses," she advises. One of the megatrends Naisbitt pinpointed in 1982 was the explosion of small business starts. The self-help trend also added a new dimension to entreprencurism.

Teague's other recommendations:

Read *Strategies 2000* by Carolyn Corbin and *The New American Boom*, Knight Kiplinger, editor. Subscribe to publications such as John Naisbitt's biweekly *Trend Letter*. This is one of the best ways to keep current.

One day a client from Detroit was sitting in Teague's office. As they discussed his declining business as a retail consultant, she pulled the latest *Trend Letter* out of her files. The lead story described how the trend toward superstores and small boutiques was squeezing out the medium-sized market. Based on this information, the client decided to restructure his marketing plan and aim it at small retail environments. Immediately he noted a marked increase in sales.

The Kiplinger Texas Letter, a biweekly publication, and *The Kiplinger Washington Letter*, a weekly newsletter, are also excellent ways to learn about local trends while they are still in their early stages. Kiplinger also publishes monthly California and Florida letters.

USA Today and *The Wall Street Journal* are always sure bets to keep you current. *Entrepreneur* is a good magazine to read regularly. In addition, subscribe to magazines and professional journals in your own particular field of interest.

Publisher's Weekly lists the leading books currently for sale and tells what is coming out next year. Next year's publications are of most interest.

Join the World Future Society, an international association dedicated to working for a better future. As a member you will receive their magazine *The Futurist*, along with various other helpful publications that deal with future trends.

The newspaper is another important indicator of trends. Newspapers attempt to select new topics on the basis of greatest interest to readers. If last month the paper carried 10 articles on female weight lifters and this month it carried 15, you can be sure the interest in women's weight training is on the rise.

Keep track of what is going on by watching news shows like *20/20* and *60 Minutes*. Learn about social issues by tuning to *Donahue* and *The Oprah Winfrey Show*.

Study the financial indicators—sales of real estate and cars, the state of the oil industry, and trends in agriculture and the stock market.

Teague recommends increasing your powers of observation and always asking yourself: What is going to be the likely result of this particular event? What does this indicate about trends for the future?

"If you can discover what people's needs and desires are going to be in the future, you can prepare yourself ahead of time and prosper by meeting those needs," says Teague. "With a little determination and some knowledge of where to look and what to look for, you can learn to predict the future."[3] Then you will be better positioned for success.

In Chapter 2, we examine cultural development in another context, the domination of the image in all aspects of society.

---

[3] Juanell Teague, The Business Coach of the Future, People Plus, Inc., Dallas, TX. Quoted with permission, "Forecast Your Own Business and Career," *Speakout*, October 1987, p. 9.

You Are What You Project . . . The Age of Image

They may forget what you said—but they will never forget how you made them feel.

CARL W. BUEHNER

The age of image is here. From corporations to individuals, the impact of image is irrefutable. By examining how the age of image impacts the individual, and society in general, we can better understand how businesses are impacted. This chapter is brief but delivers an important message while exploring the following areas:

☐ The rise of image-related seminars
☐ The high level of discontentment among men and women

☐ The frustration gap between what we want and what we can afford

☐ How Mikhail Gorbachev won the West with western public relations techniques

☐ How Oliver North used public relations for extreme advantage

☐ The need for your company to uphold the proper image to remain competitive

---

"Image is more important than ever in today's business climate," according to Seminar Information Service, Inc. (SIS). We exhibit the quest for image enhancement on many levels. Seminars on grooming, speaking, interpersonal communications, negotiations, video appearances, and wardrobe management are thriving. Why?

A doctoral student in psychology explained that "the world, to many, seems out of control. If we can manipulate our immediate environment, including how we come across, we feel a sense of control and relief."

"We have seen a dramatic increase in seminars on presentation, specifically image, just within the last year," says SIS vice president Mona Piontkowski. SIS has observed over the past seven years that as trends, and the needs they create develop in business, seminars are developed to meet these needs. Frederick Knapp Associates, Inc., of New York ("Execu-Image") and the American Management Association of New York ("Projecting a Positive Executive Image") are two of many organizations that offer image seminars. Other titles of popular seminars include "Image and Personal Power," "Influencing a Positive Public Image," "Improving Your Silent Business Image," and the granddaddy of the age of image, "Dress for Success."

According to Piontkowski, the reason for this increase is twofold. "As we have shifted from a manufacturing environment to a service-oriented society, what consumers now pay for is often intangible. The image of a company and the people who work for it has taken on new importance in buying decisions," she asserts. (More on this in Chapter 12, "The Marketing Team.") "A reassuring, professional image makes people feel more secure when buying something they can't see or hold in their hand, like a service."[1]

> **Snap judgments based on momentary cues, influenced largely by image, predominate in our society.**

Second, because we are constantly bombarded with information and images through our daily work lives, travel, and television, our minds have learned to quickly assimilate these stimuli, to rightly or wrongly make snap judgments, and to move on.

DISCONTENT WITH SELF-IMAGE

A Louis Harris Organization study found that two out of every three adults in the United States report that they "fidget, fuss, take furtive glances in windows and mirrors, and study other people's reactions to the way they look." Harris concludes that a solid majority of Americans are almost "obsessed with their physical appearance." The term "other-directed," coined by sociologist David Reisman, Ph.D., describes vast numbers of the American population. Other-directed refers to individuals who are more concerned "with what others think of them than what they think of themselves." We are extremely concerned with how we look to others.

Fifty-four percent of men say that they frequently think of their physical appearance, while 75 percent of women say the same; 40 percent of all adults say they spend a great deal of time on how they look. Segments of the population who tend to spend more time on their looks than others include young people, residents of large urban areas, residents of the Northeast, people with high incomes, people who are well educated, singles, Blacks, and, as mentioned, women.

"Perhaps the depth of Americans' obsession with and insecurity over their looks," says Harris, is revealed by people's responses to the question, "Would you change your appearance if you could?" Nearly 96 perent of respondents to a D'Arcy Masius Benton & Bowles' ("Fears and Fantasies of the American Consumer," D'Arcy Masius Benton & Bowles, New

[1] Mona Piontkowski. "Image Is More Important to Executives in Their Companies This Year." *Speakout*. June 1988.

York, March 1985, among a national cross section of 1,550 adults) consumer panel said they would. Specifically, here is what men would change:

What American Men Would Like to Change about Themselves

56%	change in weight
49%	change in waistline
39%	have more muscle
36%	have better teeth
36%	have more hair
34%	be taller
27%	not appear to be aging
21%	change in overall physique
20%	change in complexion
19%	change their noses

Among women, 78 percent would like to lose weight, with a majority desiring to lose 25 pounds or more, many seeking to lose 16 to 25 pounds, and a smaller group wanting to lose between 11 and 15 pounds. Harris pollsters found that American women are close to being obsessed with weight, while not doing a very effective job of fulfilling their desires.

What American Women Would Like to Change about Themselves

70%	have a smaller waistline
48%	not appear to be aging
46%	have a change in thighs
38%	have slimmer buttocks
37%	have better teeth
35%	change their hair
34%	change their legs
33%	reduce wrinkles
32%	change their busts
29%	change their entire physique
28%	change their height (most to be tall)
26%	change their complexion
21%	change their noses
21%	change their hands
19%	have less muscle
18%	have smaller feet
16%	change the shape of their faces
9%	change their ears

Cosmetology and Personal Appearance

Not surprisingly, the cosmetic surgery industry is booming. Its growth has more than doubled since 1980. A cosmetic surgical procedure now exists for virtually every area of the body. As widely reported by newspapers, *Newsweek*, and *U.S. News and World Report*, the age at which people first consider cosmetic surgery is decreasing. For some, it is frustrating to not appear perfect.

One cosmetic surgeon reported that he turned away an attractive 28-year-old seeking to remove wrinkles on her forehead. A Dallas-based surgeon reported that nearly 40 percent of his patients are now men, a dramatic increase in an industry that once primarily served women. It will soon be the rare individual who has not had some form of cosmetic surgery. Similarly, it will be the rare individual who has not had a color and wardrobe analysis and image management instruction.

R. H. Bruskin Associates[2] conducted a survey in November 1985 among a national cross section of 1900 adults and found that to some extent "these attitudes suggest the positive and healthy attributes of caring about one's person." They warn, however, that many people may have an insecurity about being rejected for "not looking right physically," and have fallen prey to the "artifact of advertising designed to capitalize on these fears and apprehensions."

Harris points out that in the 1970s there was a movement of mass numbers of people who wanted to obtain the natural look—women who used less makeup, did not dye their hair, and were happy with modest fashions. During the 1980s, however, the desire for the natural look fell away.

> **To have others admire one's looks now ranks high on the list of both men and women, especially the young, even if those looks are only superficial and wildly deceiving.**

The strongest desire among the population now is to be acceptable, to have the right look, whatever that means. "The race to make one's physical appearance stunning in order to be admired is on in full force

---

[2] America in the Eighties, survey research conducted by R. H. Bruskin Associates, New Brunswick, New Jersey, among a national cross section of adults, 1980.

in America," says Harris.[3] There is no sign that this trend is going to
let up soon.

The Fitness Myth

Focusing on the area of weight, Harris, in a study conducted for *Prevention*
magazine, found that while 76 percent of the population claimed to get
regular exercise, only 33 percent vigorously exercised three times or
more per week. He also found that a majority of adults, 53 percent,
were basically sedentary and infrequently undertook light exercise at
best. Sixty-five percent of all American adults are overweight. Harris's
surprising conclusion from this? "The basic facts sadly do not bear out
all the press notices of a nation on a big health, nutrition, and exercise
kick. If anything, the results indicate that exercise may be falling off,
and overweight going up."

I Came, I Saw, I Want

The U.S. population harbors strong materialistic desires. A megaphe-
nomenon is occurring among us, however. This phenomenon, not featured
on the CBS Evening News, is having a profound effect on our lives.
Anthony Casell, director of new research for *USA Today* and author of
Tracking Tomorrow's Trends, observes that "advertising has created the
desire" for an affluent life-style, even among those on a limited budget.
Based on 1986 data, only 4 percent of all baby boomers, for example,
earn incomes of $45,000 or more; only 15 percent have annual incomes
of $30,000 or more. The "typical" life-style the media depicts for us is
a reality only for a small minority.

Images influence what we want, how we act, and the way we feel
about ourselves. The images impact us in both obvious and subtle ways.
What we would like to own, achieve, and enjoy versus actual income
has created a widening frustration gap. Many people today harbor the
"psychographic" profile—the life-style and values—of more affluent,
but actually underrepresented counterparts. We typically do not earn
enough to keep up with the life-style we have been conditioned to want.

[3] Anthony Casell, *Tracking Tomorrow's Trend*, Kansas City, MO: Andrews, Parker
and McMeel, 1987.

Fine Things

In pursuit of the "good life," we find ourselves racing the clock in increasing numbers (as discussed in Chapter 1). We seek to handle our jobs, move up the corporate ladder, maintain a social life or raise a family, and achieve some semblance of balance. We are more debt-prone and our average indebtedness is higher now than at any other time in our history. Our average savings, adjusted for inflation, are lower than those of previous generations. Yet, in the ultracompetitive workplace, job security is rare for most people. Many people are living hand to mouth—literally counting on the next paycheck, and completely dependent on uninterrupted earnings in the present position, while being influenced by images of affluence that are out of reach.

American Demographics magazine reports that we are working longer hours and taking second jobs in order to invest in real estate or stocks, or to buy a car or health spa membership. And our credit cards are charged up to the limit so that we can have what we want, *now.*

Curiously, in a study by American Sports Data, reported in *Sales and Marketing Management,* 50 percent of those who buy tennis shoes don't play tennis; 49 percent of those who buy running shoes don't run; and 43 percent of those who buy leotards never work out in them. Imagine an industry in which 43 of every 100 buyers never use the product for its intended purpose. Nevertheless, this is becoming a common occurrence.

USING IMAGE FOR EXTRAORDINARY GAIN

As a result of the promotional mastery with which people and events are presented, our ability to judge effectively is often all but quashed. Moreover, our own responses to the messages we receive hamper our ability to make free choices and to maintain balance. Effective public relations help shape public opinion and mold our culture. Public relations techniques can exert global influence.

When Soviet General Secretary Mikhail Gorbachev visited the United States in December 1987, he came highly skilled in western public relations techniques. Although he may prove to be a world leader of great vision, as a nation we changed our attitude about him in three days, almost entirely based on image. At one point during his motorcade through Washington, he jumped out of his limousine and shook hands with several bystanders along a roped-off area. This public relations gesture served its purpose well. The incident was broadcast on all of the evening news programs. It was also replayed frequently on local news broadcasts, news briefs, and news and information talk shows.

The week after his visit, Mr. Gorbachev's approval rating among Americans shot up to the highest level that any Soviet leader has ever enjoyed in this country, based on a Roper Organization public opinion poll. Those surveyed offered an unprecedented increase in affirmative responses to the question, "Can the Soviet Union be trusted to keep its part of the bargain in nuclear arms control agreements?"

Similarly, a larger than ever percentage of respondents agreed that the Soviet Union "seeks only to protect itself against the possibility of attack by other countries," while fewer believed that the Soviet Union "seeks global domination."

MINICASE
THE OLIVER NORTH PHENOMENON

Our increasing familiarity with Gorbachev over a lengthy period was enhanced by his use of western public relations techniques during his visit. The transformation of Lt. Colonel Oliver North's public image, though, illustrates how an effective public relations strategy can swiftly and profoundly alter our views.

North's performance at the Senate subcommittee hearings during a one-week period in July 1987 turned him into a folk hero. During his testimony, North daily received thousands of telegrams from well-wishers. Though he is married, hundreds of women sent him marriage proposals. Major newspapers reported that men "were moved by his magnetic presence." He was the popular topic of discussion at lunch counters and dinner tables across the country.

The viewing audience was not aware of the behind-the-scences work which made North a striking, admirable figure to Americans. North's personality and appearance in his Marine Corps uniform with all of his ribbons were part of a public relations "coup of remarkable proportions" according to Jonathan Blum, vice president and general manager of the Chicago office of Ogilvy & Mather Public Relations.

Few people may realize it, but "North benefited by astute public relations counseling," says Blum, "helping him to reverse a largely negative public image to one of warrior, defender of liberty, and patriot." Notwithstanding, one former National Security Agency advisor expressed the sentiments of dozens of government officials when he said that North essentially conducted "a one-man U.S. foreign policy program," usurping Congress and the law.

Blum points out several examples of astute public relations during North's testimony:

Personal Appearance. North wore his Marine Corps uniform with ribbons, a symbol that evokes feelings of history, duty, service, and sacrifice in Americans.

Personality. North generally projected sincerity and frankness, while being respectful and attentive. Also, he generally kept cool while under fire.

Visuals. A photo of North had the distinct advantage of directly communicating through "live" television.

Blum suggests that *anyone* can employ some of the same public relations techniques that North did, such as use of:

Personality. David Ogilvy, founder of the Ogilvy & Mather Advertising and Public Relations Group and dean of the image makers, considers personality the key to successful image building. "Be enthusiastic and well-briefed on the subject matter. Maintain eye contact, scan the audience, and periodically focus on a friendly face in the crowd. Avoid gratuitous comments such as, 'It's a pleasure to be here.'"

Media management. Attempt to establish rapport with reporters. During testimony, avoid "off-the-cuff" remarks. Answer questions in a straightforward manner and don't be goaded into responding if you are unsure of the correct answer. Emotional displays are counterproductive, even if justified.

Visuals. Use graphics sparingly, and only if they are colorful and are needed to make an important point. However, be aware of television's

highly visual nature and make "visual statements" when appropriate.
The public considers television the most credible news source because
viewers can "see it for themselves."[4]

These are but a few of the elaborate prescriptions for dramatic and
effective image building. Many people do not know what to make of
Oliver North. "When I learned how North's television image was con-
cocted, I felt manipulated," said one Capitol Hill staffer, "but from the
President on down, I remember that receiving public relations counseling
is a common practice." "Washington is now divided into two classes,"
says Capital supergossip Diana McLellan, "people who are trained in
personal presentation and video savvy, and *others.*"

The image-making industry that benefited North impacts us strongly.
Because of its effects, we tend to focus on a person's image, while
regarding his values as less important. We tend to uphold an underlying
message that all is well if it plays well. Raised in the age of image, we
are surrounded by those who have been able to successfully transform
their images, particularly politicians, business leaders, and celebrities.
What is the key to successful image management?—the resources to
create and maintain one. While a public image can be developed without
it, money helps enormously.

Whether it be Lee Iacocca or Ronald Reagan before the Iran-gate
revelations, the resources and the ability of a leader to exploit a direct
and uninterrupted relationship with a constituency are important factors
in market positioning. Columnists observe that Reagan's ability to gain
popularity had far less to do with his acting ability than with his ability
to project the qualities of a best friend. He was a likable man who gained
the personal trust of much of the population. Why? He was comfortable
on camera. He knew who he was, and he was himself.

The Age of Image and Your Business

In the age of image, image is crucial to marketing effectiveness.

Now the question becomes, does America's obsession with personal
image impact what businesses in the 1990s must do to be successful?

---

[4] Jonathan D. Blum, "Astute PR Transforms Ollie North's Image," *Marketing News*,
Mar. 27, 1987, 27.

You bet. In *Marketing Your Consulting and Professional Services* Richard A. Connor, Jr., and I define image as "the sum total of all the perceptions your clients and all others have about you and your practice."[5]

We are firmly in the throes of the age of image and will not easily find release. Forty years of television (first with three channels, then escalating to 185), with an average of 2500 (but up to as many as 20,000) commercial messages bombarding the average individual each day, has taken its toll.

The very survival of your business, whether large or small, is contingent upon how you position yourself and what you project. As consumers, we now have image-related expectations regarding virtually every aspect of the establishments with whom we do business. We are ready to reject establishments that do not fit our preconceived, though perhaps unvoiced, notions of proper location (see Chapter 7, "Location and Positioning"), store layout, product packaging, color coordination, print styles, pricing, ingredient labeling, level of service, temperature level, lighting level, and so forth.

Often, we "know" in seconds whether a store or product is right "for us," simply through fleeting perceptions and other data we draw upon to make instant assessments. A bit of litter outside the building, a sun-faded carton, a sales staff kidding and joking among themselves—anything may serve as the cue that says this establishment "is not right for me."

In Chapter 3, we discuss key factors for aligning your companies with the expectations of those you wish to serve profitably. Later, in Chapters 5 through 8, we discuss aspects of advertising, public relations and promotion, location, and even financial image as they relate to positioning.

[5] Richard A. Connor, Jr. and Jeffrey P. Davidson, *Marketing Your Consulting and Professional Services*. New York: Wiley, 1985, p. 85.

3

Redefining Your Business

Fanaticism consists in redoubling
your effort when you have forgotten
your aim.

SANTAYANA

Effective position marketing begins with re-
defining your business and marketing effort solely in terms of the benefit
to the niche or niches that you serve. This represents a somewhat radical
shift from the ways in which businesses have traditionally defined themselves and their marketing efforts.

In this chapter, we will explore:

☐ How to define your business the way the customer sees it

☐ Why focusing on a precise niche is essential

☐ Why it is dangerous to target too many markets

☐ Why a name change can be detrimental

☐ How a radio station positioned itself in a crowded market

To get started on your definition, or redefinition, of what business you are in, Henry Vanderleest, associate professor of marketing at Ball State University, suggests first contemplating these questions:

- What business are we in?
- What products or services do we offer and why?
- What are our major strengths and weaknesses?
- What has our company achieved?
- What will the future be like for our company?
- In what direction are we headed?
- Where should we be headed?
- How and when will we get where we are going?
- Who is responsible?

JOCKEYING FOR POSITION

The computer manufacturers intensely define and redefine their positions. John Scully, president and chief executive officer of Apple Computers, says, "The role of Apple is to be the innovator in the industry, and the role of IBM is to add credibility to that and offer a broad line of products." Consequently, Scully often finds that the moves that IBM makes are right not only for IBM, but also for Apple. Scully believes that the introduction of some IBM products strongly endorses Apple's approach to computing.

Positioned as the innovator in the industry, Apple continues to enjoy sales among early adopters—consumers who enjoy being the first to try something new. Traditionally, Apple has been able to carve out a two-to-three-year lead—the amount of time it takes IBM and others to catch up.

Herb Baum, president—U.S. Division, Campbell Soup Company, observes that in the consumer product market, almost 6000 new products enter the market each year, with 80 percent of them failing. With high barriers to entry, Baum says that the way to be successful today is to "track emerging trends and your competitive leverage (read 'position') in the form of manufacturing, brand names, distribution innovation, to generate marketing opportunity."

Pop Quiz

If you were quizzed right now as to what business you are in, what would the answer be?

> **If the answer is long and involved, then you have not properly defined your business or its products and services so as to support or establish a position in the minds of those you wish to serve.**

As discussed in Chapter 1, today's consumers, including your best potential customers or clients, are being bombarded with too much information. Your success is dependent on your ability to understand your position and support it (or alter it, if need be) so that your targets have an easy time remembering you. When you try to be something to everyone, or too much to too many people, confusion results. Focus on key groups that you can serve readily and profitably.

Defining Your Business as Your Customers See It

At seminars, prolific business author Herman Holtz stresses defining your business "as the customer sees it." Holtz says you must provide "convenience, security, prestige, ego gratification, economy, opportunity, or any of many other *emotional* benefits." (See Jack Cohen's corroborating advice for salespeople in Chapter 12.)

What Does "Customer Driven" Really Mean?

Management consultant and author Michael F. Baber points out that many people today use the term "customer driven" without really knowing what it means. As an answer, Baber provides:

20 CHARACTERISTICS OF A CUSTOMER DRIVEN ORGANIZATION.

1. Stays close to market trends.
2. Communicates effectively with customers.

3. Listens to customers, especially industry leaders.
4. Gets feedback from customers.
5. Tailors products and services to market segments.
6. Knows the benefits of its products and service.
7. Is sensitive to customer needs.
8. Innovates based on customer and industry needs.
9. Responds rapidly to customer needs.
10. Solves customer problems.
11. Is highly committed to quality, reliability, and service.
12. Learns how customers think.
13. Performs as if it were on the verge of losing every customer.
14. Has senior management involved with customers.
15. Motivates workers down the line through customer involvement.
16. Realizes that sevice objectives inspire ordinary people.
17. Changes service incentive often.
18. Makes all employees accountable in some way for customer service and results.
19. Stresses customer service to its people.
20. Becomes a partner with its customers.[1]

If you can find the motivation or benefit that energizes the customer then, in reverse manner, you have discovered what business you are in. Holtz emphasizes never to define your business from your own viewpoint. If you think that you are selling quarter-inch drills, you are wrong. The customer is buying quarter-inch holes or, as Holtz says, "more likely, the economy and satisfaction of the do-it-yourself approach."

The notion of allowing customers to define what business you are in is, upon first hearing, a bit scary. After all, you are the entrepreneur. You are the one with the guts, determination, drive, and foresight. Why let anyone else shape the future and direction of your business? Luckily, the trauma soon passes, and you begin to realize that how your customers see your business *is* what your business is.

FINDING A *SELECT* NICHE

Each year, *Forbes* profiles and analyzes 200 of the country's best small companies. The analysis points to the ability of these companies to *find*

---

[1] Michael F. Baber, *Integrated Business Leadership through Cross-Marketing*, St. Louis, MO: Green, 1986, p. 34.

a specialty and stay with it. In short, they develop a highly refined niche. As observed in *Forbes*, "Once there was ice cream. Now there is ice cream, superior premium ice cream, and, elbowing in between them, premium ice cream. The ice cream aficionado knows the difference."[2]

A similar situation exists with pizza. There is sit-down pizza, there is take-out pizza, there is pizza by the slice. Lord knows, there is pizza delivery. There are companies that sell uncooked pizzas to supermarkets and supermarkets that sell raw pizza in their deli departments. As our fascination for pizza grows, more types of pizza have been created. It is impossible to predict what new toppings may be found on tomorrow's pizza. The point is: *Successful companies define themselves* (or redefine themselves) *in very precise terms*. The company that caters to the exotic pizza market more easily attracts the consumer who wants exotic pizza.

Then there is the *hit-by-a-truck approach* to establishing position. One evening I had dinner with the publisher of Dow Jones-Irwin, Inc., Richard Staron. Richard told me that the most successful authors are "those who stand in the road for so long" that they "get hit by a truck." What he meant was, long before anyone else notices, companies or individuals who have positioned themselves—who take a stand, have a cause or a mission—and maintain that position (standing in the middle of the road) will eventually be embraced by the market (get "hit by the truck," that is, be in demand by the niche).

Tom Peters and Robert Waterman, authors of *In Search of Excellence*, were talking "excellence" long before their book hit the shelves. Karl Albrecht and Ron Zemke were talking "customer service" long before their book *Service America* became a best-seller. Similarly, Soho sodas established a national distribution system before the market for healthy soft drinks broadly expanded. Celestial Seasonings herbal teas, a mainstay at health food stores for years, have been embraced by the masses and can be found in virtually every supermarket.

Taking on All Customers

Too many businesses attempt to serve too many markets or to handle all business that comes their way, fearing that they will suffer a poor sales period, too much downtime, or slack production capacity. They

---

[2] Steve Kichen and Mathew Schifrin, "Niche List," *Forbes*, November 3, 1986, p. 160.

end up scattering their efforts in all directions. Except in retailing, where you may have little choice, there are certain types of customers or clients that you would be better off not serving.

Suppose you are an EDP systems installer and there are four distinct markets that could use your services. Market A represents the corporate world of large organizations, market B consists of small- to medium-sized firms, market C consists of government agencies, and market D is the international market. You have studied the situation and found that all four represent potentially lucrative markets. You are well qualified to provide service to any of the four markets. What then is the most appropriate strategy in this situation?

The answer lies in what you want to do, how the market views your business, and how you have defined yourself. The answer is not attempting to launch marketing efforts in all four markets.

Dan W. could not decide whether to focus on developing his consulting business or to develop a custom software service. Though somewhat related, each required a different focus and served a different market. Not able to choose between them, Dan ended up offering both. He decided by not deciding; he defined his business by not defining it. To this day, his penetration in each market has been mediocre.

Only by establishing a targeted niche, working from that base, and becoming highly visible can you hope to penetrate the other markets successfully. To do otherwise is jumping the gun or, as they say in politics, "planting your feet firmly in midair."

The best strategy is to focus on the area that you can serve most readily and profitably, and to stay with that area. When you are well entrenched and have an established, outstanding reputation, you can then expand your focus.

Similarly, if you offer products or services E, F, G, and H, the optimum strategy is to go with the one product or service that you can offer most readily and profitably.

Concentrate rather than dilute your efforts.

Many businesses operate as if no single market, however large and well defined, will be sufficient in size and scope to engage them fully. This may be a disguised form of the fear to commit to one focus.

INSTITUTIONAL REDEFINITION AND POSITIONING

Many institutions, not just businesses, are recognizing the need to redefine and reposition themselves. In the field of associations, for example, the International Association for Financial Planning (IAFP) gained 300,000 new members in one year without advertising. It did this by positioning itself as the agency that speaks for the profession.

The IAFP undertook an energetic publicity campaign that yielded more than 13,000 print and broadcast stories. It recognized that there was still uncertainty about this young industry, and chose a public relations approach to promote awareness of financial planning services. This involved establishing a position for its client members as professional, cost-saving, and income-protecting resources, and then highlighting these benefits for clients. The key to the IAFP strategy was ensuring that the messages offered useful and consistent information to their readers.

By redefining its role in the service of its members—financial planners—the IAFP secured a strong position within the profession and will reap the rewards of this ambitious campaign for years to come.

Utility companies are mastering the art of redefining themselves. The Dayton Power and Light Company decided to launch a new program to increase its profitability and to help the community it serves. A marketing analyst with the utility observed that "the marketing force behind the project was to increase employment in the Ohio community." Positioned as not just a utility company but, rather, as a partner in economic progress, Dayton Power offered discounts to existing businesses that created new jobs, and to new businesses bringing jobs to the Miami Valley area.

The program consisted of the utility devising a simple system in which existing customers could show that they had indeed created new jobs. To encourage new businesses to expand or move into the area, Dayton Power designed full-color brochures explaining the program and then undertook a targeted mailing campaign. It subsequently encountered as much activity in one week as it normally saw in one month. In essence, Dayton Power was experiencing four times as many sales as usual.

REPOSITIONING WHEN THE MARKET WON'T LET YOU

Sometimes the position of business is so ingrained in the minds of customers, it is nearly impossible to change it. The extent to which your business or service lives up to the position developed in the minds of those you wish to serve aids overall marketing efforts. However, if your marketing efforts are not aligned with your position, or if you are trying to change position but the market still regards you the old way, you will lose business.

In recent years, Sears Roebuck, the largest retail chain operation in the world, made the decision to upgrade its image, all outlets, and the quality of merchandise offered. The problem with this is that for all of our lives, we have known Sears as a reliable vendor of low- to mid-level-priced merchandise. While Sears retained its place as first in total revenues, on a profitability basis—sales per square foot and sales per average cash register ring up—Sears has been losing ground to competitors such as K Mart and, particularly, WalMart.

Sears's delivery systems continue to be excellent. Its approach to the marketplace, the position it would like to have, however, is not aligned with the position it maintains in the minds of those people it would like to serve. Would you go into Sears to buy a suit or a dress? Sears's decades-long position conflicts with the position it would like to have. So, too, on a smaller scale, your business benefits to the degree that you are consistent with and live up to what the customer or client base has come to expect and demand from you.

WHEN NAMES GET IN THE WAY AND WHEN THEY DON'T

For all the hoopla made several years ago by Bob's Big Boy about whether to change its name by letting customers vote on it, I believe the game was rigged. Bob's could not have wanted to change its name even if the customers' "votes" were overwhelmingly for it. The corporate changes resulting from a name change would have been very costly in out-of-pocket outlays and in market position. And too many customers looking for beehive-hairdo waitresses in the 1980s might have been confused.

The experience of many companies has been that renaming the company ends up being detrimental to marketing. One study showed that only 12 percent of 1000 adults surveyed correctly gave USX as the new name for U.S. Steel, though the change is now several years old. Only 8 percent of adults know that Unisys is the name for the merger of Burroughs Corporation and Sperry Corporation. Only 6 percent knew that Navistar is the new name for International Harvester Company. Only 2 percent of those surveyed knew that the Allegis Corporation is the parent company of United Airlines, Westin Hotels, and Hertz.

Higher income respondents—representing a concentration of managers and investors—were generally more likely to know the new corporate names. For example, among persons with household incomes of $40,000 or higher, 13 percent were able to correctly identify Navistar, but among those with incomes under $15,000, only 3 percent were able to do so.

Like "ABC" type names, nondescriptive or nonsense names should be avoided in naming or renaming a product, service, product group, or even a strategic business unit. The biggest drawback to these types of names is that they do not communicate any valuable or discernible message about what is being named. Thus, for purposes of positioning, you are out in left field.

Occasionally a carefully constructed nonsense name can express to the customer an important message about a product or service. The experts say that names borrowed from "the American experience"— from idiom, mythology, or historical background—can convey a message about you or your product. These literary or image words may stand alone, or they may be joined together with a common word. For example, to market a tough, durable type of glass, Plexiglass works well. To impart a message of permanence with softness in a contact lens, Permasoft does nicely.

MINICASE
HOW A RADIO STATION POSITIONED ITSELF FOR SUCCESS IN A CROWDED MARKET

Holland Cooke, operations manager for WTOP Radio 1500 AM, offers a vivid account of how his station caters to the needs of Washington, D.C., metro area residents, in particular commuters.

"This industry is incredibly competitive. In the 1960s all the AM radio stations were playing top 40 music. FM radio was something that rich people listened to in their Cadillacs and supermarkets played in the background. FM had no commercials."

Commercials Are Our Life Blood

"At WTOP, commercials are the life blood of what we do—they are our products, our inventory. The ratings we earn enable us to sell our commercial time at higher prices. It used to be that somebody who owned an AM/FM station kept the FM on the air because the AM was making money. Now it is very, very much the opposite.

"Most AM stations are being supported by their sister FMs. An AM station that does not have a sister FM may soon wind up in the red. The AMs that do well by themselves have developed a niche, offering some special format. It is not hip to be playing music on AM radio considering the impact FM has made, unless you appeal to a very narrow niche."

The WTOP Difference

"What we offer at WTOP is called in the industry 'All News.' We play no music. You push the button for us and you get the weather, traffic reports, the news, and other information features. We offer traffic reports during rush hour.

"Washington is one of a handful of markets in the radio industry where a station like ours can survive—our overhead is very high, we are very labor intensive. Unlike an FM station, which hires six disc jockeys to play a bunch of records that come free in the mail from record companies, we have to maintain a staff about five times as large because we are constantly generating information.

"A city like Akron cannot support an all-information station. Washington can support one, New York has two, Los Angeles has two, Chicago just got a second, San Francisco has one and a half. You need a large listening audience to afford the high overhead—the reporters and newscasters behind the scenes. In short, we are in a risky business."

We Don't Call It "All News"

"WINS in New York invented the all news in the mid-1960s. They said, 'Give us 22 minutes and we'll give you the world.' Who has 22 minutes anymore? Things are much faster, people want information instantly.

"We used to think in terms of 'broadcasting'; now we think in terms of 'narrowcasting.' What we do is sufficiently narrow that we have to ensure that consumers understand our product in terms that they relate to, rather than in terms we relate to. People might be very interested in something that happened today, but not think of themselves as news consumers, not have branded themselves as 'all news' listeners."

"We are very much 'inside the box'; the consumers are 'outside the box.' It is not surprising that a lot of businesses fail because they are speaking Sanskrit—they are speaking their own lingo. What we say on the air is, 'where you get the top news instantly,' because that is how the audience likes it.

"We say, 'We won't keep you waiting.' We shape and sell what we do in the terms that the consumer uses.

"People do not turn us on all day because we would sound a bit repetitive to them. By promising the top news instantly, we assume that at any instant they may be tuning in. Which means you have to keep repeating the news. What we do continues to recycle. We will not obtain a high rating through long listening spans. We are not even hoping for it. We will settle for a number of 5-minute visits."

Accommodating Shorts Visits

"Every hour we say, 'Listen first thing in the morning and then check back two or three times a day for an instant update.' And our listeners respond. That is the way we position our product in the consumers' minds by relating it to their consumption of it."

SUMMARY

WTOP has been able to capture a significant share of the Washington, D.C., radio market by:

1. Providing instant news and updates such that any consumer can turn on the dial any time throughout the day.

2. Delivering key benefits not based on how many different stories they feature, but on the frequency of what they do feature.

3. Constantly reinforcing these key benefits with on-air position statements.

Customers Come in Many Varieties

Don Bagin,* publisher of *Communication Briefings*, tells the story of a 22-year-old man who "entered the college dean's outer office and told the secretary that he was there to see the dean. He then gave the secretary his name. She rather abruptly told him to take a seat and reminded him that the dean was a very busy person.

"About two minutes later the dean appeared, rushed over to the 22-year-old, shook his hand, put his arm around him and said, 'Come on into the office.' The dean explained to the secretary that the young man was a close friend. The secretary apologized—she thought—by saying, 'Oh, I thought you were just another student.'

"Someone has to communicate to all employees that customers—be they students or others—should be treated in a way that let's them know that we care about them," says Bagin.

A CUSTOMER BY ANY OTHER NAME

Advertising agents call them accounts.

Airlines call them passengers.

Automobile sales reps call them prospects.

Bankers call them depositors.

Beauticians call them heads.

Brokers call them investors.

Bus companies call them riders.

Cabbies call them fares.

Clergy call them parishioners.

Credit card companies call them cardholders.

Doctors call them patients.

Evangelists call them parishioners.

Health clubs call them members.

Hookers call them johns.

Hotels call them guests.

Lawyers call them clients.

Manufacturers call them dealers.

Meeting planners call them attendees.

Merchants call them customers.

Museums call them visitors.

Nursing homes call them residents.

Publishers call them readers.

Realtors call them buyers.

Resorts call them vacationers.

Restaurateurs call them diners.

Seminar leaders call them participants.

Sports franchises call them fans.

Theater managers call them patrons.

Tour guides call them tourists.

Universities call them students.

Vendors call them purchasing agents.

---

* Don Bagin, "This True Story Offers a Lesson," *Communication Briefings*, Pitman, NJ, July 1987, p. 5.

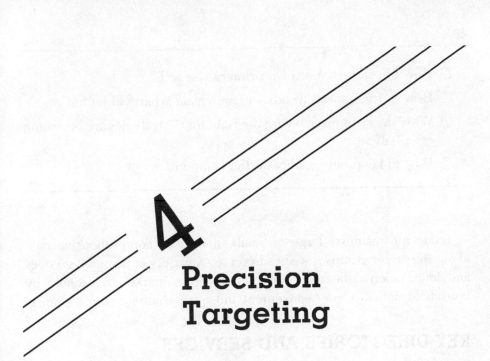

4
Precision Targeting

It is not enough to aim, you must hit.

ITALIAN PROVERB

$\mathbf{A}$ substantial benefit of effective positioning is that you can more inexpensively attract targeted customers and clients, and then keep attracting others with similar needs. No matter how well established you are in the marketplace, to ensure that your marketing efforts continue to meet with optimal returns, you will need to understand as much about your targets as you can. In this chapter, we will explore the following:

☐ How *any* business today can immediately gain a wealth of information about *any* target market

☐ What the popular business data bases offer

☐ How to find and use free sources of information

☐ How to conduct your own primary research

☐ How to track social trends and anticipate what will be hot

☐ Why "the right place before the right time" strategies are becoming essential

☐ How to keep tabs readily on the competition

Today no business, large or small, need lack comprehensive data about the target groups it wishes to serve. A variety of business services and information data bases can pinpoint your market, household by household, if that is most convenient and appropriate for your business.

KEY DIRECTORIES AND SERVICES

Whether you are a one-person business or a corporation of thousands, you can gain virtually immediate, comprehensive prospect data on any market conceivable, from consumers and households to the most sophisticated technological research and development corporations.

> **Whether you have opened up a small boutique and will be selling items retail to just a few selected neighborhoods or whether you will be distributing your product nationwide or worldwide, up to date, comprehensive, definitive data exist for your market.**

In this section we will walk through a couple of the leading directories and services which, for several hundred dollars, will provide you with valuable data. Throughout the remainder of the chapter we will discuss other options for data gathering, including well-established business data bases, government information services, publication indexes, library sources, and key newsletters.

A Sampling of Directories

U.S. Manufacturers Directory.   This handy guide, published by American Business Directories, lists over 200,000 manufacturers by company name, address, zip code, and phone number, plus employee size, sales

volume, owner, manager, and chief executive officer's names, and up
to three SIC codes per company. It also cross indexes manufacturers
by city and state, by industry, by the number of employees, and alphabetically. For more information call (402) 593-4600.

Corporate Technology Directory.   Published by CorpTech in Wellsley
Hills, Massachusetts, this volume provides the names of 25,000 companies,
including 14,800 emerging private companies, and also lists 7500 key
executives and 85,000 high-tech products. The publication contains 4000
pages in four volumes. Information is also cross indexed by company
name, geography, technology, product, and other useful criteria. Further
information is available by calling (800) 843-8036.

Findex.   This publication identifies more than 1100 research reports
in 12 categories: business and finance, health care, consumer durables,
consumer nondurables, defense and security systems, media and publishing; also energy utilities and related equipment, data processing and
electronic systems, construction materials and machinery, basic industries
and related equipment, retail and consumer services, and transportation.
Findex advertises that "millions of dollars worth of market research is
being produced every year, but if you can't find it . . . you can't benefit
from it." Call (800) 227-3052.

Contacts Influential and LeadSource.   These two separate business
entities offer essentially the same information for selected metropolitan
areas throughout the United States. *Contacts Influential* is divided into
eight major sections. For example, in the Dallas area, the names of
Dallas-based businesses are presented by alphabet, SIC number, zip
code, on a street-by-street basis, product, telephone number, alphabet
according to SIC code, and zip code according to the street index.

A *Contacts Influential* directory enables you to identify businesses
within a two-block radius of your own business. It literally enables you
to produce a targeted list of businesses by building, by street, or by any
number of criteria. *Contacts Influential* offers you Cheshire labels, pres-
sure-sensitive labels, 3 × 5 cards, computer printouts, magnetic tapes,
or computer diskettes with which to approach the marketplace. Figure
1 reveals the level of detail offered by *Contacts Influential.* For further
information call (913) 677-2240.

LeadSource works much the same way. It provides volumes on 20
major metropolitan areas in the United States (areas not covered by
Contacts Influential) and offers data on selected target markets in the

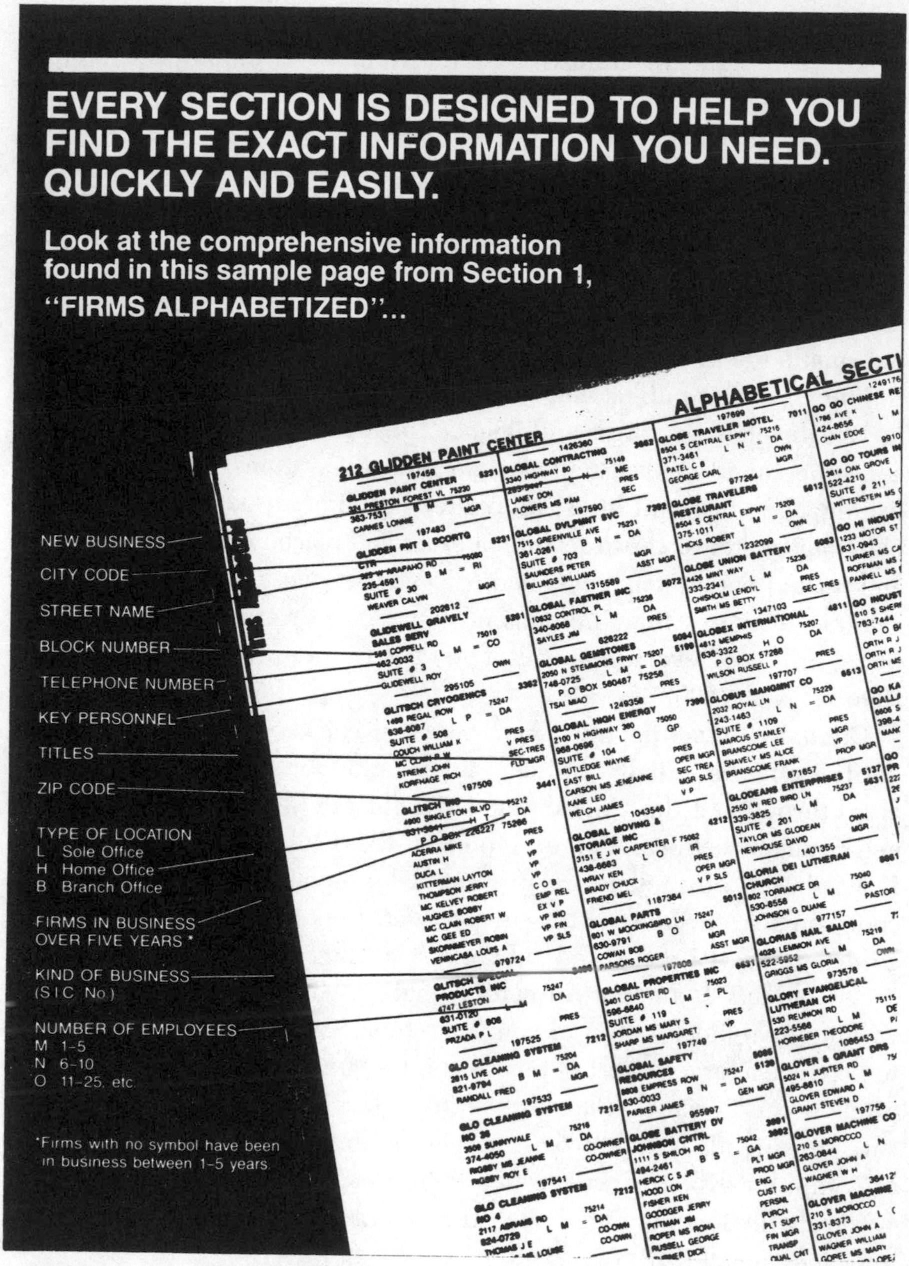
EVERY SECTION IS DESIGNED TO HELP YOU FIND THE EXACT INFORMATION YOU NEED. QUICKLY AND EASILY.
Look at the comprehensive information found in this sample page from Section 1, "FIRMS ALPHABETIZED"...
ALPHABETICAL SECTI
212 GLIDDEN PAINT CENTER
NEW BUSINESS
CITY CODE
STREET NAME
BLOCK NUMBER
TELEPHONE NUMBER
KEY PERSONNEL
TITLES
ZIP CODE
TYPE OF LOCATION
L Sole Office
H Home Office
B Branch Office
FIRMS IN BUSINESS OVER FIVE YEARS *
KIND OF BUSINESS (S.I.C. No.)
NUMBER OF EMPLOYEES
M 1-5
N 6-10
O 11-25, etc.
*Firms with no symbol have been in business between 1-5 years.

Figure 1. Sample page of *Contacts Influential.* (Reprinted with permission.)

same array of formats as *Contacts Influential*. For more information call (703) 370-1655.

Note: The metropolitan areas served by *Contacts Influential* and *LeadSource* do not overlap. Thus to take advantage of this type of service for a particular metropolitan area, one needs to determine whether *Contacts Influential* or *LeadSource* provides the data.

The List House.   This publication supplies data on businesses and consumers in five formats, including mailing labels, 3 × 5 cards, magnetic tapes, PC diskettes, and prospect lists. As with many national mailing lists, *The List House* provides an array of data: 14 million businesses in the United States, 3.2 million in Canada, 515,000 physicians and dentists, and 415,000 lawyers, for example. On the consumer side, it can provide a breakdown of 4.1 million high-income Americans, 78 million households, 9 million high-school and college students, 300,000 new homeowners, and almost any other type of list requested. These lists can then be broken down further by region, state, county, town, zip code, section of city, and neighborhood. For more information call (800) 634-1949.

Key Contacts.   A national business and executive data file, it gives access to information on the full name and title of decision makers, SIC codes, company size by the number of employees, location of local branches and headquarters, department titles, years in business, and other key prospecting information.

Key Contacts' Dun & Bradstreet data also enable you to tap into Dun's *Market Identifier* service at an affordable cost and, like *Contacts Influential* and *Lead Source*, target specific businesses based on a variety of key criteria. For more information call (301) 340-9197.

Other leading directories, primarily industrial, include:

- *Million Dollar Directory*
- *News Front*: 30,000 leading U.S. corporations
- *North American Register of Business and Industry*
- *Standard Directory of Advertisers*
- *Thomas Register of American Manufacturers*
- *Corporate 1000*
- *Standard and Poor's Register of Directors and Executives*
- *Dun's Middle Market Directory*

Research Industry Markets through Powerful Data Bases

For those serving industry, there are questions that must be answered. For example, "How big is the industry?" "How many firms are in this industry?" "What are the operating characteristics?" "What are the trends?" "What channels of distribution are necessary to reach the market?" All of these questions can be answered by data bases.

Articles, abstracts, briefs, and industry reports (all of which are provided by data bases) can give key information on buying habits of industrial representatives and agents. Data bases can also help determine at what frequency industrial companies buy, how much they buy, and the types of delivery and service as well as the type of quality and quality control they expect.

Vendors offering a wide selection of data bases include BRS, Lockheed, SDC Orbit, and Mead Data Central. Together, these system yield several hundred data bases with which to gather information on industrial markets.

BRS [Bibliographic Retrieval Service, 1200 Route 7, Latham, NY 12110, (518) 783-1161].   For a monthly subscription fee, discounts are offered for any data base maintenance by BRS in its system. Also, the search language is popular among librarians and lay users alike, and is considered an easy language to learn.

Dialog [3460 Hillview Avenue, Palo Alto, CA 94304, (415) 858-3785]. Offers more than 200 data bases representing an array of technical and general-interest fields. Volume discounts for high-volume users; user oriented.

Nexis [Mead Data Central, P.O. Box 933, Dayton, OH 45401, 1-800-227-9597].   Mead also produces a data base well known in law firms and law school libraries, called Lexis. Contains entire articles and a large newspaper selection; easy to use.

Dialog, Nexis, and virtually all other data bases can be located by using one or more of the following directories:

Computer-Readable Databases
American Library Association
50 East Huron Street
Chicago, IL 60611
(312) 944-6780

The North American Online
    Directory
R. R. Bowker
245 West 17th Street
New York, NY 10011
(800) 521-8110

Data Base Directory
Knowledge Industry Publications
701 Westchester Avenue
White Plains, NY 10604
(914) 328-9157

Here are brief summaries of data bases for business and marketing research purposes.

ABI Inform.   A general business data base with lengthy abstracts of articles from over 650 business press publications. Dates back to 1971. Available on many systems, including BRS, SDC, Dialog, VU/TEXT, and others.

The Computer Database.   Provides indexing and abstracting of articles from about 500 computer publications. Superb source for information on hardware, software, telecommunications, and networking. Available on Dialog and BRS, among others.

Disclosure II.   Contains business and financial information extracted from documents filed with the Securities and Exchange Commission by over 10,000 publicly held companies. Available on many systems, including Dialog, CompuServe, and Dow Jones News Retrieval.

Dow Jones News.   Contains new stories from *The Wall Street Journal*, *Barron's*, and *Dow Jones News Service*. Over 10,000 U.S. and Canadian companies in 50 industries are covered dating back to 1979. Available on Dow Jones News Retrieval.

Dun's Market Identifiers 10 +.   Provides marketing information and company history for U.S. businesses, both public and private, which have more than 10 employees. Coverage includes parent companies, subsidiaries, headquarters information, products, and services. Available on Dialog.

Investext.   Contains the full text of industry and company research reports produced by financial analysts of leading investment firms in the United States, Canada, Europe, and Japan. Available on several systems, including the Source and Dialog.

Magazine Index. Provides indexing for articles from over 400 popular magazines. In many cases the full texts of the articles are provided. This includes information on many subjects, including consumer information, restaurants, and travel. Available on Dialog, Mead's Nexis system, and BRS.

Management Contents. This general business data base contains information from over 500 business publications. Available on Dialog, Mead, BRS, SDC, and others.

National Newspaper Index. Contains indexing for articles from such national newspapers as *The New York Times, The Wall Street Journal, The Christian Science Monitor,* as well as the *Washington Post* and the *Los Angeles Times.* Available on Mead, BRS, and Dialog.

PTS Prompt. This is a must for industry information and includes data on both private and public companies. It includes abstracts with citations to the full text, covering thousands of publications since 1972. It is international in scope. Available on several systems, including Dialog, BRS, and VU/TEXT.

Software That Supports Your Marketing Efforts

A considerable field of marketing support software now exists. In fact, there are so many different types of software to support your sales, prospecting, marketing management, mapping, telemarketing, and follow-up efforts that a multivolume text would be needed to describe them all. Fortunately there are two excellent sources that have attempted to corral and define the vast array of marketing software available.

The first is from *Marketing News* (a sample page is shown in Figure 2), which provides one large alphabetical list of software supporting marketing and marketing research, and is categorized according to product name, application, industry or activity served, hardware and/or operating system required and minimum memory required, and price. The index has been arranged according to the following categories:

- Advertising, ad agencies, public relations
- Analysis
- Customer service

Marketing News   Jan. 4, 1988

Software directory update

SEND DIRECTORY ADDITIONS, CHANGES, and corrections to Gregg Cebrzynski, Managing Editor, **Marketing News**, 250 S. Wacker Dr., Chicago, IL 60606. Information in directory entries is categorized by numbers one through five. (N/A means not applicable or available). 1. product name; 2. application; 3. industry or activity served; 4. hardware and/or operating system required and minimum memory required; and 5. price. (Note: In multiple entries, ''same as above'' means the information for that number is the same as that listed for the same number in the supplier's first entry.)

KEY SYSTEMS INC.
512 Executive Park
Louisville, KY 40207
(800) 223-5637
(502) 897-3332
1. Prospecting Plus
2. lead gathering, literature request fulfillment, telemarketing, direct mail, outside sales, & customer support
3. sales & marketing
4. laptop, desktop, & multi-user PC systems
5. $495 for the first installation, $198 for each add-on.

B AND B SYSTEMS
P.O. Box 171
Waukesha, WI 53187
(414) 234-4038
1. B&B SaleLead
2. on-line product information reference & letter/label producer, tickler follow-up, sales/commissions/expenses tracker, Nth sampling; Flexi-Sort & Flexi-Report features allow sorting & reporting on any field of data
3. sales & marketing
4. IBM PC/XT/AT or compatibles, hard disk: 640K
5. $199.

FIRST INTERSTATE CENTER FOR SERVICES MARKETING
College of Business
Arizona State University
Tempe, AZ 85287
(602) 965-6201
1. SERVMARK
2. electronic bibliography of services marketing literature containing more than 3,500 references & 500 abstracts, with multiple keyword search capability
3. all service industries
4. IBM PC XT/AT or compatibles, 256K
5. $295.

MARKET ACTION
Business Technology Center
Bradley University
Peoria, IL 61625
(309) 677-3299
1. STRATMAP, Student Version
2. supplement for marketing research classes, shows many applications of table data to strategic planning & easy way to cross-tabulate data & display relationships among categories
3. research students
4. IBM PC/XT/AT or compatibles; 640K
5. $12.95

Figure 2. Sample page of *Marketing News* Software Directory. (Reprinted with permission from *Marketing News*, published by the American Marketing Association.)

- Data base management
- Desk organizers, automated address books
- Direct marketing, mail order, telemarketing
- Forecasting, modeling
- Graphics, mapping, report generators
- Logistics, inventory, physical distribution, transportation management
- Marketing research and analysis, questionnaire design, tabulation, processing of survey data
- Miscellaneous
- Name generators
- Planning, strategic planning, media planning
- Sales, sales analysis, forecasting, retail, evaluation, training, planning, territory planning
- Statistics, statistical testing, analysis

For more information write to the American Marketing Association, 250 South Wacker Drive, Chicago, IL 60606-5819.

Sales and Marketing Management magazine also publishes a directory of PC-based sales and marketing applications software. This directory is arranged by function, then alphabetically by vendor name, name of the software, applications, minimum internal memory required, price, and necessary hardware. For more information write to Sales and Marketing Management, Bill Publications, 633 3rd Avenue, New York, NY 10017.

RESEARCH 101

Let us explore some low-cost methods for conducting research that supports your marketing efforts.

Researching the Competition–Competitor Intelligence

More of your competitors employ corporate "spies" than you may realize. The Society of Competitor Intelligence Professionals reports that more of their members work for marketing departments than for any other functional area within business: 21 percent of SCIP members indicated that they work full time on competitive intelligence; 42 percent said they spent more than half of their time investigating what competitors are doing. But as you might have guessed, you cannot tell it from the their job titles—78 percent have job titles that do not include words such as "competitor" or "competitive."

The consensus among SCIP members is that their employer's interest in what competitors are up to is "serious" or "extreme." As a profession, competitor analysis is growing steadily.

To conduct your own competitor intelligence inexpensively there are many sources available. Information expert Leonard M. Fuld cites 10 excellent sources for gathering *competitor intelligence* from his book of the same name:[1]

1. *Company Financials*
   • Dun & Bradstreet reports—financial credit ratings

[1] Leonard M. Fuld, *Competitor Intelligence*, New York: Wiley, 1985.

- SEC 10-K, 10-Q reports
- Annual reports—available
- State filing
- Published articles
- *Moody's*
- *Wall Street Transcript*

2. *Market Share*
   - Literature searches
   - Simmons Market Research Bureau
   - A.C. Nielsen Company
   - Market studies
   - EIS
   - F&S *Predicasts*

3. *Company Background*
   - F&S indexes
   - *Standard & Poor's*
   - Dun & Bradstreet reports
   - Newspaper indexes
   - Published articles
   - *Wall Street Transcript*

4. *Industry Background*
   - Published articles
   - Trade magazines
   - *U.S. Industrial Outlook*
   - Investment reports
   - *Value Line*
   - Special annual issues of industry handbooks

5. *Directories*
   - *Standard & Poor's*
   - *Thomas Register*

- Industry buyers' guides
- *Yellow Pages*
- City directories
- Key magazines
- Associations

6. *Industry Experts*
   - Articles
   - Key magazines
   - *Directory of Directories*
   - Associations
   - Stockbrokers
   - Consultants
   - Government experts
   - University professors

7. *Management Personnel*
   - *Who's Who (General Industry)*
   - Local newspapers
   - PR departments
   - College alumni associations
   - *Wall Street Journal*
   - *New York Times*
   - Chamber of Commerce

8. *Foreign Information*
   - Consulates
   - Embassies
   - American (foreign) Chamber of Commerce
   - International Trade Commission
   - Special libraries
   - International D&B

9. *Advertising Information*
   - *Advertising Age*

- *ADTRACK*
- Local newspapers
- Advertising agencies

10. *Government Experts*
  - Washington Researchers' guides
  - Federal Communications Commission
  - Department of Commerce
  - Bureau of Labor Statistics
  - Environmental Protection Agency
  - Federal Trade Commission

Tapping Social Research

Many of the sources suggested by Juanell Teague in Chapter 1 can be used to monitor contemporary social trends. There she offers recommendations for creating your own tracking system, including habits, lifestyles, irritants, wants, and desires of those you are interested in serving.

A variety of recently published texts as well as other periodicals will further enable you to tap quickly and easily into available social research. For example, Louis Harris's book *Inside America* provides a wealth of information regarding the current state of our population's habits, wants, desires, and concerns. *100 Predictions for the Baby Boom Generation* by Cheryl Russell, and *Tracking Tommorrow's Trends* by Anthony Cassell are valuable texts to help you understand current consumer behavior.

Metro Insights published by Data Resources in Lexington, Massachusetts, provides a wealth of information on 100 key U.S. metropolitan markets, including demographic and labor force profiles, consumer spending, and income statistics. For more information about this 1100-page directory call (617) 863-5100.

Many other studies by think tanks and social research organizations are identified through the *Findex* catalog. For example, SRI, formerly the Stanford Research Institute, publishes the *Values and Lifestyles Report*, which charts the American consumer based on eight basic social economic consumer types, offering detailed descriptions on the wants, needs, and values of each group. On a monthly basis, *American Demographics* provides in-depth, detailed articles on population trends.

Its back issues are also valuable reference tools. *American Demographics* can be found in any library.

Newsletters

A key source of market research information is provided by the newsletters that are published by nearly all trade associations, government agencies, industry groups, political groups, and every major corporation. The *Oxbridge Newsletter Directory* lists several thousand newsletters, arranged by functional areas. The *National Trade and Professional Association Directory* (NTPA) indicates which of the thousands of associations listed maintain newsletters. The *Newsletter Yearbook* is also a valuable guide. By accessing these directories and others your local librarian may suggest, you can gain access to late-breaking news and information of concern to your business and your industry. Many newsletters today are available via data base. The above cited directories are commonly held by reference librarians at municipal and school libraries.

Wealth of Data

A wealth of free data are available through municipal and college libraries. The aforementioned *Magazine Index* and *Newspaper Index* offer comprehensive article bibliographies in microfiche. If you need to research an article or information on a corporation that appeared in your local newspaper, use the library's newspaper index, which abstracts newspaper articles by topic and cross references this listing by date. Your metro area may also be served by one or more area business publications. You can write to the Association of Area Business Publications, 202 Legion Drive, Annapolis, MD 21401, for the complete list. Also, *The Wall Street Journal Index* is available in many public libraries in major cities.

Three hardcopy indices, the *Business Periodicals Index*, the *Reader's Guide to Periodical Literature*, and the *Reader's Guide to Scientific Literature*, will allow you to scan for the latest articles in selected topic areas.

The *Business Periodicals Index* offers a listing by topic of all the articles in the last month, quarter, year, or several decades that appeared in such nationally known business journals as *Business Week*, *Fortune*, *Forbes*, and *Harvard Business Review*, as well as numerous other business periodicals.

Among the most insightful marketing and marketing management periodicals are:

* *American Demographics*
* *European Journal of Marketing*
* *Incentive*
* *Journal of Marketing*
* *Marketing & Media Decisions*
* *Marketing Executive's Digest*
* *Marketing News*
* *Sales & Marketing Digest*
* *Sales and Marketing Management*

Juanell Teague suggests calling the reference department of your local library and asking whether they have an on-line data base search service. Many larger libraries have access to the *Dow Jones News Retrieval Service*, which indexes such publications as *The Wall Street Journal*, *Barron's*, and the *Washington Post*.

Some libraries have access to the *Datatimes Vendor System*, which picks up various regional newspapers such as the *San Francisco Chronicle*, *Dallas Morning News*, *St. Petersburg Times*, *San Diego Union*, and *Oklahoman*. In addition, your librarian may be able to suggest other data bases that index news publications.

The fee your library charges for this service will depend on the length of time their computer is connected to the data base. There is usually a per-minute connect fee and there may be a per-reference print charge.

Reading What the Niche Reads, and Read about Them

One of the easiest ways to keep abreast of the changes, trends, and other factors affecting a target group is to identify the major publications serving the niche and read what they read.

The publications read by any target group can be identified by using the directories listed below. They collectively list over 10,000 publications in every field of endeavor and enable you to identify 90 percent or more of all publications serving a group: *Writer's Market*, *Working Press of the Nation*, *Bacon's Publicity Checker*, and *Standard Periodicals Index*.

Once you identify and obtain several publications, get the most from them:

Table of Contents. In addition to normal feature articles, look for the following: book reports, trend watch, columns, reader surveys, letters to the editor or opinion pieces, people in the news, new products and services, and classified advertising. Classified ads are often a good indicator as to the needs of the readership.

Readership Demographics. All publications maintain information on their readership, including average age, income, sex, job title, and other valuable data. Write to the advertising department and ask for a copy of the advertising-rate card and readership demographics. The advertising-rate card, available on request, describes the costs and procedures for placing a single or a continuous ad within the publication. You can also use *Standard Rate and Data*, which contains information on all major U.S. publications and a directory of advertising-rate cards.

Editorial Guidelines. Most editors maintain a published set of editorial or authors' guidelines. These are also available on request. These guidelines define the nature and scope of the material the editor is seeking to interest his or her readers.

Special Issues. Many publications periodically offer a special issue that highlights developments and trends in the industry. For example, *Inc.* produces a special issue entitled the "The Inc. 100," which lists and describes the fastest growing small businesses in the United States. Other publications, such as *Forbes*, *Fortune*, *Business Week*, and *Venture*, are noted for their special issues. The calendar outlines the topics and issues for the following year. The editorial calendar will pinpoint when a special issue will be published. Here are 10 publications that offer special issues:

- *Fortune*: The 500 Largest U.S. Industrial Corporations
- *Inc.*: The Inc. 100
- *Business Week*: R&D Scoreboard (McGraw-Hill)
- *Chain Store Age—General Merchandise*: Top 100 Chains
- *Dun's Review*: Best Managed Companies
- *Advertising Age*: 100 Leading National Advertisers
- *Black Enterprise*: The Top 100 Black Enterprises
- *Dun's Review*: Top Corporate Performers

- *Forbes*: Annual Directory Issue
- *Journal of Commerce*: Various
- *The Wall Street Journal*: Various
- *Financial World*: America's Top Growth Companies

Subscriber Mailing Lists. Most publications have subscriber mailing lists for sale. Although some publications sell their entire list of subscribers (representing overkill to you if you only want subscribers in a particular locality), others offer a more targeted list. In addition, many publications sell their subscriber lists to the direct-mail catalog houses, who often can offer them to you at a lower cost than the publisher because of high-volume sales.

Research through Association Resources

Association directories can be found in any library and offer the names, addresses, and phone numbers of trade and professional associations. *Gale's Encyclopedia of Associations* and the *National Trade and Professional Association Directory* collectively offer 12,000 association listings. Associations themselves provide trend information, surveys, publications, monthly newsletters and magazines, and in many cases directories of their memberships.

The *Directory of Conventions* tells you where associations and professional groups are actually meeting, how many people will be attending, and the name of the meeting planner. This book is valuable for pinpointing meetings and conventions that may be important to your business.

A Gold Mine of Government Data

Through the Bureau of the Census of the Department of Commerce you can obtain sales and revenue data on virtually any industry by state, county, and standard metropolitan statistical area, and general demographic data on population down to the block level. Although the Bureau of the Census is primarily known for its population reports, a census of business is taken in the second and seventh years of each decade and is available 18 months later.

Census information is available on more than 800 of the approximately 1000 industries, businesses, and products classified according to the SIC system. Expense and production-type information is assembled for about 1000 material categories, and quantity and value data are given for 16,000 product classifications. Separate censuses are conducted for manufacturers, mineral industries, construction industries, retail trade, wholesale trade, and service industries.

Computer file tapes can be obtained directly from the Bureau of the Census. The Bureau of the Census also produces many special industry reports and offers several ways to access their files. To obtain a list of the bureau's publications, write to Bureau of the Census, Washington, DC 20233.

SIC: The System Explained

The *Standard Industrial Classification* (SIC) facilitates the analysis of data on all industries in the United States.

Within the system, each major area of activity is first assigned a range of 2-digit classification codes. For example, the manufacturing division includes SICs 20 to 39, with each 2-digit designation denoting a *major group*, such as SIC 20—Food. These in turn are subdivided into more than 150 3-digit *industry groups*, such as SIC 208—Beverages. At the next level of detail, 4-digit *specific industries* are identified (SIC 2082—Malt beverages or SIC 2086—Bottled and canned soft drinks).

The 4-digit classification codes are most widely used by marketers, although extended codes of up to 8 digits are starting to see significant use.

The basic reporting unit in the SIC system is the *individual establishment*, defined as a "single physical location where business is conducted or where services or industrial operations are performed." Establishments are equal to entire companies, which may consist of one or more separate establishments, depending on the number of actual physical locations involved. Where "distinct and separate economic activities" are performed at a single location, each is treated as an establishment, in accordance with the guidelines on classification in the government's *Standard Industrial Classification Manual.*

For a more detailed listing of all industries, their codes, and their definitions, the *Standard Industrial Classification Manual* is available from the U.S. Government Printing Office (GPO), Washington, DC 20402. The 1977 Supplement, which incorporates some minor revisions and additions, is also available from the GPO.

Excerpted courtesy of *Sales & Marketing Management* © 1987.

The Department of Commerce annually publishes the *U.S. Industrial Outlook*, which traces the growth of 200 industries and provides five-year forecasts for each industry. Write to *U.S. Industrial Outlook*, Bureau of Economic Analysis, U.S. Department of Commerce, Washington, DC 20230.

The *U.S. Statistical Abstract* is a useful compilation of data and reports and contains over 1000 charts from the Department of Commerce, the Department of Labor, the Department of Transportation, the Small Business Administration, and other federal agencies. Much of the research information you may be seeking can be found in this one volume. The Abstract and many other major publications produced by the federal government are on sale at the U.S. Government Printing Office. The federal government is always conducting studies on industries, on new technology, and on social trends.

A sampling of government data follows:

- Bureau of the Census. *Annual Survey of Manufacturers*. Washington. Annually.

- Bureau of the Census. *Census of Retail Trade*. Washington. Years ending in 2 and 7. Every 5 Years.

- Bureau of the Census. *Census of Selected Service Industries*. Washington. Years ending in 2 and 7.

- Bureau of the Census. *Catalog*. Washington, U.S. Government Printing Office. Annually.

- Bureau of the Census. *County and City Data Book, 1984*. Washington, U.S. Government Printing Office. Annually.

- Bureau of the Census. *Supplementary Reports, Population and Households by States and Counties*. Washington. 1980.

- Bureau of the Census. *U.S. Census of Housing*. Washington. 1960, 1970, 1980.

- Bureau of the Census. *U.S. Census of Population*. Washington. 1960, 1970, 1980.

- Bureau of Labor Statistics. *BLS Data Bank Files and Statistical Routines*. BLS Rept. 507. Washington. 1984.

- Bureau of Labor Statistics. *Employment and Earnings, BLS 790 Data*. Washington. Monthly plus annual supplement.

- Bureau of Labor Statistics. *Handbook of Labor Statistics*. Washington. Annually.

- Congressional Information Service, Inc. *American Statistic Index*. Various years (computerized bibliographic search). Washington. Monthly.

Generating Your Own Research

There are several reasons for undertaking your own market research. There is no substitute for accurately determining who is interested in your product or service, or for assessing the perception of your clients or customers. Primary research—that which you generate yourself—is a building block for effective marketing and effective positioning. Here are the basics.

Telephone Surveys. Both qualitative and quantitative data can be obtained through a telephone survey. You can ask yes/no or multiple-choice questions, or you can ask for elaborate answers, providing a more complete picture than numbers alone would give.

A telephone survey is less expensive than on-site interviewing and more expensive than a mail survey. The main advantage to a telephone survey is the concentration of personnel and resources. For example, you could have 30 people working a bank of phones from one or two rooms. You also get the added responses to your questions that interviewees' may not offer in written responses to mail surveys.

The increasing number of telephone interruptions that people are exposed to almost daily is an obstacle to surveying by telephone. Because of less than reputable companies, people have become suspicious. If feasible, publicize your telephone survey of customers in advance by mail. When interviewing, be sure to explain the purpose of the survey and provide a general overview of how the research will be used.

Interviewing. Conducting a series of face-to-face interviews provides more complete information, but is costly. Personal interviews are generally more comprehensive since it is possible for an interviewer to detect if a person's body language and gestures agree with his or her verbal statements. Hire a research firm to undertake the research or train your personnel in the proper techniques. Sloppy methods by untrained interviewers result in useless data. Interview questions must be standardized, with some probing allowed for interviewers.

A medical clinic hired a consultant to conduct interviews to determine its image and its attractiveness to a selected target market. One-on-one interviews are most useful on subjective questions, such as the ones sought by the clinic. In addition to their telephone survey, a university also conducted interviews with high-school seniors to get a feel for what they are looking for when picking a college.

Focus Groups. Focus groups, one of the newest and most popular techniques for market research, are used to gain insights and directional data. "You are seeking gut feelings and thoughts," according to Gary L. Berman, president of Market Segment Research, headquartered in Miami, Florida. "Focus groups need a trained, professional moderator who understands group dynamics."

Focus groups can be used to develop creative strategies and evaluate the effectiveness of current marketing programs. Although focus groups are used for all types of market research, their primary effectiveness is in evaluating the attitudes and underlying beliefs held by the respondents and in identifying the key issues that must be dealt with. An average focus group costs between $2400 to $5500, although costs vary across the nation and depend on the target groups necessary to accomplish the research goals.

Focus groups take advantage of group dynamics, encouraging participants to react to and build on one another's ideas. "Unlike paper and pencil questionnaires, focus groups allow respondents to expand on their views," says one research specialist. "If you ask people why they don't belong and they say the dues are too high, you can go into the reasoning behind that response."

Mail Survey. A mail survey is the least expensive way to reach the greatest number of people, but it is also the least effective research method. Average response to a well-designed mail campaign of 10 to 20 percent is considered acceptable. You can increase the odds by including a postage-paid return envelope, or by making the response instrument an easily returnable, tear-off postcard. "Response rates greatly increase," according to Berman, "when the respondents have a vested interest in the questionnaire." As with the telephone survey, explain why you are asking for the information and how you intend to use it.

A Typical Research Strategy

ABC Company is interested in determining the consumer attitudes regarding its products. The target market is just under one-half million, ethnically mixed, with divergent income levels. What methods would a research company use to gauge the attitudes and how much would it cost? Although Berman cautions that costs vary greatly throughout the nation, the following is a typical approach.

The first step to the hypothetical research strategy would be to set up focus groups. He would use them to glean key insights into product usage. The qualitative responses from the focus groups would become information on which to base development of the questionnaire. An average focus group includes 8 to 10 people. Four different focus groups might be used for ABC Company. To minimize any communication barriers, groups would be segmented by demographic characteristics, including age and sex.

Next, a total of 900 telephone interviews would be conducted among a cross section of consumers. Each interview would last from 10 to 12 minutes since people become tired easily and may abort answers to hasten completion. The questions would be structured, with one or two opportunities for respondents to expand their answers. Qualitative responses are harder to condense into statistical categories. However, they yield very useful information when they offer the reasoning behind answers.

"Face-to-face interviews yield the most reliable and complete data," denotes Berman, "since a respondent is more likely to complete the interview and give valid responses, and less likely to evade questions when speaking to an interviewer in person." Mail surveys are the least reliable since there is no personal contact. An important limitation of telephone research, however, is that certain groups may be under-represented.

When undertaking research yourself it is hard to be objective. Also, it is difficult to design a research project so that the research is representative of the groups you want to include. Market analysis can be used to evaluate everything from the image people have of an organization to why brand X is selling so well.

APPLYING INFORMATION YOU'VE GATHERED

Businesses that reach targeted niches through effective positioning often incorporate a "free form" marketing perspective. Particularly for consumer markets, this involves taking a long and protracted look at the research and data gathered, and then employing innovative ways to capture the attention of targeted niches based on the predictable course of their day, week, month, etc.; based on the hardship, struggles, stresses, and strains they encounter; based on the time pressure, social pressures, family pressures, and economic pressures that confront them; and on any other identifiable factor which translates into a need.

The consumption of goods and services can often follow a pattern that is the guide to customers' "rights of passage." Tracing likely events in the course of the typical individual's life reveals the following "purchasing" occasions:

- Renting an apartment or buying a home
- Starting a new career or a new job
- Marriage, separation, or divorce
- Childbirth, rearing of children
- Illness, accident, continuing health needs
- Adult education, workshops, seminars
- Vacations, travel, leisure-time activities
- Relocation
- Children going to school
- Children's sports clubs and activities
- Graduation
- Anniversaries, reunions, periodic gatherings
- Empty nest, retirement, slowing down
- Dysfunctioning, death

Entire industries are created to accommodate the needs of large masses of people experiencing the same life-cycle-related needs. The current rise in diaper and day-care services, for example, mirrors "the baby echo"—baby boomers having children in large numbers. Similarly, the rise of home grocery deliveries and personal services reflects the growing number of two-income families (where husband and wife are both working) and the rise in the number of singles who have no "domestic" partners.

Another major framework for applying the "human element" to the data that you have generated on a particular market is to consider the psychological and emotional needs of your markets. Researchers tell us that common human desires for love, safety, shelter, security, and avoidance of pain are strong buying motivators. So too are guilt, anxiety, and fear. The need to keep up with the Joneses has probably never been more pronounced in our society than today. Market researchers and sociologists have found that among our outer-directed populations (see Chapter 2) the strong desire to convey the image of success, or at least of "making it," compels many people to make heavy investments in material goods.

Today, for many people what they buy is "who they are."

In our outer-directed society materialism is likely to remain strong well into the 1990s.

The Right Place before the Right Time

It is disconcerting to hear that in today's economy to be successful you have to be at the right place before the right time; yet this is becoming the reality. More and more, we are seeing the practice of "anticipatory" marketing, even on the small business level. National and multinational manufacturers and advertisers have long been in the practice of investing millions of dollars in a product or project before knowing whether the payoff will ever come.

On a smaller scale, advertising agencies and consultants routinely "buy into" contracts by as much as 20 percent before knowing whether they have a good chance at winning. In advertising, for example, countless labor hours and resources are consumed in the preparation stage just to make a presentation. The client then says "yea" or "nay," and the work will either pay off with a nice contract or will be written off as a loss.

I call this type of investment "running without the ball" because it is analogous to the good basketball player who positions himself to receive the quick pass for a lay-up.

Effective positioning requires some initial maneuvers that don't appear to contribute to overall prosperity!

One very successful international consultant whose small firm earns revenues in excess of $1 million per year observed that his "calculated buy-in" to help secure a new contract is often as much as 20 percent of the total face value of the contract. I have observed that entrepreneurs in other industries also had mentally preestablished the size and percentage of a calculated buy-in to secure a new product or to help secure their position. Most said that a risk of between 10 and 20 percent of the contract total is something that they have to live with, and often do.

Elements of the Right Place before the Right Time Thinking

The Ace-in-the-Hole Approach. Using this approach, let us say we have studied a particular market and have found that in several months product X will be in demand because of shortages of product Y. Your strategy would be to buy as much product X as possible, even though right now the market for it may be somewhat soft. The ace-in-the-hole approach requires a keen understanding of the needs of your targeted niche and sufficient capital for the acquisition of the goods and resources which you predict will grow in value. The ace-in-the-hole approach is not to be confused with speculation, because your ace in the hole will pay off or you can bail out and break even.

Ready, Fire, Aim. This approach requires that you constantly test the waters. Instead of developing a product or service (the ready stage), undertaking some test marketing (aiming), and then launching a full-scale campaign (firing), in the ready, fire, aim approach you accelerate the process by firing soon and then immediately making course corrections. This concept was popularized in Peters and Waterman's *In Search of Excellence*, but has historically been the modus operandi of many successful entrepreneurs.

The One-in-Ten Phenomenon. This approach, which could also be called one in five or one in fifteen (you pick the number), presumes that out of any given number of approaches to a market, only a very small number, but at least one, will pay off in a big way. Therefore one may presume that a series of failures, particularly when undertaking the right place before the right time thinking, is normal. The trick, then, is being able to move quickly as one approach proves to offer right place, right time benefits.

The need for right place before right time thinking mandates the death of sacred cows. What worked yesterday has less and less to do with what will work today and what will work tomorrow. In the 1990s, more than ever, "business as usual" may well mean "out of business."

PART TWO

POSITIONING APPROACHES

5

Advertising for Position

The best argument is that which seems merely an explanation.

DALE CARNEGIE

Much has been written about the use of advertising in developing a corporate or business image. For the purpose of position marketing, we will discuss selected elements of advertising that help to define, establish, and refine your advertising image within your desired target market. This chapter will examine:

☐ Why so few advertising messages ever get through to the desired targets

☐ Why all businesses must use an advertising agency

☐ How to evaluate and select an agency

☐ Using promotional publications to attract commercial buyers.

☐ Methods for determining your advertising budget

☐ Tips on placing an effective *Yellow Pages* ad

☐ Actual ads that help establish position

Each day, the targets you are seeking are exposed to thousands of messages from different sources. Through the processes known as selective exposure, selective attention, and selective retention, only a handful of messages ever actually get through. The people you wish to attract see or hear only a tiny portion of the messages to which they are exposed—selective exposure. Then only a small portion of those messages are actually given any attention—selective attention. Of the relatively few messages that receive selective attention, an even smaller number are processed and integrated by the brain with other information already stored for potential future action—selective retention. The art of producing advertisements that impact your target and maintain or enhance an effective image cannot be left to amateurs—including yourself.

ESSENTIAL FOR *ANY* SIZE BUSINESS— ADVERTISING AGENCIES

It is widely known that the advertising industry has grown into a lucrative, influential institution in our society. Scores of successful firms can be found in every city. Whether we like it or not, the ability to capture the attention of targets has grown more difficult. The risks in managing your own advertising program have become inordinate.

In the sophisticated marketing environment of the 1990s, even the smallest of enterprises will find it necessary to retain the services of a capable advertising agency. Developed by pros, advertising can enable you to attract new customer interest; regain former customers; position your company and its product or services; even reposition your competition, including their products and services. Advertising can enable you to stand apart from the crowd or discourage or scare away would-be competitors. Most important, advertising can create a climate of receptivity to what you are offering.

You can have strong opinions regarding how you wish to be perceived and presented, but these ideas must, of necessity, be turned over to an advertising professional who understands the nuances of advertising and its impact. Bob Battenfield,[1] owner of Bob Battenfield and Associates, Marketing, Advertising, and Public Relations, believes a "necessary evil of doing business is working with an advertising agency. At best, an ad agency is like a working partner, sharing your concerns and helping guide your growth and long-term success. At worst, the ad agency seems to lack an understanding of your product and service goals." Since the selection of and cooperation with a good agency is crucial to your positioning, let us first look at Battenfield's 10 steps for the evaluation and selection of an advertising agency.

1. No other currently competing accounts. In most situations, an agency will have only one client in a product category. There are some specialized agencies that do handle several accounts in a product category, such as hotels, restaurants, or computers. However, it is generally in your best interest not to have your ad agency working for your direct competitors.

2. Strong creative track record. The most visible output of an advertising agency is its finished creative work. Depending on your own needs, you will want to see what kind of advertising the agency has created for its other clients. For instance, if you need help with trade advertising or with audio/visual materials, you should ask about the *results* the agency has achieved in those areas—creative materials can win prizes from the advertising industry and not win customers for the client.

3. Strong collateral materials capability. Collateral materials are the brochures, product fliers, direct-mail sales aids, and counter displays that most advertisers find they need about two weeks into an ad campaign. They agree to the agency's advertisement and media schedule and then find, to their dismay, that their salespeople have no printed materials that relate to the new campaign, or that the retailer needs a display to better identify the product referred to in the advertisement.

There is more to advertising than just creating an ad. Usually you have to have something appropriate on the shelf to respond to those

[1] Bob Battenfield, Bob Battenfield & Associates, La Mesa, CA. Reprinted with permission.

new customer inquiries. You have to inform and motivate your salespeople, distributors, and retailers.

4. Broad media experience. Again, depending on your needs, you will want an agency that knows radio, television, or electronic trade journals. In addition to considering media experience, you might be able to eliminate some agencies by checking into their reputation for paying their bills on time. An agency with a cash-flow problem can create problems for you when you try to reach your customers through paid media advertising.

5. Market research experience. In today's marketplace, with the uncertainties of the future brought on by the world economic situation, you cannot afford to develop, manufacture, distribute, and hopefully sell a product without a foundation based on market research.

You should seek an agency that uses marketing research techniques to measure and evaluate your product's acceptance and potential as well as the effectiveness of the advertising program it would create for you. Look for an agency with a demonstrated capability to apply research findings to the advertising it does for its clients.

6. Account service depth. No agency will have a team of top-rated people sitting idly in the back room waiting for your account to walk in the front door. However, you should be wary of an agency that plans to hire all new people ("staff up") to service your account.

Most medium- to large-sized agencies will have a "new business team" of smooth-talking, entertaining senior people who attract new clients, make the presentation, and then turn the account over to junior people for the day-to-day activities. Be aware that this is likely to happen, and get to know the senior people well enough to set your demands before them directly, in order to obtain the results you expect.

7. Compatibility. If your company is conservative, you may find an agency of ex-rock singers incompatible. By the same token, if your operation is pretty basic, you may have difficulty working with an account executive who wears expensive suits and drives a Mercedes. You will work best with an agency that reflects your own attitudes and values.

8. Compensation systems. Agency compensation is becoming increasingly important. Many agencies set minima for fees or commissions. It simply is not profitable for them to service an account for less than a certain amount per month.

Commissions given by radio and television stations, and by most magazines, amount to at least 15 percent of the gross rate. Most agencies add 17.65 percent or more to advertising production costs. Other agencies do not charge commissions at all and work for a set fee instead. The fee is usually renegotiated every year.

9. *Readiness to work.* How quickly could the agency "come up to speed" on your account? You should have an idea of how soon you need the agency's output. Obviously, it needs some time to learn your business. Also, it will likely need to hire and possibly train a few people. But in making your final decision, you may find that one agency appears to be "more ready" than another, and that may be important if you need a quick strike.

10. *Speculative presentations.* Big advertisers with multimillion-dollar accounts can ask an advertising agency to invest its own time, talent, and money in developing creative concepts, marketing strategies, research plans, and media schedules to "show what it would do" if it were awarded the account. It is actually unfair for smaller advertisers to ask small- and medium-sized agencies to develop speculative presentations.

In your initial review of potential agencies, you should ask to see their work for other clients. Transfer those ideas to your own product line and market situation. Finally, Battenfield advises that if you are unable to make a decision without asking for the finalists to make a creative presentation, develop an agreement that compensates them for at least their out-of-pocket expenses.

THE HIGHEST PRINCIPLES OF ADVERTISING

The creative code of the American Association of Advertising Agencies (AAAA) conveys standards of professionalism to which the industry itself strives to have all its members adhere (Figure 3). Not coincidentally, this code serves as an excellent set of principles by which to develop your own advertising messages. By following the code, you enhance your marketing position from the standpoint that you will never knowingly deceive a customer and you will be offering exactly what you are claiming to offer.

Despite your best intentions and those of your advertising agent, however, the chances are high that on occasion your printed advertisement

CREATIVE CODE

American Association of Advertising Agencies

The members of the American Association of Advertising Agencies recognize:

1. That advertising bears a dual responsibility in the American economic system and way of life.

To the public it is a primary way of knowing about the goods and services which are the products of American free enterprise, goods and services which can be freely chosen to suit the desires and needs of the individual. The public is entitled to expect that advertising will be reliable in content and honest in presentation.

To the advertiser it is a primary way of persuading people to buy his goods or services, within the framework of a highly competitive economic system. He is entitled to regard advertising as a dynamic means of building his business and his profits.

2. That advertising enjoys a particularly intimate relationship to the American family. It enters the home as an integral part of television and radio programs, to speak to the individual and often to the entire family. It shares the pages of favorite newspapers and magazines. It presents itself to travelers and to readers of the daily mails. In all these forms, it bears a special responsibility to respect the tastes and self-interest of the public.

3. That advertising is directed to sizable groups or to the public at large, which is made up of many interests and many tastes. As is the case with all public enterprises, ranging from sports to education and even to religion, it is almost impossible to speak without finding someone in disagreement. Nonetheless, advertising people recognize their obligation to operate within the traditional American limitations: to serve the interests of the majority and to respect the rights of the minority.

Therefore we, the members of the American Association of Advertising Agencies, in addition to supporting and obeying the laws and legal regulations pertaining to advertising, undertake to extend and broaden the application of high ethical standards. Specifically, we will not knowingly produce advertising which contains:

a. False or misleading statements or exaggerations, visual or verbal.

b. Testimonials which do not reflect the real choice of a competent witness.

c. Price claims which are misleading.

d. Comparisons which unfairly disparage a competitive product or service.

e. Claims insufficiently supported, or which distort the true meaning or practicable application of statements made by professional or scientific authority.

f. Statements, suggestions or pictures offensive to public decency.

We recognize that there are areas which are subject to honestly different interpretations and judgment. Taste is subjective and may even vary from time to time as well as from individual to individual. Frequency of seeing or hearing advertising messages will necessarily vary greatly from person to person.

However, we agree not to recommend to an advertiser and to discourage the use of advertising which is in poor or questionable taste or which is deliberately irritating through content, presentation or excessive repetition.

Clear and willful violations of this Code shall be referred to the Board of Directors of the American Association of Advertising Agencies for appropriate action, including possible annulment of membership as provided in Article IV, Section 5, of the Constitution and By-Laws.

Conscientious adherence to the letter and the spirit of this Code will strengthen advertising and the free enterprise system of which it is part.   *Adopted April 26, 1962*

Endorsed by

Advertising Association of the West, Advertising Federation of America, Agricultural Publishers Association, Associated Business Publications, Association of Industrial Advertisers, Association of National Advertisers, Magazine Publishers Association, National Business Publications, Newspaper Advertising Executives Association, Radio Code Review Board (National Association of Broadcasters), Station Representatives Association, TV Code Review Board (NAB)

Figure 3. Creative Code of the American Association of Advertising Agencies, 666 Third Avenue, New York. (Reprinted with permission.)

will not be understood. A study conducted by the AEF Corporation revealed that, on the average, a single reading of one magazine communication resulted in 63 percent of correct answers to the questions on its meaning. 37 percent of written communications were either misunderstood or totally lost to readers. According to Alfred J. Seman, chairman, "21 percent of the meanings were clearly misunderstood, and 16 percent of the respondents answered 'don't know.'"

DETERMINING YOUR ADVERTISING BUDGET

Though the agency you select will have some specific numbers in mind, determining how much you should spend on advertising is never a clearcut decision. *The Business Report*, published in Monterey, California, says that "deciding how much to spend on advertising is an uncertain business at best, even for those with experience." They outline six different methods for determining advertising expenditures.

1. Under the *percentage method*, the advertising budget is set as a percentage of sales—either past, future, or combined past and future. This is a popular method as it is defendable by management. Because the overall advertising budget is fixed, however, dollars can be taken away from the most profitable products (those having the highest rate of return from advertising). Setting the advertising budget by sales also assumes that sales are the cause of advertising rather than the reverse. Further drawbacks include an inability to accommodate changes in market conditions, competitive situations, and media costs.

2. The *competitive method* sets advertising expenditures in relationship to competitors' advertising budgets. Companies use this method in an attempt not to spend more than the competition. The competition, however, is always setting the pace. A company that just reacts ignores its own competitive strengths and does not take into account its real needs. Companies also compete in several product categories and industries, all of which have different rates of sales growth. Similarly, not all industries have the same advertising growth rates.

3. The *fixed-sum method* sets the advertising budget using quantity times a monetary unit. This method is most commonly used by companies where products are well established or with small companies holding a

specialized segment of a market. The budget is normally higher when compared to other methods, but often ignores appropriations on a product-by-product or territory-by-territory basis, or other market differences.

4. The *affordable method* funds advertising only after all the company's other expenses are budgeted. It offers close control of expenditures so the company's cash flow is not drained. This method, however, disregards the relationship between advertising costs and advertising effects.

5. The *profit margin method* can produce an advertising budget two different ways: (1) by using gross profit (sales less cost of goods) and (2) by using gross margin (gross profit divided by sales). The gross profit way is considered an earning maintenance strategy. The budget is created by multiplying the previous year's gross profit by the average ratio of advertising to gross profit in the industry. The gross margin variation pursues an investment matching strategy based on potential gross profits. The company's projected sales are multiplied by the gross margin which is then multiplied by the average advertising-to-profit ratio in the industry.

6. The *budget by objective method* sets specific advertising objectives, plans activities to meet them, and estimates the cost of performing these tasks. The total sum of these activities becomes the advertising expenditure level. This approach is considered the best because it is most likely to put advertising dollars to work where they will do the most good. Objectives, however, must be realistic, and it is difficult to calculate costs accurately. Too often the budget ends up being based on some percentage.

The *Business Report* also suggests these advertising rules of thumb:

- For every four dollars spent to buy space or time, one dollar is spent to produce the advertising.
- The advertising budget is not a luxury. Once set, an advertising fund should not be used to make up for other budget shortfalls.
- Companies should worry as much about underspending as about overspending. Overspending is usually less of a threat to a company, as it may produce higher sales and yield a more advantageous competitive position.

- During periods of inflation, the advertising budget should be increased as a company's product prices increase.

- The rate of sales change is compared to the rate of change in the advertising spending. Company results are measured using historical data on the product, the market, and the competitor's activities.

- Campaigns are changed as they wear out. Companies increase their rate of return on advertising by putting advertising dollars into new, creative ideas.

DECIDING TO CHANGE AGENCIES?

What if you already have an agency and believe it is time to make a change? Battenfield suggests four steps to help you think through this decision.

1. Define the problem. You and your agency are not getting along. Is it a problem of communications? Examine the channels. Check personalities. Lack of response? What about fuzzy direction? Falling short on the results? How realistic are your goals? Make sure the problem has been defined and that your own house is in order.

2. Allow the incumbent agency to adjust. Often the client–agency relationship can be helped by a change of personalities in the account team, a fresh new approach by a new account executive, or new creative talent. No matter how exciting the product line is, agency people can "burn out" or grow stale.

3. Allow time for a full review. Realize that if you do decide to change agencies, you will lose momentum in the process. You will probably not want to continue to spend money on the old agency's campaign, and the new agency will need time to develop and place a new campaign. Your product will be "out of the market" in the interim. You may lose market share, so do not make a hasty decision. Allow time for a full review of the problem with your incumbent agency.

4. Responsibility and authority. If you are the president of your company, you probably have the responsibility and the authority to make the decision to change agencies, or to initiate a new agency search. If you are the marketing manager or the sales director, you may have the responsibility of working with the agency, but actually lack the authority to carry out a termination. A written presentation, perhaps following your outline, can stregthen your argument to top management. It is wise to check the contractual relationship between your firm and the agency to determine who has the authority to terminate the relationship before you stick your neck out too far.

ATTRACTING THE COMMERCIAL BUYER

If you are marketing to other businesses, as opposed to to consumers, your advertising image is no less important, though it may take other forms. Compared to consumer products, business products and services are "more complex and require a relatively lengthy promotional message to convey adequate information for prospects to make a buying decision," according to James V. Laabs,[2] managing partner, Douglas & Laabs Associates.

Advertising specialist Robert Bly says that all companies large and small need some kind of printed sales literature because industrial buyers "insist on seeing product literature before they will put a manufacturer on their list of approved vendors." Bly notes that your prospects ask for sales literature, your sales people want it, your competitors have it, and if you sell through manufacturing reps you will also have to have it.

Laabs believes that although they have a larger volume of information to communicate, most business-to-business marketers, are armed with small promotional budgets compared with their consumer marketing counterparts.

"A strong, but underused tool for business-to-business marketers," say Laabs, writing in *Marketing News*, "is the promotional publication. With a well-planned publication, marketers with smaller budgets can effectively communicate a larger volume of information than with traditional advertising media."

Using an editorial-type format for promotional communications is not a new idea. "Several well-known advertising authorities have been long-

---

[2] James Laabs, "Promotional Publications Can Be Valuable Business to Business Tool," *Marketing News*, November 7, 1987.

time proponents of editorial formats for display advertising," says Laabs.
"An effective promotional publication, however, must go much further
than looking like editorial matter. It must be editorial material, containing
information that readers do not perceive as advertising, but as useful
and worthwhile reading."

The material also must educate prospects about key selling points of
the product or service, so that the reader benefits from the information
while the marketer communicates a sales message. Laabs says, "Business-
to-business marketers find that publications offer several major advantages," including:

1. *Promotional publications overcome advertising clutter.* As we have
seen, the average American is exposed to far too many advertising messages. Even direct mail has become a cluttered medium. A survey in
Direct Marketing News reported that the typical executive receives 44.5
pieces of unsolicited mail every week. As a result of exposure to this
tremendous volume of advertising, most people develop a mental system
(selective attention, exposure, and retention) to screen out all but a
small percentage of advertising messages. Promotional publications
overcome these psychological defenses by combining sales messages
with relevant information. Although people read because of the information
value of the publication, they are exposed simultaneously to promotional
messages.

2. *Promotional publications help establish credibility and Expertise.* For targets such as technical product managers, hospitals, medical
groups, and accounting firms, promotional publications help establish
an image of credibility and expertise.

> **By providing helpful information, the publication's sender is positioned
> in the reader's mind as an expert.**

3. *Publications are helpful in cross selling.* Many organizations are
surprised to learn that their clients or customers are not aware of the
full scope of products they offer. Present customers or clients are the
strongest potential buyers, and a promotional publication educates them
about other offerings in a professional, nonoffensive manner. Although
such a publication is well suited for manufacturers, catalogers and other

product-oriented businesses as well as professional services can also use it profitably.

YELLOW PAGES ADVERTISEMENTS

Although *Yellow Pages* advertising has long been a mainstay among businesses, and many clients and customers first become acquainted with your business through the *Yellow Pages*, the task of producing a quality ad that positions you appropriately is not easy. In my book *Marketing on a Shoestring* I offer a long and extended chapter on proper telephone and *Yellow Pages* advertising. Here are a few highlights, specifically in regard to position marketing.

A Whirlpool Corporation study showed that, next to the recommendations of family and friends, people most often turn to the *Yellow Pages* when they seek information on where to find the products and services they have already decided they need. More than 90 percent of adults use *Yellow Pages* directories for a total of four billion references each year.

Yellow Pages are directional media, showing people where to buy once they have already made the decision. Your basic decisions include:

• Whether to advertise in the *Yellow Pages*
• What heading(s) to place the ad under
• How large an ad to run
• What layout to use

With the increased number of directories available in many markets, a result of the divestiture ruling, advertisers also must choose which directory to use.

Your *Yellow Pages* publisher or sales representative should be able to give you usage data for the directory. Remember to ask about the type of distribution system the publisher uses. Do they mail copies or deliver door to door? Do they give businesses one copy for each telephone on the premises? Also, where are your competitors advertising? Have they been long-term users of that directory? If so, it is a good bet they are getting results.

An often forgotten essential in planning a *Yellow Pages* advertisement is to keep in mind the purpose, or purposes, of the ad. How do you want to be positioned? Do you want the ad to help you distinguish yourself from the competition? Do you want it to announce the availability of certain products or types of services that are not available elsewhere in your general area?

Here are some dos and don'ts from the American Association of Yellow Pages Publishers when establishing your *Yellow Pages* advertisement:

DO:

- Think from the reader's point of view. For your business, does the customer need more than just the telephone number?
- Include hours of operation, lines carried, and your location.
- Make it easy for the reader to find you. A local landmark may help: "One block west of the Palace Movie Theater."
- Distinguish your business from the competition. Are your years in business important to customers?
- Keep the ad clean and simple.

DON'T:

- Use the company name as the heading unless it is descriptive.
- Use the company name as the heading unless it is descriptive.
- Use more than two different typefaces.
- Use detailed line drawings.

USING REAL PEOPLE

One of the emerging trends in the design and production of advertisements in general is the use of "real people." Many studies indicate that there is little reason to continue to feel compelled to exhibit only the young or very attractive in advertisements for the majority of products and services being offered. Despite America's obsession with image, the reality is that most people are not glamorous.

One advertiser found that using a beautiful woman to sell coffee did not produce the desired effect. Others have found that because the young and beautiful and Main Street-type characters have been used so often within ads, they lose the ability to gain attention. People who are just ordinary or even unusual can command more attention. Corporations such as Westin and Woolco have achieved significant results using people who are not particularly remarkable in any way.

Also consider the demographics—ours is a nation that is aging. The median age is well over 30 and rising. Minority groups continue to gain in overall percentage in the population. Over 20 million people are physically disadvantaged in some way. To be sure, the young and the beautiful will always be in demand among advertisers. However, a more flexible, diversified use of people "types" in your ads will help establish your position in a very competitive business environment.

NOVELTY IS STILL THE SPICE OF LIFE

It must have been pleasantly shocking and somewhat amusing for the 1,000,000 *Newsweek* magazine readers who opened the pre-Christmas issue and were serenaded by tiny, penny versions of "Santa Claus Is Coming to Town" and "Jingle Bells." That is the strategy taken by Absolut Vodka to capture the imagination or attention of the targeted readership.

Novelty, the spice of life, is also the spice of advertising for strategic position. In a recent issue of *Newsweek*, Toyota Motor Sales USA included a cardboard 3-D viewfinder in the magazine to promote the Toyota Corolla. In the spirit of innovation, Estée Lauder and Revlon provided eye shadow and blusher minisamples as part of advertisements in popular women's magazines. Years ago, four-inch 45-rpm records adorned the pages of some magazines and were particularly popular with children.

To be sure, this sort of advertising can be expensive. But it prompts us all to think—what can we do on not so grand a scale that has a similar impact? For example, I am a member of the National Speakers Association headquartered in Phoenix, Arizona. To remind me to attend their annual winter workshop, I received the following card in the mail (Figure 4):

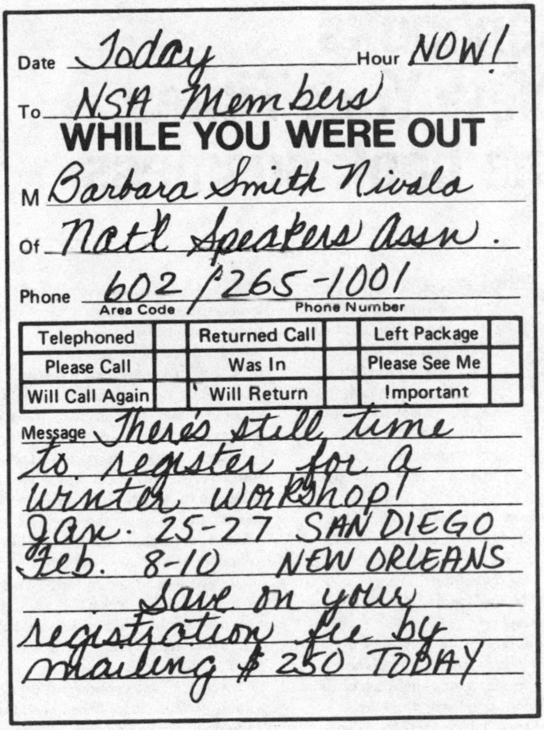
Date Today Hour NOW!
To NSA Members
WHILE YOU WERE OUT
M Barbara Smith Nivala
Of Natl Speakers Assn.
Phone 602 / 265-1001
Area Code Phone Number

Telephoned		Returned Call		Left Package	
Please Call		Was In		Please See Me	
Will Call Again		Will Return		Important	

Message There's still time to register for a winter workshop! Jan. 25-27 SAN DIEGO Feb. 8-10 NEW ORLEANS Save on your registration fee by mailing $250 TODAY

Figure 4. While you were out. National Speakers Association, 3877 North 7th Street, Phoenix, AZ. (Reprinted with permission.)

I have belonged to many associations over the years and have attended many conventions. Each month I receive dozens of advertising fliers and convention kits urging me to attend conventions. This card, however, is the only memorable one.

EXAMPLES OF ADS THAT HELP ESTABLISH POSITION

The following are examples of how corporate image and advertising image are nurtured through paid advertisements.

The first is in the form of a letter from Harry Hoffman, president and CEO of Waldenbooks (Figure 5). This message appeared in *Publisher's Weekly* and was directed toward the entire publishing industry, including book and magazine publishers, distributors, book sellers, and book sup-

Waldenbooks, The New York Times, and the book business.

On November 9, 1986, The New York Times Magazine published an article entitled "The Supermarketer of Books". The reader of this article might reasonably conclude that Waldenbooks' ambition is to dominate both the bookselling and publishing industries. An ambition characterized by arrogance, fired by greed, and indifference to the product it sells.

Accepting the increasingly inimical attitude of the press toward business, and ignoring its inaccuracies, this article's staggering failure to capture the reason for Waldenbooks' success, the spirit of its people, and its contribution to the bookselling and publishing industries demands a response.

Waldenbooks is the world's leading bookseller. It has become the leader by changing the face of the industry. This oftentimes meant attacking established attitudes and practices, in an industry with a great many established traditions. It has sometimes meant working against these traditions, frequently a requirement of progress. Our success can be attributed, in the main, to two factors: the quality of our people, and never forgetting to listen to our customers.

From these two factors a management style developed at Waldenbooks. A style characterized, not by greed or arrogance, but by creativeness and innovativeness. Over the years it has forged a collective purpose among Waldenbooks' employees. There is a pride among our employees that is unique to the industry. A pride that is tempered by a strong sense of fairness, to our customers and to the industry. It is a management practical enough to be concerned about profit, but that is not our only concern.

Waldenbooks is conscious of its responsibility to all its constituencies: customers, employees, suppliers, the communities we operate in and society at large. In July of this year we sponsored a nationwide "banned books" campaign to raise awareness of First Amendment rights, at a time when those rights were coming under increasing pressure. We sponsor children's reading hours, fund raising on behalf of Reading is Fundamental, music programs and other social and cultural causes. We encourage and fund participation by Waldenbooks' people in the social life of the communities in which they live.

We intend to maintain our leadership position. We will continue to show a willingness to try new things, to innovate to meet the demands of the marketplace. We will continue to seek a closer working relationship with the publishing industry, something we believe to be to our mutual benefit. And we will continue to listen to our customers.

Above all, we will continue to nurture the collective purpose of Waldenbooks' employees. Just as with all of our past triumphs, any future success we may enjoy will come from this remarkable group of people.

Harry Hoffman

Harry Hoffman
President & CEO
Waldenbooks

Figure 5. Letter from Harry Hoffman. Waldenbooks, 201 High Ridge Road, Stamford, CT. (Reprinted with permission.)

pliers. In one fell swoop, Hoffman and Waldenbooks were able to convey the message that the company intends to maintain its leadership position. Note the key paragraph:

> *We intend to maintain our leadership position. We will continue to show a willingness to try new things, to innovate to meet the demands of the marketplace. We will continue to seek a closer working relationship with the publishing industry, something we believe to be to our mutual benefit. And we will continue to listen to our customers.*

The Bekins advertisement in Figure 6 is so skillfully crafted that one need not read the copy to understand why Bekins is a "better buy for your moving dollar" than others. The advertisement specifically discusses Bekins's capabilities in arranging moves to accommodate trade shows and exhibitions. The man on the left, quite obviously not an employee of Bekins, is out of shape, a bit sloppy, and perhaps does not exhibit the right attitude. The man on the right is as professional a mover as you could ask for. His shirt is immaculately pressed. He wears a bow tie. The symbol of Bekins Van Lines is clearly displayed. His clipboard is in hand. He is lean, but muscular.

This ad helps Bekins to position itself as a highly professional, responsive, confident moving system. You can rely on them to handle your high-technology equipment, because they obviously know what they are doing.

The one-page corporate chart of Figure 7, part of the overall advertising and promotional materials of Asija Associates, also accomplishes its mission. Pal Asija is an independent entrepreneur who provides custom training, technology transfer, software protection, and advice on software patents, computer law, and personal performance. Asija's corporate chart, intended to amuse, also conveys that he is a solo entrepreneur offering a wide variety of services, and that he is a pleasant individual with whom to work.

OUTDOOR VISIBILITY—BILLBOARDS AND SIGNS

Depending on your type of business, billboards, posters, and point of activity displays (such as a photo collage of customers) can be effective vehicles for conveying a message. Slogans and logos are particularly appropriate for billboards and posters since the message must be comprehended quickly.

The advantages and disadvantages of these transmission methods, as discussed in *Marketing for Public and Nonprofit Managers*, by Christopher H. Lovelock and Charles B. Weinberg, are summarized below.

[3] Christopher H. Lovelock and Charles B. Weinberg. *Marketing for Public and Nonprofit Managers*. Redwood City, CA: Scientific Press, 2nd ed., 1989.

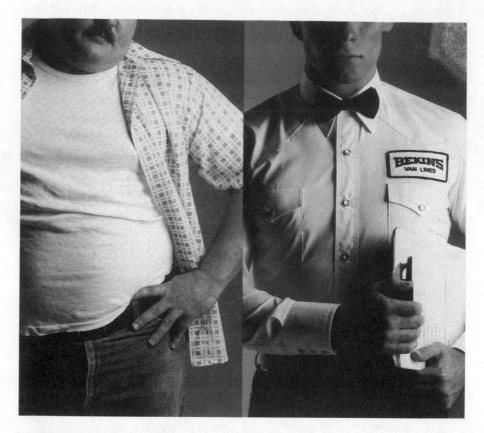

Which outfit would you trust to move your exhibit?

You wouldn't choose a carrier strictly on the appearance of its people. Yet, it is a good indication of a carrier's attitude toward service, its expectations of its people and its understanding of your needs.

At Bekins we do everything possible to put your mind at ease. Neat, uniformed trade show handlers are just the beginning.

Only experienced display and exhibit specialists get to wear the Bekins uniform. They're professionals who understand the concerns, constraints and logistics involved in managing an exhibit.

Bekins' trade show experts will handle the entire job. They'll arrange scheduling, pick-up and delivery, storage between shows, and help you comply with local regulations and drayage rules anywhere in the U.S. or the world.

Our people will also be on the site to supervise. And they'll stay there until you're satisfied.

Even our trade show fleet is different. It's used exclusively for transporting exhibits and displays, unlike most other carriers.

Bekins' trade show experts can also help you plan an entire year's program in advance, including scheduling and a firm annual budget. We'll even custom engineer a system to meet your specific needs.

There are a lot more reasons why Bekins looks better than all other carriers, and why we should be your choice. Let us custom design a proposal for you. Send for our free trade show Logistics Analysis Kit. Write: Bekins Trade Show Service, High Technologies Division, P.O. Box 109, La Grange, IL 60525. Or call toll free: **1-800-451-3989.** In Illinois: **1-312-547-3113.**

High Technologies Division
Reader Service #163

Figure 6. Bekins' advertisement. Bekins Van Lines Co., Hillside, IL. (Reprinted with permission.)

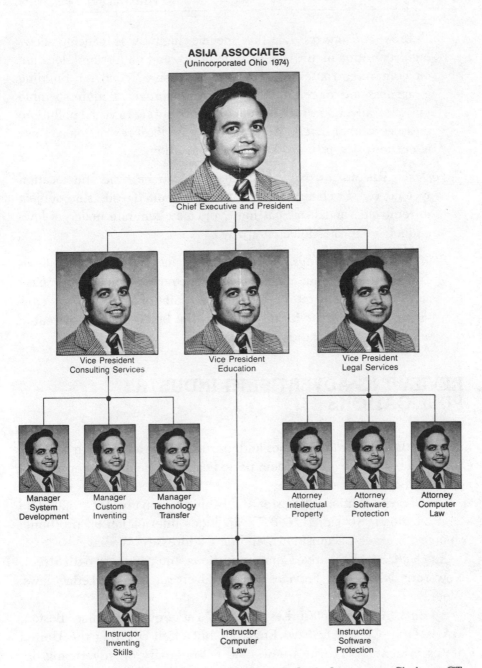

ASIJA ASSOCIATES
(Unincorporated Ohio 1974)

Chief Executive and President

Vice President
Consulting Services

Vice President
Education

Vice President
Legal Services

Manager
System
Development

Manager
Custom
Inventing

Manager
Technology
Transfer

Attorney
Intellectual
Property

Attorney
Software
Protection

Attorney
Computer
Law

Instructor
Inventing
Skills

Instructor
Computer
Law

Instructor
Software
Protection

Figure 7. Corporate chart of Asija Associates. Asija Associates, Shelton, CT. (Reprinted with permission.)

Billboards. Advantages: Location specific; highway sequencing allows high repetition of message; easy to notice and understand; location on commuter routes ensures high exposure; good for building awareness and for reinforcement. *Disadvantages*: Requires simple message; advertiser may be seen as contributing to visual pollution; message cannot be clipped; there may be local restrictions on use of outdoor ads in the most desirable locations.

Posters. Advantages: No media charges; can be time and location specific; very low budget. *Disadvantages*: Limited readership; subject to removal, vandalism, pasting over; may generate image of low-budget, nonprofessional company.

Point of Activity Displays. Advantages: Serves as direct action follow-through to preselling in mass media; encourages impulse purchase and behavior; generates excitement at point of activity. *Disadvantages*: Must compete for display; may not be possible to guarantee scheduling and duration of display.

REVIEWING ADVERTISING INDUSTRY PUBLICATIONS

Some of the standard magazines and journals of the advertising industry are listed below. Reviewing them periodically can help you keep abreast of advertising innovations,

Ad Change (National Register Publishing Company, Inc., 5201 Old Orchard Road, Skokie, IL 60077). Includes information on personnel changes, mergers, acquisitions, and new addresses. Weekly.

Ad Day/USA (Executive Communications, Inc., 400 East 54th Street, New York, NY 10022). Provides current advertising and marketing news. Weekly.

Ad East (Ad East Enterprises, Inc., 907 Park Square Building, Boston, MA 02116). Geared to New England, but often covering the United States in general. Provides news and commentary on advertising developments. Monthly.

Advertising Age (Crain Communications, Inc., 740 Rush Street, Chicago, IL 60611). Offers news of the advertising world, major advertising events, articles by leaders in the field, statistics, special features, and illustrations. Also publishes several annual surveys and reports on advertising agencies, expenditures, sales budgets, and markets. Weekly.

Advertising Age/Europe (Crain Communications, Inc., 740 Rush Street, Chicago, IL 60611). The European version, published 10 times per year.

Advertising Techniques (ADA Publishing, Inc., 10 East 39th Street, New York, NY 10016). Focuses on specific techniques of successful ad campaigns. Monthly.

Adweek (A/S/M Communications, Inc., 820 Second Avenue, New York, NY 10017). Regional editions: East, Southeast, Midwest, Southwest, and West. Each edition covers advertising, public relations, and media news. Offers a blend of national and local information. Eight special reports are published each year: creativity, consumer magazines, newspapers, business-to-business advertising, salary survey, market watch, broadcasting, and cable-video. Also, four bonus directories are published for regional subscribers: agency billings, client budgets, media by market, and creative services. Weekly.

Agency Directory (Adweek, 514 Shatto Place, Los Angeles, CA 90040). A special publication of *Adweek* magazine. Separate directories for the different regions of the country. Provides information on leading advertising agencies, media buying services, management, annual billings, and clients. Annual.

Marketing & Media Decisions (1140 Avenue of the Americas, New York, NY 10017). Covers the advertising world in depth, with stories about trends, people, strategies, campaigns, case histories, and developments in all media. Designed specifically for the large national advertisers and their agencies, with a controlled circulation. Publishes an annual directory of the top 200 brands. Monthly.

Media Market Guide (322 East 50th Street, New York, NY 10022). Highlights the availability, costs, and coverages of the major media opportunities. Offers cost/audience ratios for broadcast media, updates the cost and household coverage results for newspapers, and combines them in summary fashion for daily and weekend papers. Also includes data on city magazines and outdoor and transit media. Quarterly.

Putting the Squeeze on Olympic Hopefuls

You may not like it, and I certainly don't, but "the right time before the right place" thinking has already prompted national advertisers to seek endorsements from Olympic athletes before they have actually won gold medals.

Three days after figure skater Brian Boitano won a gold medal for the United States in the 1988 Winter Olympics at Calgary, Disneyland featured an advertisement where a gleeful Boitano announced backstage, "I am going to Disneyland!"

Disney had actually set up the endorsement long before Boitano won the medal. Disney had also made deals with other Olympic athletes in case they, too, were able to win a gold medal. Did the pressure of a multiple-figure contract dangling before her eyes cause skater Debi Thomas to falter? We will never know. But for Disneyland, Brian Boitano's potential represented the right person just before the right time.

6

Public Relations and Promotion for Positioning

Never argue with people who buy
ink by the gallon.

TOMMY LaSORDA

One of the primary modes by which corporations communicate their activities and interests to their public is through public relations. "Public relations is the conscious effort to motivate or influence people, primarily through acceptable performance and two-way communication, to think well of an organization, to respect it, to support it and to stick with it through trial and trouble," according to Dr. Michael V. Reagen, County Administrator of Human Services in Onandaga County, New York.

In this chapter we will examine the following:

☐ The objectives of good public relations

☐ Why you are what they read

☐ Choosing a public relations agency

☐ Promotion in magazines, journals, and newsletters

☐ Establishing good media relations

Anthony M. Franco, former president of the Public Relations Society of America, observes that all organizations have a posture, culture, or mission that needs to be shown. "Public relations is closing the gap between what you think you are and what the public thinks you are. Companies or organizations that communicate properly succeed. Those that don't, fail."

The objectives of a good public relations campaign are to:

• Help establish a position in the minds of those you wish to serve

• Keep customers aware of existing products and services

• Build awareness for new products or services

• Overcome customer indifference or confusion

• Convey how a company's efforts benefit the community

EFFECTIVE PUBLIC RELATIONS DURING THE WORST OF TIMES

The Johnson & Johnson Company is regarded as a corporate leader in the area of community responsibility. The company was besieged with problems several years ago when the Tylenol crisis became a national headline. Always a class act, Johnson & Johnson swiftly and boldly removed all Tylenol from the shelves across America, even though there was a very high probability that the product tampering was local, confined, and done by an outsider. Time proved them to be not at fault, but the public never forgot how this respected company reacted in an emergency.

Within three days of "Black Monday," October 19, 1987, when the stock market dropped by a record 500 points, Merrill Lynch was on the television airways with commercials designed to alleviate anxiety among their client investors. The fact that a disgruntled investor entered a branch of the brokerage house in Florida and shot and killed the financial advisor does not diminish the astuteness of the company's advertising and public relations directors. Polls three months following the crash indicated that fewer than 2 percent of all investors considered the crash to be significant and fewer than 12 percent had sold stock as a result of the crash.

Even the Lowly Corn Chip Can Be Used to Generate Effective PR

"Doritos," a corn chip produced by Frito-Lay, sported packaging which illustrated the company's desire to support the "Just Say No" to drugs program across America. Figure 8 shows the company's program to pledge up to $300,000 to the antidrug "Just Say No" program. This is another example of a company using a product, in this case just a corn chip, to create strong positive customer and community relations.

Not Just for the Giants

In an ever-tightening economy, the entrepreneur, too, must make extended efforts to achieve the proper image. "A sound public relations program," according to public relations practitioner Larry Kim Garvey, "often thought of as something only the giant corporations can afford, can give the added strength needed for the entrepreneurial business to become known and recognized by those people who use and need its product and services."

What are you projecting? Are you a local operation? Is your company's inventory more complete than that of the competition? Do you provide more dependable service? Is your staff better trained and equipped to serve the customer? Have you been in business longer than the competition? Garvey says that your firm's image should reflect something unique about your business, something that makes you stand out from the competition.

DORITOS® BRAND TORTILLA CHIPS
CHIP IN FOR "JUST SAY NO"

DORITOS® brand Tortilla Chips is proud to support The Just Say No Foundation. That's why we're making a donation to "Just Say No" when bags of DORITOS® brand Tortilla Chips are purchased between July 10th and August 6th (up to $300,000.00). But it takes more than money to create a drug-free America. It takes a commitment by you to be a good role model and help create a positive atmosphere.

That's why we're challenging you to chip in for "Just Say No." Young people look up to you as a role model. Here's a few ways you can help:

- Be the kind of friend you'd like to have.
- Let them know you don't approve of drugs.
- Talk to them about peer pressure — and teach them how to say No.
- Show them how to have fun and win acceptance without using drugs.

Another important way you can chip in for "Just Say No" is to become a Teen Leader in a "Just Say No" Club. For more information write:

"Just Say No" Teen Leader Program
1777 No. California Blvd., Suite 210,
Walnut Creek, CA 94596

Or call ⋯ ⋯ ⋯ ⋯. (California and Alaska call ⋯ ⋯ ⋯).

Together we can make it easier for everybody to — **"Just Say No" to drugs.**

Figure 8. Doritos Chips and "Just Say No." Frito-Lay, Inc., Plano, TX. (Reprinted with permission.)

PR AS A STRATEGIC WEAPON

"Successful public relations," according to George Haber,[1] director of business and development with G&R Associates, "unlike successful advertising, obtains media exposure for companies, their products or services, and their management for the cost of the PR development alone. Used properly," Haber observes, "it can be an extremely cost-effective marketing tool. Of course, it is not without drawbacks. While an advertising message can be controlled for the timing, placement, and size of its appearance, the public relations message cannot." Articles scheduled may be canceled, news releases may not be used, journalists may decide not to interview company management. "Nevertheless, in times of tightly controlled advertising budgets," he says, "PR can be an important productive addition to any company's total marketing program."

Four major components that make up the foundation of a successful PR program according to Haber include:

Press Releases. These are "news" oriented, usually run one or two pages, and have a *professional format* that enables the editor to determine quickly what the release is all about and whom he or she may contact for further information.

Feature Article Development. The feature article is longer than a press release and usually focuses on the user of the company's products rather than on the company itself. In addition, it constitutes a valuable marketing tool when it is obtained and distributed as a reprint.

Executive Statements. These are industry-oriented statements attributed to a company executive which help establish the executive as an authority and leader in his or her field. Meaningful and perceptive statements of this nature enable both the company and the executive to obtain visibility and prominence.

Special Events. These may include press conferences, trade shows, seminars, and other gatherings.

[1] George Haber. "PR, the Cornerstone of Your Business Image." *Connektions 50*, July 1983, p. 24.

CHOOSING A PR AGENCY

Although many firms today can provide service as both an advertising agency and a public relations firm, the functions are distinct enough to discuss how to choose a PR firm. Haber says, "Looking for a PR agency is a little like looking for a doctor or lawyer—but only a little. When you need a doctor, you usually take a recommendation from a friend or a referral from another doctor. You visit the doctor, receive treatment, look at the bill, gulp, and reach for your checkbook. "But," he says, "when you are looking after the health of your marketing program, it is not considered gauche to ask a prospective PR agency, 'Whatsitgonnacost?' and sit back, while the agency's representative comes up with a figure that will net a fair profit while not making you gasp and hustle her or him out of your office."

"Public relations being a somewhat vague art," he says, "you should, nevertheless, try to pin down what you will get for your monthly retainer fee." Typically, an agency's fee will cover the cost of meeting with the client, preparing a media mailing list, writing and disseminating news releases on a regular basis, generating story ideas to editors for the purpose of including the client as a major source for the story, suggesting and coordinating client participation in special events, preparing or editing public addresses, and rehearsing speakers.

"Providing for ongoing consultation on any public relations or marketing communications matter (with the agency leaving an after-office-hours telephone number for those weekend press inquiries) may also be included," says Haber. "The agency should provide the client with an activity report—once a month is best—describing what has been accomplished and what is ongoing."

When selecting a PR firm, Haber offers these guidelines:

1. Determine who will actually work on your account, not just who your contact with the firm will be. If your company manufactures electronic components, you will most likely be better served by an agency staffer who spent time as an editor of an electronics magazine that by a copywriter who specialized in cosmetic product releases.

2. Ask to see actual placements that agency staffers have obtained for clients, and make sure the kinds of media the agency seems to deal

with most often are the kinds of media that can do your business the most good. An impressive portfolio of placements in *The New York Times* and *Business Week* and regular appearances on the Carson show say nothing about the agency's ability to place a two-page technical feature on electronic warfare in *U.S. Naval Institute Proceedings*.

3. Ask to see a client list with names of specific companies, and find out how long these clients have been with the agency. That the agency has retained three clients since 1973 speaks better for the quality of its service than if it boasts 10 clients, none of whom appeared on the roster 18 months ago.

After hiring an agency, Haber advises not to expect results in two weeks. "Developing relationships with editors on specific topics related to the client's field; proposing story ideas to client management and 'selling' them to editors; researching, producing, and distributing news releases and monitoring their appearances in publications all over the country—these all take time. You should not have to wait six months for something to happen, but you will have to wait one or two months."

Once the firm is "on board," make them a real part of your company. "Tell your PR firm about contract awards, include them on the routing list for strategic plans, appraisals, reviews, and quarterly assessments," says Haber. "Don't let your PR firm find out about top management changes by reading 'Who's News' in *The Wall Street Journal*. Companies must realize that public relations agencies are only as good as the information they have to work with. If a strike is looming, if your leading product is being recalled, if your executive director is being indicted, put your PR firm in the loop. The firm may have been down this road before, and may be able to show you the detours and the best way around the potholes."

YOU ARE WHAT THEY READ

For the smaller enterprise, very often the image that you project is based on paper. Many of your potential customers will make a complete evaluation of your business based on what they read about you—your project literature, your advertising, and so forth. Not surprisingly, entrepreneurs increasingly view being written about or getting published in newspapers, magazines, and newsletters, or writing a book, as an appropriate and effective marketing vehicle for enhancing their business.

Getting published in today's media society means much more to authors than fees or kudos. An attractive reprint, from either a 2,000,000 circulation magazine or an 1800 circulation newsletter, is a powerful tool when used in combination with other strategies to influence targets. For example, an attorney who writes an article on wills and gets it published, regardless of the type of publication in which it appears, can use that article to generate new business more effectively than any brochure that explains the scope of his or her services in the area of wills. Similarly, most businesses can benefit by getting into print.

Many entrepreneurs believe that developing an "in print" image is important, but the majority are deficient. While getting into print generally is not perceived as mandatory for success, the most successful entrepreneurs among us, nevertheless, are skilled in this area.

WHY THE RIGHT PHOTOGRAPH IS WORTH MORE THAN A THOUSAND WORDS

Great photos can help your positioning efforts. Kevin E. Foley, president of KEF Media Associates, Inc., in Chicago, says, "A vibrant photograph in a newspaper's business section, an important trade journal, or a major news magazine can say much about a company's own vibrancy to customers, employees, and investors."

Ken Love, a freelance photographer, notes that "the news media, and in particular the publications read by those who can influence a company's growth, need good photos." Love places hundreds of pictures every year with wire services and they never tire of them.

What does Love photograph? R&D labs, assembly lines, production facilities, reception areas, inspection points, and other manufacturing or research areas; anything that can carry the underlying theme of quality. In addition, he also photographs, aerial views, supply areas, and quality control areas. Love's goal is to humanize the technology in a way that is "visually stimulating."

PUBLIC RELATIONS AND PROMOTION IN MAGAZINES, JOURNALS, AND NEWSLETTERS

To keep abreast of the latest in the field of public relations, here are some of the leading publications:

Publicity Break (Public Relations Aids, Inc., 330 West 34th Street, New York, NY 10001). A trade journal for publicists and PR executives; provides how-to-articles, case histories, agency and media news, and other items of interest. Bimonthly.

Public Relations Journal (Public Relations Society of America, 33 Irving Place, New York, NY 10003). Covers ideas, trends, and new techniques in use in both the management and the communications aspect of PR; includes book reviews. Monthly.

Public Relations Quarterly (44 West Market Street, Box 311, Rhinebeck, NY 12572). Written for PR executives; features articles written by practitioners and social scientists in the field; covers new research, education, trends, and publications of use in public relations. Quarterly.

Public Relations Review (Communication Research Associates, Inc., 10606 Mantz Road, Silver Spring, MD 20903). Provides articles on public relations and public relations research written for both practitioners and academics in the field; includes book reviews. Quarterly.

Jack O'Dwyer's PR Newsletter (J.R. O'Dwyer Company, Inc., 271 Madison Avenue, New York, NY 10016). Covers news of interest to the public relations industry, such as personnel and account changes, special events, and publications of interest to PR people. Weekly.

PR Aids' Party Line (Public Relations Aids, Inc., 330 West 34th Street, New York, NY 10001). A newsletter providing a weekly summary of what editors in magazine, TV, and radio media need in the way of feature and story material; reports on opportunities for the placement of publicity in these media. Weekly.

PR Reporter (PR Publishing Company, P.O. Box 600, Dudley House, Exeter, NH 03833). Includes information on issues and trends in public affairs, communications, and public relations, and provides case studies of PR events and programs; includes book reviews and special reports on new PR techniques. Weekly.

Public Relations News (127 East 80th Street, New York, NY 10021). Provides case studies of successful PR programs in business, industry, government, and other sectors, and includes news of personnel and account changes, awards and honors, book reviews, and PR trends and new techniques. Weekly.

MINICASE
GETTING INTO PRINT

Pick up the Sunday edition of your newspaper and flip through the magazine section. Then get a copy of the latest city magazine (the *Bostonian* in Boston, the *Washingtonian* in Washington, D.C., *D* in Dallas, *San Francisco* in San Francisco, and so forth) and peruse the table of contents. Or buy one or two of the area business publications serving your community.

Any issue of these publications is likely to contain an interview of a local entrepreneur. What you may not have known before is that *more than three-quarters of these stories are placed by public relations firms and who have been paid by the person whom the story is about.* Those interesting profiles you just happen to come across are part of a carefully designed program initiated and paid for by the entrepreneur, worked out months in advance with a public relations firm or agent.

The reason why it seems that everyone else is being covered by the press while you are not is that in the majority of cases, the people being written about are paying for it. How does this work? What is it worth? Suppose you build modular homes in the Atlanta, Georgia, area, and funds available through city and federal housing programs continue to be earmarked for traditional construction. One well-placed interview in the Sunday "Home" section of the local newspaper on the benefits offered to the community by modular homes is likely to command the attention of virtually every politician, developer, program coordinator, and anyone else concerned with local housing issues.

A Pittsburgh-based cosmetic surgeon wanted to increase his visibility in the community and thereby attract a continuing stream of patients. As a dramatic gesture, the surgeon, who already appeared to be much younger than his 50 years, announced he would undergo a "face lift" to demonstrate his commitment and belief in the service he was providing. Before and after the surgery he kept a daily diary and had "before" and "after" photos taken. A publicity agent was in on the promotion from the beginning and crafted an interesting, detailed account of the venture.

Within a few weeks following the operation, a major story about the surgeon appeared in one of the city's most prestigious monthly magazines, under the byline of the publicity agent.

To the average reader it would have appeared that the publication either contracted with the writer to produce this story or accepted the story over the transom. In either case one would assume that the writer was paid by the publication for this substantial work. However, magazine and newspaper publishers very often get their material for free because there are healthy numbers of people in their community who wish to be written about and who have the funds to commission an article.

In essence, the surgeon and the modular home builder are paying for advertisements. However, the ways in which their products or services are publicized do not appear as advertisements but rather as articles or items of community interest. Any public relations agent can tell you that an article about someone is far more influential than an ad taken out by that same person.

"But wait," you say, "isn't it much more costly and much more difficult to get an article written and placed than to simply take out an ad?" Not necessarily. The cost of getting an article written, which may span several pages and include photos, is likely to be far less than that of a single-page ad in the same publication. Clearly, the advance planning, coordination, and acceptance of the self-generated article require more effort than the mere placement of an advertisement, but it is a very sound investment. Indeed, one well-placed article in a prestigious or widely read publication can have a greater impact than an entire year's worth of advertisements.

Getting on the Front Cover

What about getting on the front cover? Understandably, the front cover costs more. A good public relations agent may get your mug on a prestigious front cover in stair-step fashion. For example, he or she may first have an article on you placed in a mediocre publication and use the reprint with a subsequent article to get on the cover of, or at least be one of the lead stories in, a more visible publication. He or she may then use that placement to buy your way onto the front cover of the publication you had targeted from the beginning. This strategy requires much more time and effort, and could end up rivaling the costs of a year's worth of advertisements in that same publication. But remember, the impact will still be far greater. What are the costs?

A large firm is likely to charge a minimum of $600 per day and to accept only jobs of a certain size. A seasoned public relations agent or publicist may ask for anything from $2000 to $4000 or more per month and sign you up for 30, 60, or 90 days' worth of services. However, a freelance public relations agent (or a marketing consultant with writing capabilities and far lower overhead) may charge only $300 to $600 per day and be able to complete the project for $800 to $1800. Again, this compares quite favorably to the costs of buying even one ad in the same publication, especially when considering the impact of the article versus that of the ad.

The next time you pick up your favorite area magazine, think for a second. Are the profile articles based on people who were so interesting or contributed so much to the community that the publication felt compelled to write about them? Or did those profiled arrange and pay for it?

Establishing Good Media Relations

Taking the time to plan your communications strategy and to establish good relationships with the press will prove invaluable in your positioning effort. For many businesses today, developing good press relations is not optional; in our media society it is something that businesses of all sizes must undertake. It helps to know the publisher or managing editor of the local newspaper, and the owners of the radio and television stations.

The individuals who are most important in your efforts to build a good public image are the news editors and working reporters. Help them, and you can usually count on cooperation in return. Make sure any reporter who covers your business has your business and home phone numbers. Give reporters the name and number of someone else to call when you are unavailable.

Avoiding communication with the press or public does not solve a problem, it merely puts it off until later. If your company has made a mistake, admit it to the press, emphasizing the lessons you have learned from the mistake. Ignoring an issue only leads to criticism and perhaps the irreplaceable loss of public trust. Christopher Lovelock says, "Never try to whitewash a problem with a public relations effort. People can recognize this."

Here are three tips for dealing with the press.

1. *When the news reporter cometh.* Be truthful and maintain integrity in dealing with the news media. When questions cannot be answered for legal reasons or because of uncertainty of the answer, this should be explained. Promise to get the answer promptly if it can legally be given. It is appropriate to ask reporters if they have spoken with others about the story they are working on.

2. *If your company is mentioned in the press*, don't complain about a story unless a serious error has been made. Call the reporter who handled the story, but do not go to the publishers unless it is absolutely necessary.

3. *Remember to say thank you.* It pays big dividends to let members of the media know you appreciate their efforts. If someone does a particularly good job of reporting, a simple thank-you note will be appreciated and remembered. When you are thanking a reporter, send a copy of your note to the editor or news director.

Cooperating with the Media

A battle was in the making. Reporters from the local paper were accusing JKL company officials of withholding information. JKL felt besieged and responded by stopping its usual flow of news releases. While the battle raged, employee morale plummeted, special projects were abandoned, and a general air of mistrust pervaded.

Company PQR, on the other hand, emphasizes a keen understanding of public reations. PQR realizes that cooperation with the press serves PQR's purpose, especially when times are tough. PQR's president holds regular press conferences and regularly issues news releases. The company regards communication with the press to be a joint effort.

These two examples point out that a company's position is best preserved or upheld when it cooperates with the press—not when it approaches the press as an enemy.

Executives of a social services organization wanted to improve communications by holding monthly meetings. The meetings were promoted extensively in the city newspaper. The meetings were held at night to make it easier for people who worked during the day to attend. Each meeting began with a 10-minute professionally produced slide show. These well-attended meetings lasted 90 minutes and received favorable press coverage. In addition to improving the communications link between the organization and its patrons, the organization received valuable input on several pressing service issues.

Working with the media is an idea whose time is here.

MINICASE
COINING YOUR OWN TERM

"Could you hand me the Scotch tape?" "Did you get a chance to Xerox that?" "I think I will Simonize my car this weekend."

Over the years, popular brand names and registered trademarks have made their way into our vocabulary. Until we reach the age of 10 or 12 many of us believe that the terms "tissue" and "Kleenex" are synonyms. Even when we buy a box of Dove tissues or Scottie tissues we are still likely to call them Kleenex tissues. If your product name is used so often that it becomes part of common vocabulary, you lose exclusive rights to the name. Until then, and it only happens infrequently, coining your terms and having them catch on is a PR masterstroke.

John Naisbitt was going to name his book *High Tech*, *High Touch*, but after several rounds with the publishers at Warner, settled on the name *Megatrends*. The book went on to sell 6,000,000 copies worldwide and literally changed Naisbitt's life.

How was the term derived? In the first few chapters of the book, Naisbitt used "megatrend" to describe trends, occurring nationally or globally and of huge proportion, for which he could find no other descriptive term. Warner Books, recognizing the marketing value of a coined term that conveyed instant meaning, chose it for the title.

A particularly popular method for coining your own term is to use acronyms. Light amplification by stimulated emission of radiation was dubbed "laser," just as "sonar" and "radar" before it are but acronyms of long, complicated names.

What product or service do you offer and how could it be named in a way that captures the imagination of the intended target while readily conveying meaning? One company literally coins terms for its clients' products and services. Finding the proper phrase, or coining the right term, is serious business.

What are the underlying principles in successfully coining your own term? It helps if you have an original product or service. You must create a term or phrase that is catchy and easy to remember, and that is associated with you or your venture. Also, the term should not conflict with or sound like anything else either currently in the language or in the marketplace.

A coined term can readily become your most valuable asset. In a world where people are bombarded by thousands of bits of information each day, a coined term could be exactly what the position-marketing doctor ordered.

DEVELOPING THE "OPEN LETTER"

Marily Mondejar is a successful fashion and image consultant and executive director of the Image Industry Council International based in San Francisco. Figure 9 shows Mondejar's "open letter" to Senator Paul Simon, which she reprinted in the council's newsletter. Whether or not the senator ever responded, in using such a tool, she positioned herself as a wardrobe authority willing to support (or eschew, we may infer) the dress of public figures.

Her letter reprint draws attention to her and her expertise. Its impact is several times that of a bylined article. Using Simon's picture is the crowning touch. She can now use reprints of this letter to hand to prospects and to gain an exposure by newspapers that see its value as a public interest piece.

WHEN YOU WANT TO INITIATE PR

The *Magazine Industry Marketplace* or *Bacon's Publicity Checker*, both available at most libraries, are useful for finding the names and addresses

A Letter to

    Senator **P**aul **S**imon

May 27, 1987

Senator Paul Simon
Senate Office Building
Washington, D.C. 20510

Dear Senator Simon:

  I read in the *New York Times* that you have been advised to abandon your bow tie and wear four-in-hand ties instead. You are reported to have rejected that advice by those image consultants.

  I agree with you. Do not change your look. You feel comfortable with your bow tie and horn-rimmed glasses and you have been wearing them for years! All you need to take into consideration is that your clothes should be coordinated to create a harmonious effect.

  The bow tie as a fashion accessory is found in several contexts. Historically it is a component of formal evening wear usually worn during evening functions with elegant dinner jackets. That is why care should be taken when wearing the bow tie during the day.

  Comic performers have used the formal bow tie out of context in the manner of Charlie Chaplin's tramp character. Pee Wee Herman uses it for humorous effect. Steven Jobs, however, wears it with a button down shirt and jeans. This wardrobe expresses his ultra casual attitude towards IBM that he can beat them at their game.

  You wear the bow tie with professional horn-rimmed glasses. You convey an image of scholarship which is supported by your writing. Thought must be the prerequisite to action. To balance your academic appearance you must convey the message that you are a man of action, not just thought. You should be careful to avoid Adlai Stevenson's error of speaking over people's head and appearing to be indecisive.

  Abraham Lincoln is often pictured in a bow tie. I would respond to bow tie critics using his images although he is the first Republican Party President. Historians will remember that in his day, Lincoln championed liberal progressive ideas and national unity.

  More recently, a prominent regional politician and now Chief Justice of Michigan, G. Mennen Williams, used the bow tie symbol successfully in his campaigns.

  If I were your Image Consultant, I would confirm your "look" by using your style as a great marketing tool heralding a return to basic values which the American public yearns for.

                                           Marily Mondejar

Figure 9. A letter to Senator Paul Simon. Marily Mondejar, Mondejar and Associates, San Francisco, CA. "Open" letter appearing in *The Image Report* of the Association of Fashion and Image Consultants, May 1988. (Reprinted with permission.)

of publications in support of your publicity efforts. Be sure to get the full names of department editors, staff writers, and regular contributors. Also, every magazine and newspaper maintains a demographic breakdown, available upon request, of its readers, circulation figures, and often a breakdown of where subscribers live. The demographic breakdown of the subscribers includes age, income level, education, and, depending

Table 1. Publications of Professional Associations

Professional Association	Publication (Subscription)
1. *Management and Business*	
National Management Association 2210 Arbor Boulevard Dayton, OH 45439 (513) 294-0421	*Manage* (75,000)
Association for Quality and Participation 801-B West 8th Street, Suite 501 Cincinnati, OH 45203 (513) 381-1959	*Quality Circles Journal* (6000)
American Society of Association Executives 1575 Eye Street, NW Washington, DC 20005 (202) 626-2723	*Association Management* (14,000)
National Employee Services & Recreation Association 2400 South Downing Westchester, IL 60153 (312) 562-8130	*Employee Services Management* (5500 companies)
Federal Research Service, Inc. 370 Maple Avenue, West, Suite IV Box 2538 Vienna, VA 22180-2538 (703) 281-0200	*Federal Career Insights* (20,000)
American Society for Public Administration 1120 G Street, NW, Suite 500 Washington, DC 20005 (202) 393-7878	*Public Administration Review* (20,300)
International Personnel Management 1617 Duke Street Alexandria, VA 22314 (703) 549-7100	*Public Personnel* (9700)
2. *Business and Professional Women*	
American Society of Professional & Executive Women 1429 Walnut Street Philadelphia, PA 19102 (215) 563-3501	*Successful Woman* (104,000)

(Table continues on p. 114.)

Table 1. (*Continued*)

Professional Association	Publication (Subscription)
Professional Secretaries International 301 East Armour Blvd. Kansas City, MO 64111-1299 (816) 531-7010	*The Secretary* (50,000)
Women in Communications, Inc. Box 9561 Austin, TX 78766 (512) 346-9875	*The Professional Communicator* (12,000)
Women's Council of Realtors 430 North Michigan Avenue Chicago, IL 60611 (312) 329-8483	*Referral Roster* (16,000)
Nine to Five National Association of Working Women 614 Superior Avenue, NW #852 Cleveland, OH 44113-1306 (216) 566-9308	*Newsletter* (12,000)
National Association of Women Business Owners 600 South Federal Street, #400 Chicago, IL 60605 (312) 346-2330	*Newsletter* (2500)
3. *Health Professionals* American Association for Counseling and Development 5999 Stevenson Avenue Alexandria, VA 22304 (703) 823-9800	*Journal of Counseling and Development* (55,000)
American Psychological Association 1200 17th Street, NW Washington, DC 20036 (202) 955-7600	*Journal of Applied Psychology, Psychology Today, APA Monitor* (90,000)
National Association of Social Workers 7981 Eastern Avenue Silver Spring, MD 20910 (301) 565-0333	*Social Work, NASW News* (107,000)

Table 1. (*Continued*)

Professional Association	Publication (Subscription)
American Psychiatric Association 1400 K Street, NW Washington, DC 20005 (202) 682-6240	*American Journal of Psychiatry* (44,000)
American Society for Training and Development 1630 Duke Street, Box 1332 Alexandria, VA 22313 (703) 683-8100	*Training and Development Journal* (33,000)
American Association of University Professors 1012 14th Street, Suite 500 Washington, DC 20005 (202) 737-5900	*Academe: Bulletin of AAUP* (55,000)

on the publication, number of children. See if the publication's subscribers match your desired target audience.

Local newspapers will print news releases without cost. Newsletters can reach many targets at low cost. Publications of professional associations (Table 1) are often eager to get your "copy."

In Chapter 7, we discuss the effects of your business location on your position.

7

Location and Positioning

It is only the shallow people who do not judge by appearances.

OSCAR WILDE

The personality of your business, to a large degree, is reflected by your location. Whether we like it or not, prospective customers and clients may form a vast array of opinions about a business based on what they see from the outside. In this chapter we will examine key components of business locations and specifically address the following questions:

☐ What is retail compatibility and how does it affect your business?

☐ What strengths can be mustered in association with surrounding merchants?

☐ How do factors such as responsiveness of your landlord and local zoning and planning affect your marketing efforts?

☐ What are other important elements to consider in a business location?

☐ What important considerations are there for manufacturing and wholesaling locations?

☐ What is entrepreneurial location fever?

☐ What are important considerations for professional service firm locations?

Particularly for retail and business services, but increasingly so for professional services, wholesale industry dealers, and even manufacturers, your location says much about who you are and the quality of products and services you provide.

Choosing an appropriate business location—whether in retailing, wholesaling, manufacturing, or business services—is one of the most difficult tasks. For professional service firms, the question of location is of lesser importance because of the relative mobility and ease with which professional service firms may relocate. It has been said that the three most important factors when considering residential real estate are location, location, and location. The same holds true for retail operations and business services.

RETAIL AND BUSINESS SERVICE LOCATIONS

When choosing a retail or business service location (business services include shoe, watch, and appliance repair; barber shops and beauty salons; laundry, mailbox, and storage services; and equipment, video, and other rental shops), it is helpful and necessary to appropriately define or redefine the business (see Chapter 3) and determine long-term objectives. These tasks should be undertaken when preparing the business plan.

It is not sufficient to merely obtain information on the demographics of the population in the trade area, that is, age, income, and size of family; competition; and traffic data. These factors are important, and all retail and business services locational analyses should properly include them. However, once a tentative location has been sited, and given that the traditional demographic analysis reveals many positive factors, there are still a host of other areas that must be checked before a final commitment to a location is made.

MINICASE
RETAIL COMPATIBILITY

Steve Wayman opened his small restaurant on the far left end of an H-type neighborhood shopping center off Route 18—one of the major roads in town, which included a median. Since Steve's business was the last one on his side of the strip, Steve had no neighbors to his left. To his right, in order, were a pet shop, a hardware store, a convenience goods store, a Post Office branch, and an appliance repair shop.

Located directly across from Steve was a barber shop, a quick-print shop, a toy store, a medical aids and devices retail outlet, and a Radio Shack store. Steve's research revealed that hundreds of vehicles entered the common parking lot each day. The shopping area itself had adequate name recognition among consumers in the trade radius. Most of the other merchants were doing well, many having been in the present location for three or more years.

Steve felt certain that, with the amount of traffic the shopping center was already pulling in, some good advertising, good word of mouth, first-rate decor, and great food, it would only be a matter of time before he would be doing a bustling business. However, he was not attempting to offer a four-star restaurant at this location. Steve had considered a location up the road in the regional mall, but the lease was nearly three times as costly, and he feared getting "lost" among the surrounding competing restaurants.

In the weeks that followed the grand opening, Steve quickly observed that business was pretty good from 11:00 A.M. to 2:30 P.M; fair from 2:30 to 5:00 P.M., and threadbare after 5:00 P.M. Though his menu included some special dishes that Steve felt were sure to please, very few customers were ordering them.

Originally Steve had not wanted to do any take-out business; he felt that this would conflict with his intended image. However, it became apparent to Steve that unless he offered take-out, revenues would suffer greatly. He also rolled back the prices on his menu and eliminated some of the more costly specialty dishes.

His clientele, which consisted largely of the regular patrons of surrounding stores, were impulse diners. They stopped in Steve's restaurant because they were in between errands and needed a break, they were in a hurry and just wanted to pick up something for the road, or they worked in the area and found it to be convenient.

Though Steve had spent a bundle on fixtures and decor, he began to realize that as a small restaurant in a convenience goods neighborhood shopping area, "fancy" was not needed, and certainly was not sought by patrons.

At a seminar on marketing, Steve learned that business compatibility is a key factor in the collective draw of retail businesses in the immediate area, that being located next to a pet store and an appliance repair shop, for example, actually had negative impact on his business.

While he had settled in comfortably and was doing moderately well, to achieve his original goals Steve would need to be located in a shoppers' goods location. Had Steve elected to be located near movie theater, other restaurants, men's and women's clothing stores, home furnishing stores, and office buildings, building a four-star restaurant might have been possible.

Convenience versus Shoppers' Goods

How important is retail compatibility? For a small retail store in its first year of operation, with limited funds for advertising and promotion, retail compatibility can be the single most important factor in the survival of the store.

Will you be located next to businesses that will generate store traffic for your business? For example, if you are offering shoppers' goods items, such as men's and women's clothing, major appliances, or expensive jewelry, it is best to locate near other stores carrying shoppers' goods items. Conversely, as Steve discovered, if you are located in a convenience goods shopping area, including such stores as a supermarket, a hardware store, a bakery, a liquor store, or a drugstore, the best way to take advantage of business compatibility would be to open a convenience goods store also.

Examine the shopping centers in your own area and invariably you will find a clothing store or a shoe store located in an otherwise all convenience goods shopping area. The number of days these stores have in that location are limited. They simply will not generate the traffic, vehicular or pedestrian, necessary to be successful.

With the advent of supermalls and regional shopping centers, often shoppers' goods and convenience goods outlets will be found coexisting under the same roof. In this situation it is important to be located in a section of the shopping complex that is conducive to what you are offering. For example, a gift shop is generally well located if it is next to a general merchandise or department store, a theater, an eating place, or anywhere lines of patrons from (and thus have several minutes to observe the front window display). A pet store should not be located immediately adjacent to a restaurant, a dress shop, or a salon—it will not help either merchant.

Merchant Associations

A strong merchants' association can be effective in promoting and maintaining the business in a given area. When considering any retail location, the presence (or absence) of an effective merchants' association is a very important factor.

What if there is no merchants' association? Generally, but not always, a shopping center with no merchants' association (or an ineffective one) is often on the decline. This is characterized by excessive litter or debris in the area, vacant stores, or a parking lot in need of repair. It is best to avoid any locations with these symptoms, and with a little investigation this can be done. However, the desire of some to start a business transcends common sense.

A good merchants' association can strengthen your position and save you money through group advertising programs and group insurance and security measures. Some associations have even induced city planners to add highway exits near their shopping centers. Other associations have lobbied for and received funds from the city to remodel or renovate their shopping centers, including extension of parking lots, refacing of buildings, and installation of better lighting. In addition, merchants' associations can be particularly effective in the promotion of the stores based on a common theme, holiday, or event. The collective draw can be several times that of a single merchant.

How can you determine if the retail location you are considering could benefit from an effective merchants' association? Ask other store owners in the area who the officers of the association are, how often the group meets, what the yearly dues are, and what specifically has been accomplished in the last 12 months. Also ask to see a copy of the last meeting's minutes. Determine what percentage of the members were in attendance.

Perceived Safety

Many women have told me that one of their most important considerations in choosing to patronize a business or not is the feeling of being physically safe. If you are a man, you probably cannot understand this issue with the same passion that a woman does. Women like to feel that they will be safe from their cars to your front door, to the inside of the store, back to the front door, and back to their cars.

Consider that if you are open in the evenings and you do a high volume of business with women, the chances are excellent that you are doing something right in the area of perceived safety. It may be your lighting, the presence of security guards, the proximity to other stores, or simply the fact that you are in a good neighborhood.

If you are drawing a high percentage of female customers and the products and services you offer are not particularly geared toward females, you are doing something right, and something that probably could be highlighted or emphasized to attract others who are concerned about safety.

Responsiveness of the Landlord

Directly related to the appearance of a retail location is the responsiveness of the landlord to the individual merchant's needs. Unfortunately many landlords hinder the operation of the business and are responsible for the demise of their own properties.

In countless instances, landlords have thwarted business owners' attempts to generate more business by restricting the placement and size of signs, by foregoing (or ignoring) needed repairs and maintenance, or by renting adjacent retail space. Some indiscriminately rent to businesses that are not compatible, or that are in direct competition with present tenants. Often landlords lack the funds to maintain their properties, and rather than continuing to "invest" in their holdings by maintaining a proper appearance and supporting the tenants, they instead try to "squeeze" the property for whatever they can get.

To determine whether the landlord is responsive, you must talk to the tenants before moving in yourself. Does the landlord return calls within a responsible time period, and are service people dispatched in a timely manner? Or is the landlord simply collecting the rent and then disappearing? Does the landlord have any policies that hamper marketing innovations? Many do.

You must also contact the previous tenants of the location you have in mind. This will provide invaluable information. Find out what business they were in and why they left. Did they fail or move, and why? What support or hindrances did the landlord provide? Also, if the opportunity presented itself, would they be the retail tenants of the landlord again?

Zoning and Planning

Your town's zoning commission will be happy to provide you with the latest "mapping" of the retail location that you are considering and its surrounding area. Find out if there are restrictions that will limit or hamper your operations. Will construction or changes in city traffic routing serve as barriers to your store? Will any locational advantages you may currently have be diminished by changes in zoning? Most zoning boards, along with economic/regional development committees, do several years' advance planning, and can provide valuable insights for an entrepreneur considering locations.

Related to zoning, what is your intended length of stay and your lease agreement? Do you plan to operate the business in your first location indefinitely, or have you determined a set number of years? If the business is successful, will you be able to expand at the initial location? Then, is your lease flexible so that you have an option to renew after a specified number of years? The time to consider these factors is before you settle on a location.

Lease Considerations

When seeking a lease for commercial space, Robert S. Cunningham, vice president of the real estate brokerage subsidiary of Spaulding and Slye in Boston, says to consider:

- How long will the lease run? Typically, commercial leases run from 3 to 10 years.
- Renewal capabilities. Once the present lease expires, the landlord has no legal obligation to offer the same space to you. Thus it is important that a renewal option be included in your lease agreement guaranteeing that you will have first rights to the space at the prevailing market rate when your lease expires.
- What if the landlord goes broke? To guard against this possibility, your lease should contain a standard "recognition" or nondisturbance clause.
- Are all building services spelled out? You must obtain a list of precisely what services you are entitled to in writing as part of your lease. These might include electricity; heating, ventilation, and air-conditioning; cleaning; and security.
- Who pays for improvements? This provision is usually open to negotiation and the best negotiator gets the best deal. Landlords are more prone to pay the bill for major renovation work if the items requested will attract future tenants after you move. Agreements about renovations must be put in writing and accompanied by a detailed floor plan with an estimate of costs from a contractor before the lease is signed. This document is called the work letter and should specify who *owns* any improvements. Unless agreed otherwise, the landlord can claim ownership of all improvements.

Other Considerations

Here is a quick review of considerations when choosing a retail or business service location, all of which can affect position:

- How much retail, office, and storeroom space is needed?
- Is parking space available and adequate?

- Can special lighting, heating or cooling, or other facilities be installed if necessary?
- Will external lighting in the area attract evening shoppers?
- Will increased advertising expenses be needed if a more remote location is selected?
- Is public transportation available?
- Can the area serve as a source of employees?
- Is there adequate fire and police protection?
- Will sanitation or utility service be a problem?
- Are customer rest-room facilities available?
- Is the perceived accessibility to the store adequate?
- Are external awnings or decks present to provide shelter during inclement weather?
- Will crime insurance premiums be excessive?
- Will you be providing pick up and/or delivery?
- Is the trade area heavily dependent on seasonal business?
- Is the location convenient to your residence?

Figure 10 is a checklist developed by the Small Business Administration to assist businesses in assessing a new location or in upgrading and improving an existing one.

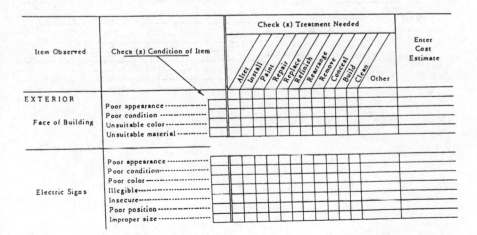

Figure 10. Small Business Administration "Retail Location Checklist," Washington, DC. (Originally published 1960.)

(Figure continues on p. 126.)

Item Observed	Check (x) Condition of Item	Check (x) Treatment Needed												Enter Cost Estimate
		Alter	Install	Paint	Repair	Replace	Refinish	Rearrange	Remove	Conceal	Build	Clean	Other	
EXTERIOR														
Window Lettering and Other Outside Signs	Poor appearance													
	Poor condition													
	Poor color													
	Illegible													
	Poor position													
	Improper size													
	Poor style													
	Letters missing													
	Obstructs vision													
Display Windows														
Glass	Cracked													
	Scarred													
	Frame too heavy													
Window Base (exterior)	Poor appearance													
	Poor condition													
	Unsuitable color													
	Unsuitable material													
Window Platform (interior)	Poor appearance													
	Poor condition													
	Improper height													
	Too shallow													
Side Walls, Ceiling, and Rear Partition	Poor appearance													
	Poor condition													
	Unsuitable material													
	Unsuitable color													
Lighting	Inadequate													
	Glaring													
	Unduly noticeable													
	Poor style													
Display Windows Ventilation	Condensation													
Awnings	Poor appearance													
	Poor condition													
	Poor color													
	Poor style													
	Improper height													

Figure 10. (*Continued*).

Item Observed	Check (x) Condition of Item	Check (x) Treatment Needed												Enter Cost Estimate
		Alter	Install	Paint	Repair	Replace	Refinish	Rearrange	Remove	Conceal	Build	Clean	Other	
EXTERIOR														
Entrance Doors	Poor appearance													
	Poor condition													
	Hard to operate													
	Wrong location or size													
	Knobs poorly located													
	Insecure lock													
	Poor lettering													
	Glass too small													
	Poor screens (if used)													
Steps	Can ramp be built?													
	Practicable to change floor level?													
Sidewalk	Poor condition													
	Unsatisfactory material													
Cellar Entrance	Insecure door													
	Not flush with sidewalk													
	Unsafe													
	No elevator													
	No steps down													
	Poor interior condition													
	Poor location													
Outside Equipment — Vending Machines	Poor appearance													
	Out of order													
	Obsolete design													
	Poorly located													
Curb Service Space	Inadequate													
	Inconvenient													
Parking Space	Inadequate													
	Inconvenient													
INTERIOR														
Floors	Poor appearance													
	Squeaky													
	Rough													
	Poorly covered													
	Unsuitable material													
	Unsuitable color													
	Hard to clean													
	Undue moisture													

Figure 10. (*Continued*).

127

Items Observed	Check (x) Condition of Item	Check (x) Treatment Needed												Enter Cost Estimate
		Alter	Install	Paint	Repair	Replace	Refinish	Rearrange	Remove	Conceal	Build	Clean	Other	
INTERIOR														
Walls and Ceilings	Poor appearance ------------													
	Poor condition-------------													
	Excessive posters, etc.-----													
	Poor color harmony---------													
	Partitions needed-----------													
	Unnecessary obstruction----													
	Bad skylights--------------													
	Leaks---------------------													
Structural Obstacles	Columns-------------------													
	Projecting columns---------													
	Offsets--------------------													
	Partition wall-------------													
	Bad angles ----------------													
	Low or varying ceilings-----													
	Varying floor levels---------													
	Floor not on street level-----													
	Elevators -----------------													
	Stairways-----------------													
Electric Wiring	Unpleasantly noticeable ----													
	Insufficiently protected ----													
	Inadequate for expansion of lighting equipment---------													
	Inadequate for present needs -------------------													
Piping, Gas	Exposed-------------------													
	Poor condition-------------													
	Inadequate-----------------													
Plumbing	Exposed-------------------													
	Poor condition-------------													
	Inadequate-----------------													
Toilet Rooms	Poor appearance ------------													
	Poor condition-------------													
	Inadequate number----------													
	Poor location --------------													
	Poor ventilation------------													
	Poor lighting--------------													
	Unhandy light switch-------													

Figure 10. (*Continued*).

Item Observed	Check (x) Condition of Item	Check (x) treatment needed												Enter Cost Estimate
		Alter	Install	Paint	Repair	Replace	Refinish	Rearrange	Remove	Conceal	Build	Clean	Other	
INTERIOR														
Wash Basins, Sinks, and Toilet Bowls	Poor appearance													
	Obsolete design													
	Out of order													
	Hard to operate													
	Unduly noisy													
	Cracks, stains, leaks													
	Unduly exposed													
Telephone Booths	Poor appearance													
	Poor condition													
	Poor location													
	Improper number													
Lighting Fixtures and Departmental Signs	Poor appearance													
	Poor condition													
	Insufficient illumination, out of order													
	Obsolete design													
	Improperly placed													
	Glaring or obscure													
Shelves and Wall Cases	Poor appearance													
	Poor condition													
	Too high													
	Too deep													
	Excessive													
	Insecure													
	Unsuitable material													
	Unsuitable color													
	Drawers stick													
	Doors hide merchandise													
Counters	Poor appearance													
	Poor condition													
	Improper height													
	Excessive													
	Unsuitable material													
	Unsuitable color													
	Faulty design													
	Long, unbroken lengths													
	Poorly placed													
Open Display Equipment	Poor appearance													
	Poor condition													
	Excessive													
	Unsuitable material													
	Unsuitable color													
	Faulty design													
	Poorly placed													

Figure 10. (*Continued*).

129

Item Observed	Check (x) Condition of Item	Check (x) Treatment Needed												Enter Cost Estimate
		Alter	Install	Paint	Repair	Replace	Refinish	Rearrange	Remove	Conceal	Build	Clean	Other	
INTERIOR														
Glass Show Cases	Poor appearance													
	Poor condition													
	Excessive													
	Faulty design													
	Poorly placed													
	Glass cracked and scarred													
Heating and Ventilation — Heating and Heating Equipment	Poor appearance													
	Poor condition													
	Inadequate													
	Poorly placed													
	Obsolete													
	Exposed pipes													
	Inefficient													
Air Conditioning	Inefficient													
	Inadequate													
Fans, regular and draught	Poor appearance													
	Poor condition													
	Inadequate													
	Poorly placed													
	Noisy													
	Obsolete													
Transoms	Poor appearance													
	Poor condition													
	Hard to operate													
	Do not fit													
	Glass broken or cracked													
Refrigeration — Mechanical	Poor appearance													
	Out of order													
	Poor position													
	Poor drainage													
	Obsolete													
	Inefficient													
	Noisy													
Other Equipment — Cash Registers	Poor appearance													
	Out of order													
	Obsolete													
	Inefficient													
	Unduly noisy													
	Unsuitable type													
	Improper number													

Figure 10. (*Continued*).

Item Observed	Check (x) Condition of Item	Alter	Install	Paint	Repair	Replace	Refinish	Rearrange	Remove	Conceal	Build	Clean	Other	Enter Cost Estimate
		Check (x) Treatment Needed												
Other Equipment														
Water Coolers	Poor appearance													
	Out of order													
	Obsolete													
	Inefficient													
	Improper number													
Burglar Alarm	Poor condition													
	Out of order													
	Obsolete													
	Ineffective													
Incinerator, Trash, and Garbage Boxes	Improper size													
	Poor condition													
	Improper place													
	Insecure													
	Fire hazard													
Fire Extinguishers and Other Fire Equipment	Improper places													
	Poor condition													
	Out of order													
	Obsolete													
	Inefficient													
	Need refilling													
	Improper number													
Other Equipment (Add as required)	Poor appearance													
	Poor condition													
	Out of order													
	Obsolete													
	Inefficient													
	Unduly noisy													
	Improper number													
	Improper places													

Figure 10. (*Continued*).

Proceed with Caution

Choosing a location is, at best, a risky undertaking. Considering the consequences of choosing a location that proves to be unsuitable, it pays to get as much assistance as possible. The local Chamber of Commerce in a city of at least 100,000 people will usually have a division devoted primarily to assisting entrepreneurs in finding a location. This is a free service of which surprisingly few people take advantage. The Small Business Administration's 108 offices throughout the United States can also provide help.

You may need to hire a consultant to analyze two or three locations that you have selected. It is far more cost effective to provide the consultant with preselected potential locations, rather than to initiate open-ended searches.

Other sources of information on potential locations include bankers and lawyers who are familiar with the previous locations of their clients. Realtors can also provide information on locations, but they may be biased since their compensation is based on commissions for renting property.

The selection of a retail or business service location requires time. It should *not* be done hastily to concur with a loan approval. If a suitable location has not been found, postpone your plans and do not plan to open until a suitable location is secured. A few months' delay is only a minor setback compared to massive problems that result from a poor location.

MANUFACTURING AND WHOLESALING LOCATIONS

While manufacturing and wholesaling locations may be less crucial from a positioning standpoint—consumers rarely visit production or warehouse facilities—location is nevertheless important for your long-term success. The complexity of evaluating a location for a manufacturing firm or a wholesaling and distributing operation far exceeds that of retail locations. You must get help from the beginning.

Real estate brokers or developers may offer various package deals. A professional real estate broker must have your best interests in mind when recommending a plant location. He or she must not be following hidden agendas, that is, trying to sell you on properties they represent exclusively, or for which they will receive additional consideration or favors from others.

There are consultants who specialize in industrial locations. For a fee they can guide you through the entire planning phase. Many leading banks, major utilities, and, in some areas, local governments provide such specialists for no fee. These professionals, who generally remain unbiased in their assessment of various locations, are invaluable.

With the emergence of organized industrial parks, many of the start-up headaches for a new manufacturing or distributing operation are diminished. Still, it is important to review the terms of leases carefully and to determine to what degree lease covenants are enforced. You have probably figured out that choosing a location also requires the services of an attorney, perhaps an engineer, more than likely a contractor or two, a banker, an insurance agent, and a good accountant.

It is not unusual to be evaluating locations for a year or more. This may seem like an inordinate wait before starting a business, yet the costs of choosing a poor location can be far greater than the cost of delaying an opening. As with any major commitment to a business location, all conditions and terms must be in writing. If it is not in writing, it does not exist.

Some Similar Analyses

Many of the steps used to evaluate a specific site are similar to those that should be undertaken for a retail location analysis. For example, check with nearby businesses to determine what problems, if any, exist and how they may be avoided. If your plans call for leasing a turnkey operation, it is important to check the reputation and experience of the architect and the builder. No building, plant, or location is perfect, and once you have settled in one, this fact will become abundantly clear.

Business compatibility is also important for manufacturers. Will you be locating next to other companies that operate somewhat similarly to yours? If so, you may benefit from existing transportation facilities and supply lines that may result in lower overall costs than could be achieved otherwise. Here is a checklist of other items:

- Is there adequate police and fire protection in your area? In unincorporated areas, this may not be a given. In such circumstances, you may incur higher insurance costs for the duration of your stay at this location.
- Are mail delivery and telephone service in this area adequate?
- Does this site include a showroom that is readily accessible to buyers and customers?
- Will you be located near support services such as banks, the post office, hospitals, libraries, and shopping facilities?
- What is the availability of utilities, including electricity and gas? Also, what about the availability of natural gas and alternative fuel sources for heating and processing?

- What is the adequacy of the water supply, the water pressure, and the water quality?

- Is there an abundance of skilled labor in your area that will support operations?

- Are there sewers, and what is their elevation?

- How is waste disposal handled?

You also will have to check local zoning ordinances. How restrictive are they? Are there restrictions that will specifically hamper your activities? What are the regulations in regard to parking and employee-to-parking space ratios?

Will your business be violating pollution control standards and prompt a tax by the EPA and other local environmental protection agencies? Remember pollution includes noise as well as air and water. In terms of community relations, will your business have at least adequate "curb appeal"? This can be useful in community standing, as well as appealing to visiting clients and customers.

In addition, is parking allowed on the street, and what are the overnight and weekend restrictions? Are the streets surrounding your plant publicly or privately operated and maintained? Will you be responsible for sweeping, repair, maintenance, snow removal, and repaving of the roadway?

Entrepreneurial Location Fever

Far too many entrepreneurs go about choosing a business location with too short a time perspective.

For retail and business service locations, some entrepreneurs fall in love with a site and collect evidence that supports their instantaneous decision, believing that they have undertaken a proper analysis. The personal preferences of the entrepreneur are "part and parcel" of any site selection, but when a site is selected for emotional reasons (the entrepreneur enjoys the status of a certain location), or for reasons of personal convenience (the location is minutes from the entrepreneur's residence), the business may suffer.

After visiting four or five locations and finding that the costs were more than one bargained for, many people rerank their priorities. They decide what they can live without in a lower cost location. Often, however, the final decision for location is made in haste, under the pressure of a deadline and, quite possibly, with less consistency toward original business objectives.

Much can go wrong in the selection of manufacturing and wholesaling operation locations, and usually it does. Since location selection in this case contains so many variables and can be so overwhelming, there is a strong tendency among entrepreneurs to "get it over with," "make do," and "take care of it later." Rather than continue to assess additional locations to find one that is closer to the ideal, anxious, bedazzled, action-oriented types (read "entrepreneurs") tend to suboptimize. They choose a location that is good, as opposed to continuing to look a bit longer for one that is excellent.

PROFESSIONAL SERVICE FIRM LOCATIONS

Author Robert L. Shook, in his book *Winning Images*, observes that, for many companies, simply publicizing longevity is a masterstroke of community and customer relations. Shook points out that as one company grew, it was able to tell the world that it had been in business since 1961. It is amazing how many companies have nothing to say about themselves except how old they are. If that is all they have, they should flaunt it because it will impress many people.

The office location of an attorney, doctor or dentist, realtor, and so on, is a prime ingredient of effective positioning. It can convey an image of prosperity to prospective clients and patients. Some of the considerations discussed in this chapter also apply to professional service locations, particularly in the areas of parking, security, accessibility, compatibility, and responsiveness of the landlord or leasing agent.[1]

In what shape is the exterior appearance of the building? Is there an outdoor sign or directory in the lobby? Is parking available? Are you located in an appropriate business district? If the building has a lobby, what is the decor? Does it need to be modernized? Is the lobby clean and well lit? Approaching your office, what is the appearance of your door and the sign or lettering?

[1] Robert L. Shook. *Winning Images*. New York: Macmillan, 1987.

When visitors first enter, do they notice shabby, worn carpeting and marks on the wall? Or is your reception area spiffy, well maintained, and contemporary? Is the layout cramped? Or are there clear open passageways to enter the office? Is the reception area located in an area where other offices are screened from initial view? This is important to convey a quality image.

In what condition are the office hallways? Are they clean, well lit, and floored with new rugs? Is the overall decor pleasing? The appearance of your office and its surroundings may well influence the fees you are able to charge, and hence your profit.

Since potential clients are buying intangibles—your services—your office location and the impression it conveys help reassure the prospect and make him or her feel at ease. Therefore take nothing for granted when setting up your offices.

The following two minicases will discuss marketing a specific site, a task faced by industrial developers, and marketing a resort facility. Both shed additional light on how location and positioning are intertwined.

MINICASE
MARKETING YOUR SITE

Can you convey your understanding of the needs of the company looking to relocate? A major regional industrial development advertising effort directly addressed industrial managers about the problem of finding a skilled, technologically sophisticated labor force for the coming decades. This kind of advertising demonstrated an understanding of the need of high-tech industries, and helped to reach the desired target market.

What Businesses Will Want to Know about Your Site

You will need to provide accurate and complete information concerning each of the following factors, according to to Phillip D. Phillips, director of corporate relations with the Fantus Company:

1. Physical Characteristics
   • Total site size, usable acreage

- Slope, drainage, and drainage problems
- Floodplain location
- Soil-bearing capacity
- Presence of undermining or caverns

2. Environment
   - Present uses
   - Zoning classification, permitted uses, restrictions under this classification
   - Compatibility of surrounding land uses
   - Expansion potential

3. Utilities
   - Electric power, natural gas
   - Water, sewer
   - Data on suppliers
   - Position of service lines, capacity and reliability, and cost and terms of any necessary extensions

4. Transportation
   - General highway access
   - Quality and capacity of specific site access roads
   - Cost and terms of road extensions or improvements
   - Rail access, position of the line's service level and service continuance, engineering feasibility of a spur line, and cost and terms of provision of a spur

5. Protection
   - Police protection
   - Fire protection
   - Fire insurance rating

6. Political
   - General political climate
   - Taxing districts, assessment rates, and assessment ratios
   - Requirements for annexation to obtain utility service

7. Ownership
   * Title
   * Easements
   * Mineral rights

8. Site Preparation
   * Clearing of vegetation, cost and terms
   * Removal of existing structures, cost and terms
   * Grading requirements, cost and terms

9. Site Cost
   * Option, cost and terms
   * Sales price, provision such as improvements, site preparation, utility extensions

Attracting outside business often includes networking through the state Department of Development, the state and local Chambers of Commerce, utility company development specialists, transportation company development specialists, local and regional real estate developers, executives of lending institutions, local legislators, and congressional representatives. Networking is a cost-effective method to market your site, particularly if you cannot afford a regional or national marketing campaign. Networking takes hard work but can pay off nicely.

MINICASE
MARKETING A RESORT FACILITY

To attract more association and business meetings, many resorts are becoming meeting planners, able to help visiting groups with all aspects of planning. More and more areas are vying for a share of the $17 billion spent annually on conventions and meetings. What can you do to increase your market share of the convention business?

Selling a group on holding a meeting or convention requires matching your resources to their needs. How many hotel rooms do you have? How many restaurants do you have and what load can each handle?

How many meeting rooms are available? What are your transportation systems like?

Many convention hosts maintain inventories of available facilities and research the needs of prospective groups seeking convention or meeting space.

Is your staff capable of meeting the service needs of a particular group? Although there is no formula that sells every group, stress your unique characteristics when marketing to meeting planners. What will make it easier, less expensive, more enjoyable, or more enlightening for them to meet in your area?

One community facilities director suggests that you determine where a group held its last meeting and what problems, if any, occurred, or what services could have been improved. Then, when making your presentation, stress your ability to handle just those situations. The best advertisement for you is the positive experiences of those who have held meetings there previously. Meeting planners talk to each other frequently, and horror stories travel quickly.

8

The Impact of Financial Image

As the general rule, nobody has money who ought to have it.

BENJAMIN DISRAELI

Your financial image plays an important role in influencing corporate purchasing agents, customers, bankers, investors, suppliers, creditors, and others who may have an impact upon your business.

In this chapter we will look at such issues as:

☐ How your financial statements affect your image

☐ Sources of capital

☐ Value of audited statements

☐ What audits involve

☐ Three rules for dealing with loan officers

☐ How to accent the positive

Your financial image goes a long way toward enhancing your market efforts. All other things being equal, a small business vendor that appears to be on firm financial footing is more attractive than one that is not. Your financial status, and the image others have of it, most definitely affect your ability to market.

Where can you get money to operate and effectively market your business to major corporations?

Where You Can Get Money

If your company is a sole proprietorship:

- Personal funds of the proprietor
- Bank loan
- Loans from an individual
- Loans from or guaranteed by a government agency
- Loans from another business

The amount of the loan and the interest rate will be determined by:

- Track record of the proprietor
- Size of inventory
- Rate of inventory turnover
- Market potential
- Profit potential

If your company is a partnership:

- All of the sources available in a proprietorship
- Contributions by each partner to the capital of the business
- Loans from partners

If your company is a corporation:

- All of the sources available in a proprietorship
- Initial stockholders
- Equities—selling additional stock, common or preferred
- Industrial revenue bonds

With the stock market crash of October 19, 1987, many sources of funds traditionally available to smaller enterprises have tightened up. To determine where businesses could turn in a fluctuating economy, *Venture* magazine recently presented 11 sources of direct or indirect start-up capital. Here is is a brief summary of their roster[1]:

1. *State Funds*
   - *Example:* Ben Franklin Partnership
   - *Amount of financing:* Up to $35,000 for research seed grants; $5000 to $50,000 for challenge grants; up to $250,000 in venture capital
   - *Type of financing:* Cash grants and equity
   - *Return sought:* Fees such as royalties from cash grants; 30 to 40 percent compounded annually from equity
   - *Required investment hurdle:* Companies should reach $15 million to $40 million in revenues over seven years for venture capital

2. *Potential Customer or Supplier*
   - *Example:* Du Pont Company
   - *Amount of financing:* From $500,000 to $10 million
   - *Type of financing:* Equity combined with contracts for joint product development or marketing
   - *Return sought:* Slightly less than traditional venture capital
   - *Required investment hurdle:* Must meet Du Pont's internal product and sales goals

3. *Small Business Innovation Research Program*
   - *Example:* National Science Foundation
   - *Amount of financing:* Up to $50,000 in phase I; up to $250,000 in phase II
   - *Type of financing:* Cash grants

---

[1] Marie-Jean Juilland, *Alternatives to a Rich Uncle.* Reprinted from the May 1988, issue of *VENTURE, For Entrepreneurial Business Owners & Investors,* by special permission. Copyright © 1988 Venture Magazine, Inc., 521 Fifth Ave., New York, NY 10175-0028.

- *Return sought:* None; designed to spur technological development and job creation

- *Required investment hurdle:* Projects must meet the agency's research and development requirements

4. *"Angels"*
   - *Example:* A successful local entrepreneur
   - *Amount of financing:* Equity
   - *Return sought:* 25 percent or more annually, with a five- to 10-year cashout
   - *Required investment hurdle:* Must show after-tax earnings capability of 15 to 25 percent

5. *Small Business Investment Companies*
   - *Example:* Bay Venture Group
   - *Amount of financing:* From $250,000 to $400,000 on average
   - *Type of financing:* Straight equity and equity/debt combinations
   - *Return sought:* 25 to 30 percent compounded
   - *Required investment hurdle:* Looks for companies that will attract top venture capital firms for second-round financing

6. *Community Development Funds*
   - *Example:* Coastal Enterprises Inc.
   - *Amount of financing:* Up to $300,000 on loans and up to $100,000 on equity
   - *Type of financing:* Debt, equity, and combinations, including subordinated debt
   - *Return sought:* Minimum of 15 percent compounded annually on equity; interest rates at or above prime on debt
   - *Required investment hurdle:* Company must create one job for every $10,000 invested

7. *Bank Loans*
   - *Example:* First National Bank of Liberal, Kansas
   - *Amount of financing:* From $20,000 to $400,000, with the average loan less than $100,000

- *Type of financing:* Some commercial loans but primarily SBA-guaranteed loans
- *Return sought:* Interest rates 3 to 4 points above prime on commercial loans, 2.25 to 2.75 points above prime on SBA-guaranteed loans
- *Required investment hurdle:* Entrepreneur must have equity in the company and collateral for the loan

8. *Accounting Firms*
   - *Example:* Peat, Marwick, Main & Company
   - *Approach document:* None needed, but a business plan is necessary to secure financing
   - *Fee:* Sometimes free or discounted from usual hourly fees of $60 to $225
   - *Contacts:* Institutional and individual venture capitalists and wealthy individuals
   - *Amount of financing:* $25,000 to $2.5 million, with average investments in the $100,000 to $500,000 range

9. *Venture Capital Networks*
   - *Example:* Indiana Seed Capital Network
   - *Approach document:* Data base response sheet, three-page summary of business plan including financials, and a formal business plan
   - *Fee:* $100 to 12 months' use
   - *Contacts:* Venture capitalists, individual investors
   - *Amount of financing:* $10,000 to $500,000

10. *Small Business Incubators*
    - *Example:* Crozer Mills Enterprise Center
    - *Approach document:* None to join incubator, but a formal business plan needed for investors
    - *Fee:* None
    - *Contacts:* Banks, wealthy individuals, and institutional investors
    - *Amount of financing:* $25,000 to $75,000, with the average amount less than $100,000

11. *Attorneys*
    - *Example:* Gallop, Johnson & Neuman
    - *Approach document:* None for attorney, but a business plan is needed for outside investors
    - *Fee:* Initial consultation is often free; $100 hourly fee after that
    - *Contacts:* Banks, venture capitalists, and individual investors
    - *Amount of financing:* $50,000 to $200,000

IDENTIFY YOUR FUNDING NEEDS

A paradox confronts successful smaller companies: the larger the contracts won, the less likely the firm will be able to sufficiently stock the required inventories and raw materials. The funding of sufficient inventories is largely a generic problem. Any business that undertakes a large project, or handles an unusually large amount of business, experiences financing problems. Only in the ideal setting, unfortunately, where a business receives an equal volume of work each month and accounts receivable and payable are in perfect harmony, can hope exist to finance a large inventory of raw materials primarily through internal cash flow.

What are the alternatives? You could try front-loaded contract billing, obtaining a revolving line of credit, and maintaining a strong working capital position.

TO BORROW OR NOT TO BORROW

Since your ability to raise the necessary funds will affect your positioning capability, and effective positioning with loan officers is necessary to get a loan in the first place, let us talk about the nuances of loansmanship. Getting a loan is an art. Much like mastering other arts, a certain amount of discipline and preparation is necessary.

When you seek to borrow money for your company, it is important to know the kind of financial assistance you will need from a bank or other lending institution. When making the decision to borrow, there are two important concerns to consider: what will the funds be used for? and what is the source of money for repayment? Short-term loans are usually repaid from the liquidation of the current assets they have financed. Long-term loans are usually repaid from earnings.

Quick Tips for Dealing with Banks

Show loyalty by dealing with one bank:

* Savings
* Checking accounts
* Loans

To enhance your chance of receiving a loan:

* Prepare a loan proposal—include:
    Amount of capital needed
    Type of loan—long- or short-term
    Terms—secured, unsecured
    Desired interest rate
    Proposed payback schedule
* Clearly explain the purpose of the loan
* Present company financial statements
    Cash flow and pro forma projections
    Balance sheets and income statements for past three years
    Collateral
    Inventory
    Fixed assets
    Life insurance
    Listing and aging of accounts receivable
* Provide related nonfinancial information
    Business strategy
    Data on company's industry
    Company's position in the industry
    List trade suppliers for references
* Other Factors
    Repay loans on time
    Make yourself known to bank officers, especially well before you need a loan
    Bring in business for the bank
    Ask—the bank can't help you if it doesn't know your needs

Generally, the longer the payback period for a loan, the higher the risk to the bank. In order to protect itself, the bank is naturally interested in the profits that you will generate. Banks are also keenly interested in knowing if you have a guarantee from the Small Business Administration because that greatly reduces the risk. If the loan is going to be applied specifically toward named assets, then the bank can take those assets in the event you default on the loan.

You must offer personal guarantees, and considering the length and complexity of some of the loan documents these days, in more ways than you will ever know. The bank will take your personal assets, if it has to. If your note has been cosigned by another person, his or her assets will also be under lien.

If your loan is specifically for the purchase of assets, the bank will take the first position, that is, it gets the assets should you default. However, it also will take the second position on accounts receivable, inventory, or other assets. This is called an assignment, and in the case of accounts receivable, would be called "a blanket position on receivables."

In positioning for loan success you must steer past sandtraps and master the art of loansmanship. This involves recognizing that:

1. Preparation for outside financing must always start far in advance of the actual need.

2. Cultivation of personal and professional relations with loan officers is essential

3. The appearance of desperation is detrimental to your quest for financial assistance.

1. Preparation for outside information must always start far in advance of the actual need. Obtaining a loan in a start-up situation requires the same kinds of skills needed to hit a moving target. The inherent lags in loan application procedures and reviews, combined with other uncertainties as to actual start-up date and distribution of funds means that even with a successful application, you may get the loan out of sync with your plans.

Whatever amount you are seeking should probably be increased significantly, and you had better get started months before you think you have to. The inherent danger of asking for too much is that you may be rejected because the financial institution does not see a way to cover itself for the full amount of the loan. The danger in asking for too little is twofold: (1) you may actually receive that amount and find it inadequate, and (2) bankers are more likely to reject applicants who ask for too little because these applicants appear to have an unrealistic view of the situation.

Which is the greater sin—asking for too much or for too little? On balance, you are better off asking for too much. The banker may knock down the amount you seek and offer you a somewhat lesser figure. If you ask for too little and it is apparent to those reviewing your financial package, you have no retreat. When someone has to say to you, "Based on your situation this amount will not be adequate," you have already indicated your inability to identify your own financial needs. If this is so, the loan officer wonders, what are your other managerial shortcomings?

When should you start preparing materials for your loan package? Three to six months before you actually need it. Your ability to offer a detailed, credible business plan is of prime importance when seeking a loan. Specifically, when seeking debt, you must be able to answer two basic questions:

- How much money do you need, over what period, and how will the funds be used?
- When and how will you pay the money back?

The most effective way to answer these questions and to provide a graphic overview of your situation is to produce both a short- and a long-term cash-flow analysis. Another aspect of your advance preparation will to be familiarize yourself with other available financing sources. On a personal basis, obviously there are your own savings, life insurance loan programs, friends, relatives, and a second mortgage on your home. Asset-based financial measures include loans secured by accounts receivable, inventories, or fixed assets; leasing of fixed assets; or transfer of accounts receivable to another party.

Debt capital can also be raised through finance companies, SBA guaranteed loans (both with and without a commercial bank's participation), federal loans for businesses in high unemployment or undeveloped areas, loans from other businesses such as insurance companies, or industrial revenue bonds.

Equity capital can be raised by sale of stock—both common and preferred, sale of part of the business to a venture capitalist, sale of part of the business to a small business investment corporation, or filing with the Securities and Exchange Commission and going public. Raising equity capital requires preparing a prospectus, which is much more extensive than a loan package.

2. Cultivation of personal and professional relations with loan officers is essential. Take a loan officer to lunch. The best time to get to know a loan officer is well before you ever ask for a loan—positioning. It makes good sense to get to know more than one at your primary bank, and to meet other loan officers at othr banks. Many entrepreneurs, upon hearing that they should invite a loan officer to lunch and discuss the highlights of a proposed or initiated plan, feel a bit sheepish.

"Why would a loan officer want to spend time with me if I am not even asking for a loan?" Particularly in this era of aggressive bank marketing, as a potential loan recipient, creator of jobs, payer of taxes, and pillar of the community, loan officers will be interested in getting to know you.

The first time that entrepreneurs usually introduce themselves is one fine day when they walk into the bank, sit down at the desk, and begin to talk about their business. The standard line is "everything is going well, can you lend me X amount?" (or "how much can you lend me?"), and "I need it as soon as possible." This is bad form and is not likely to win you any points. By making an immediate "I need it as soon as possible" request to a loan officer, you may have unknowingly placed him or her in a difficult position. You certainly do not project the image of an effective planner.

Leading financial experts agree that if you play your cards right, you can actually get favored treatment at your bank. By cultivating a relationship in advance, you can request and possibly get an interest rate that is lower than the going rate to other small businesses, and have other service costs eliminated. The better the loan officer understands your business (as typified by the more information on you in the file), the more effectively you will be represented to the bank loan committee.

Loan officers are eager to develop long-term client relationships and to provide additional services such as payroll management, financial systems, and pension management. The more the loan officer is able to get to know you, the more he or she is able to reduce the bank's risk and the greater opportunity that he or she has to build a portfolio of successful, responsible clients.

3. *The appearance of desperation is detrimental to your quest for financial assistance.* The greatest financial paradox facing the entrepreneur is being able to obtain funds without appearing to have great need for them. If you can make requests for financial assistance as part of an overall business planning process, and not because you have to have it or else, you are way ahead of the game. One must tread a very fine line in this area.

What are some of the telltale signs that bankers look for to determine whether you are in trouble? If you have too much invested in fixed assets without corresponding revenues to justify them, or if you are permanently overextended, all the alarms and buzzers will go off. Loans to officers or owners for nonbusiness purposes get you a quick rejection. Similarly, if you have a pile of unpaid bills, excessive officer salaries, or heavy inventories as compared to sales, the loan officer will be wary.

FINANCIAL STATEMENTS AND YOUR IMAGE

Financial statements are prepared from accounting records to aid management in analyzing the performance of the business. Besides loan officers and investors, purchasing agents also examine them when evaluating your firm as a prospective vendor.

Are your financial statements audited by a certified public accountant? This process serves as notice that your statements meet certain accounting tests and standards. Auditing lends credibility and professionalism, and the winners do it.

What are audited statements? Price Waterhouse, one of the big eight in accounting, defines them as documents presenting your company's financial data in a periodic, consistent, and acceptable fashion. They are very important for positioning because they present your company to outsiders in a "professional and current manner reflecting your progressive and professional organization." Audited statements are your statements. A CPA firm merely attests that "in its opinion, the financial statements present fairly the operations of your company for a given period of time, and the financial condition of your company at a given point in time."

Price Waterhouse cites five instances where having audited statements can be beneficial.

1. *Banks.* As we have discussed, banks are in business to make money by making loans that are sound investments. The bank seeks to determine the borrower's ability to repay in accordance with the terms of the loan. The banks are generally interested in a specified return for a given degree of risk. Because of market conditions or legal restrictions, banks frequently have a narrow range of possible return, but a broad range of prospective borrowers within that range. In the end, if a decision comes down to two apparently

similar companies, one of which has audited statements, a banker will most likely put greater reliability on the audited numbers.

2. *Bonding Companies.* The larger your bonding capacity, the larger the jobs on which you can bid. Your financial statements play a significant part in getting the bonding capacity you desire, and the reliability of these statements weighs heavily in the eyes of the bonding agent.

3. *State Requirements.* Incorporated businesses in several states must file, on a yearly basis, a certificate of condition. In some states if a company's assets are over a certain amount, an independent auditor's statement is required.

4. *Selling the Business and Going Public.* If you ever sell your business outright, or sell shares of the business, you must present a history of the firm to these potential investors. The Securities and Exchange Commission requires a five-year audited summary. Most buyers look askance at unaudited data.

5. *Creditor Requirements.* Often your suppliers may request financial information prior to extending credit. Depending on the size of the order and past experience, a supplier may require audited financial statements as opposed to in-house statements.

One of the basic objectives of financial statements, according to Price Waterhouse, is to provide information useful for making economic decisions. The regular audited financial statement is a measurement of the period-by-period progress of an enterprise toward its overall goals.

With the new series of auditing standards issued in May 1988 by the Auditing Standards Board, more than ever, audits of a company's financial statements, and the resulting expression of opinion by the auditor, can ensure to others that your financial data are reliable and accurate.

ACCENTING THE POSITIVE

Especially when you have had some lean years (and who hasn't?), your financial image should be presented as favorably as possible. If your firm has a steady rate of growth or an improving cash position (even if you have a long way to go before you can show a profit), emphasize the positive aspects of this improvement. Horizontal and vertical trend analyses are techniques that can be used to present your financial image favorably.

Sample trend analysis charts follow for balance sheets and income statements. With a horizontal trend analysis you set all components of your balance equal to 100 percent in the base year. Then in succeeding years you show change as it compares to the base year, that is, no change would equal 100 percent. The same analysis can be applied to income statement components.

Horizontal Trend Analysis

Base year equals 100%, subsequent years are compared as percentages to the base-year figures.

BALANCE SHEET

	Base Year	2nd Year	3rd Year
Total assets	100%	105%	104%
Current	100%	102%	108%
Fixed	100%	98%	99%
Other	100%	107%	110%
Total liabilities	100%	106%	105%
Short-term	100%	102%	101%
Long-term	100%	101%	103%
Net worth	100%	101%	104%

INCOME STATEMENT

	Base Year	2nd Year	3rd Year
Sales	100%	104%	109%
Cost of goods sold	100%	102%	111%
Gross profit	100%	102%	98%
Operating expenses	100%	102%	102%
Net profit before taxes	100%	101%	100%

With vertical trend analysis for balance sheets, the figure for total assets each year is set equal to 100 percent. Other balance sheet components are then expressed as percentages in comparison with total assets. For income statements the analysis works the same way, using "sales" in places of "assets."

Vertical Trend Analysis

Total assets, total sales equal 100 percent, with the component entries listed as percentage portions of these figures.

BALANCE SHEET			
	Base Year	2nd Year	3rd Year
Total assets	100%	100%	100%
Current	14%	11%	8%
Fixed	52%	54%	54%
Other	34%	35%	38%
Total liabilities	106%	104%	101%
Short-term	36%	33%	32%
Long-term	70%	71%	69%
Net worth	−6%	−4%	−1%

INCOME STATEMENT			
	Base Year	2nd Year	3rd Year
Sales	100%	100%	100%
Cost of goods sold	79%	79%	80%
Gross profit	21%	21%	20%
Operating expenses	20%	18%	18%
Net profit before taxes	1%	3%	2%

In summary, by:

- Keeping abreast of potential sources of funds
- Determining your funding needs in advance
- Cultivating relationships with bankers
- Having audited statements
- Favorably presenting your financial data

You will add to a stronger financial position and financial image, which will enhance you marketing efforts.

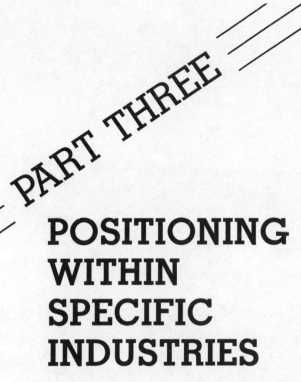

PART THREE

POSITIONING WITHIN SPECIFIC INDUSTRIES

9
Building the Professional Service Firm

Quality is not an act. It is a habit.

ARISTOTLE

The present concept for the marketing of professional services originated 15 years ago, yet only about half of all practitioners have accepted marketing as an inevitable and necessary component of the strength and longevity of their firms. In positioning oneself in the marketplace, there are several elements of importance, most of which successful professional service firms have mastered.

In this chapter we will examine key aspects of positioning for professional services, including:

☐ Being known for something

☐ Being consistent

☐ Being everywhere

☐ Maintaining a strong referral network

☐ Being uncompromising regarding quality of service

☐ Gaining and using professional certification

☐ Using more advanced strategies, such as sitting on the board of directors of a large company.

WHAT ARE YOU KNOWN FOR?

The first element is to be *known for something*. Merrill Lynch positions itself as "a breed apart." H & R Block has "29 reasons" why it should do your taxes for you. The "something" a company is known for does not have to be part of a catchy phrase or slogan. Some accounting firms develop a reputation for superior tax work, while others develop their niche in the area of auditing, and still others specialize in financial planning services.

A common mistake made by new entries in the professional services field is to try to be all things to all clients, which frequently leads to being not much to anyone. Richard A. Connor, Jr., says the goal of the professional service firm should be to "be somebody special to some special bodies." The fastest way to achieve this is to identify the one service or aspect of your background for which you can become known and strategically market that strength to appropriate targets.

MINICASE
THE BOGUS IVY LEAGUE CONNECTION

Before presenting the following minicase, I wish to discuss a caveat about it. While appropriately capitalizing on legitimate affiliations is an effective positioning vehicle, the manner in which James Loehman proceeded is, in my opinion, unethical.

James H. Loehman (name disguised), president of James H. Loehman and Associates, was a dynamic, energetic, aggressive, charismatic business entrepreneur who had punched all the right tickets and had begun reaping the rewards. As a small businessman, he was wired for many contracts on the federal and local levels for which his management consulting firm was qualified.

In one particular study, James H. Loehman and Associates successfully produced a 10-year plan for a government agency. This consulting engagement, along with numerous other successes, earmarked the firm as special in its field.

Loehman's very carefully crafted literature, which I reviewed on several occasions, lead one to believe that he had a Harvard MBA. In fact, Loehman had gotten his MBA from a small midwestern university. As a management consultant with the prestigious McKinsey and Company, Loehman was sent to Harvard's management development program and attended the six-week course along with executives from top firms across the nation. Loehman completed this six-week course and was subsequently elected president of an alumni group which was formed.

Thereafter, Loehman's corporate résumé, company brochure, and other corporate literature stated that Loehman was president of this Harvard alumni group. Yet the language used was misleading—not something anyone should emulate. One readily assumed that Loehman was both a Harvard MBA and president of the MBA alumni group. In reality, Loehman was merely a graduate of an intensive six-week course at Harvard and president of the alumni group affiliated solely with that six-week course.

There is no way to calculate what impact Loehman's clever use of his Ivy League connection had in developing his marketing materials, or how that influenced the contracting officers of the federal and local agencies whom he served. What is known is that he was able to accelerate the growth of his firm, although later he ran into several management and contract problems.

The registrar and records offices of institutions such as Harvard and Stanford report that they regularly receive requests for transcripts of individuals who never attended their institutions. Harvard University, for example, reports that fully 4 percent of the requests they receive cannot be fulfilled because the individuals in question did not attend or graduate from Harvard.

Does maintaining some type of Ivy League connection increase your marketing effectiveness? Probably so. I do *not* advocate creating misleading or bogus credentials. If you have taken an executive development course, or are affiliated with a prestigious institution in any way, legitimately highlighting and accenting this fact may cause doors to open a little sooner than they usually would.

In March 1979 I was fortunate enough to be assigned to a consulting project that my then employer was undertaking for the Massachusetts Institute of Technology Innovation Center. I was enthusiastic about the prospects of successfully completing this consulting engagement with M.I.T.

Later, particularly when applying for my certified management consultant designation (CMC) and preparing marketing materials to attract additional clients, I legitimately highlighted my work with M.I.T. and the results that I was able to achieve for them.

Think about connections that you have with prestigious organizations or institutions. Particularly when offering a professional service, properly accenting your connection can indeed be one of the best marketing vehicles you can employ.

MR. OR MS. CONSISTENT

Consistency is the second element found in abundance among professional service providers. Dave Voracek, president of The Marketing Department in Alexandria, Virginia, produces award-winning brochures for his clients that are so good his name is passed from friend to friend. Each of Michelle Lusson's presentations in her seminar series on creative wellness has been thoroughly researched and is smoothly delivered. Lusson, based in Vienna, Virginia, is known as the "Wellness Lady" and is able to markedly reduce the stress levels of those attending her courses.

What are other hallmarks of professional consistency? There are many signs—promptly responding to clients, completing jobs on time and on budget, and providing the same level of effort to all clients. Perhaps the greatest reflection of professional consistency is longevity—at the same location or within the same community.

Remember, as author Robert L. Shook pointed out in *Winning Images*, many businesses promote themselves by essentially saying nothing more than how long they have been in business. Business longevity, however, is an excellent customer draw. A new client may not have been familiar with your firm, but upon finding that you have been in business since 1976, may decide that you must be good to have lasted.

HOW TO BE EVERYWHERE

The appearance of being everywhere is the third notion professional service marketers must embrace. The illusion of being everywhere can be maintained through having articles published; undertaking speaking engagements; using direct mail; joining and volunteering with key professional, charitable, and civic groups; and influencing others to speak of you favorably.

Robert Bookman, president of Bookman Resources, a Chevy Chase, Maryland, based team productivity and training firm, continually identifies business reporters who may be tempted to visit one of his presentations and write a story on the results he achieves. In the last three years, Bookman has successfully persuaded journalists from the *Washington Post*, *USA Today*, and the *Journal Newpapers* to write about his team-building programs. This type of media coverage has enabled Bookman to receive calls from around the country, yet his is a one-man firm.

IN-PLACE REFERRAL NETWORK

Though we would like to believe that clients and patients carefully analyze several potential professionals before making a decision, the reality is that they often go with the first one or the one that their friend recommended, without doing any further checking. If you doubt that this is true, think for a second of how you selected your present dentist.

If you have lived in the same town all your life, perhaps you chose your dentist based on whom your parents chose. If you have reestablished yourself in a new town after college, or sometime during the course of your career, think back to how you first made contact with your dentist.

Did you call three to five dentists, make appointments with each of them, visit their offices, talk with their receptionists, check their degrees, speak with them briefly to get an impression of what they were like, and then weigh all these factors carefully and make a decision? If not, did you open up the phone book and call the one that appeared to be nearest you and had a halfway presentable ad? Or did you ask people at work whom they used and whether they would recommend them?

Most of us agree that our present clients are our best sources of new clients. In Chapters 14 and 15 we will further explore ways of cultivating client relationships for long-term gain.

QUALITY OR BUST

Another component of successful positioning is maintaining a policy of *never compromising on the quality of services provided.* Edward Thiel, an Alexandria, Virginia, based photographer, has been known to reshoot a sitting as many as three times if that is what is necessary to produce the end product sought by the client. Adherence to quality standards in this day and age of making a fast buck sticks out like a sore thumb.

Most consumers, when pressed, will admit that they would rather pay more for quality and enjoy long-term benefits than find a bargain and perhaps be disappointed. This is especially true in retaining professional service providers. The lawyer, the doctor, or the consultant whose performance can be counted on will retain a higher percentage of clients or patients, develop excellent word-of-mouth business, and avoid having to scramble for new business with the viscissitudes of the economy.

Not compromising on quality costs a little more in the short run, but pays off in the long run.

ENHANCEMENT THROUGH CERTIFICATION

We all look to certification and licensing as a way of judging the credentials and experience of a professional. It lets us know that the professionals we hire have passed certain examinations or qualifications set by their industry. Institutionalized license procedures such as MD tell us that the person has completed the training necessary to meet standards set by law. Dentists have DDS after their names, indicating successful completion of training and an examination. Certified public accountant (CPA) signifies a certification of quality in the profession of accounting.

This section will address the following questions:

- What is certification?
- What are some positioning benefits of being certified?
- What kinds of professions provide certification?
- How can one identify associations and societies that offer certification programs?

Certification is frequently confused with accreditation or licensing. Accreditation applies to programs rather than individuals, generally those of a school, college, institute, or university. It is granted by an association to organizations that meet standards determined through initial and periodic evaluations. Licensing applies to individuals and is granted by a political body to people who meet predetermined qualifications. Licensing is required by law before professionals can engage in certain occupations, such as medicine or dentistry.

Certification is granted by an association to professionals who meet predetermined qualifications, but is voluntary. More than 300 associations and societies offer professional certification programs. The following represent a sampling:

Certified Public Accountant

Certified Professional Social Worker

Certified Safety Professional

Certified Shorthand Reporter

Chartered Financial Analyst

Certificate in Data Processing

Certification for Occupational Therapy Assistants

Certified Association Executive

Certified Commercial Investment Member

Certified Electronics Technician

Certified Financial Planner

Certified Laboratory Assistant

Certified Military Club Manager

Certified Medical Assistant

In many professions, the certification process involves an examination, a written code of ethics that professionals must sign, and a description of the experience the professional must have to warrant certification.

If certification in any field is to signify ability and experience adequately, the process of certification is necessarily rigorous. After all, if it were easy to get certified, the certification would soon be worth very little to its recipients and their clients. Many professionals complain about certification procedures as "jumping through too many hoops," but they know that the process of applying and earning acceptance is essential for a professional designation.

When I began my management consulting career in 1975, I had no idea that I would soon start working toward certification. After a year, however, I wrote to the Institute for Management Consultants to inquire about their Certified Management Consultant designation. When I realized how rigorous the process would be, I was motivated to work that much harder for certification.

The requirements included five years' experience as a management consultant and at least one as a project manager. The applicant had to submit five client write-ups (including a detailed description of a client engagement), three client references, and three associate references. Additional requirements were an interview by a panel of three, an application fee, an initiation fee, and annual dues.

I found out that one-third of the Certified Management Consultants came from large national consulting firms such as A. T. Kearney, and Booz Allen & Hamilton. Another third came from major management advisory services, such as Price Waterhouse, and Deloitte Haskins and Sells. A few were from small firms, as I was.

As soon as I had the required years of experience, I began the application process. It took me nine months to complete the process and be granted certification; but, finally, in 1982 I was accepted. I felt I had earned my CMC designation, but I also knew that it was still up to me to reap the greatest possible benefits from it.

Certification programs offer many positioning benefits for the professional receiving certification, including:

Recognition. When you are able to use a designated certification label with your name, people within and outside your industry recognize that you have a certain degree of expertise in your field. Even though they may not know anything about the certification requirements or the certifying association, they automatically regard you as being a cut above the rest.

Networking. Certification provides occasions to become involved with the certifying association—to attend conferences, speak at meetings, or simply have a common ground for discussions with others who are also certified. Typically, this generates a professional network of colleagues who can refer business to you when they are not suited to handle the client.

Continued Development. Involvement with other certified professionals allows you to keep abreast of the latest developments in your field and establishes channels for an exchange of information that crosses organizational boundaries.

Keeping Current. Because you are exposed to top professionals in your field, you are encouraged to keep your knowledge and abilities current. This is a prime way to enhance your position. You may also do this by attending seminars and conferences offered through the certifying association or by reading the newsletters, magazines, and other publications the association may distribute.

Self-Assessment. The process of applying for certification can be a valuable self-assessment and development tool as you prepare for the certifying examination and review your achievements in writing for the application. Many certifications require periodic updating, which allows you continued opportunities to reassess your professional strengths and weaknesses.

By all means, *use* your certification. Add your designated title to your stationery and business cards. Make sure it is included when something is written about you. Take a leadership role in organizing and conducting any local meetings of professionals in your field. Get involved, stay involved, and let your certification really work for you.

Professions Providing Certification

A few certification programs whose value will be immediately recognized by people in the field are described briefly:

Certified Management Consultant (CMC). The certification process to attain the CMC has several stages. The goal of the Institute is to ensure the highest levels of competence and professional ethics. "Affiliate" memberships are available while earning the CMC. (Institute of Management Consultants, 19 West 44th Street, Suite 810, New York, NY 10036.)

Certified Financial Planner (CFP). A 9000-member group, the ICFP establishes guidelines for the CFP designation. Its goals are to define and uphold the standards of professionalism within the industry. (Institute of Certified Financial Planners, Two Denver Highlands, 10065 E Harvard Ave., Suite 320, Denver, CO 80231.)

American Society of Mechanical Engineers (ASME). Membership *is* certification for this group. The aims and objectives of ASME include producing creative solutions for technical, government, and society interface; encouraging personal and professional development; and fostering ethical conduct. (American Society of Mechanical Engineers, 345 East 47th Street, New York, NY 10017.)

Certified Association Executives (CAE). The American Society of Association Executives has developed a comprehensive certification program that focuses on all aspects of association management. Thousands have already been certified. (American Society of Association Executives, 1575 Eye Street, NW, Washington, DC 20005.)

Real Estate Consulting Professional (RECP). This certification, issued by the International College of Real Estate Consulting Professionals, is from a group that includes attorneys, appraisers, brokers, engineers, planners, property managers, and mortgage brokers. (International College of Real Estate Consulting Professionals, 1908 First Bank Place West, Minneapolis, MN 55402.)

Two directories, mentioned throughout this text, list thousands of professional, trade, and technical associations and societies. You can find them in the reference section of your local library. They are:

- *Gales Association Directory*
- *National Trade and Professional Association (NTPA)*

Find the group in your field and write to them for detailed information about any certification programs available. You are a professional and you have every right to try for certification.

ADVANCED STRATEGIES

Sitting on the Board

"There is no shortage of people who want to get on boards," says Robert K. Mueller, chairman of Arthur D. Little, Inc. writing in *Fortune*. Every day people write to him asking how they can get on boards.

While there is a strong element of prestige associated with being a board member, particularly of a large corporation, the basic reason professionals seek to become directors is that it enables them to exchange ideas with top people in the business world. Membership enhances one's visibility and exposure, and offers a marketing shot in the arm. The networking that occurs among directors is likely to foster business and social opportunities that would otherwise not be available.

The typical board of a Fortune 500 corporation meets nine or ten times a year. Each director spends from 175 to 200 hours per year, or nearly five 40-hour weeks, serving in this capacity. Directors are paid generally between $16,000 and $22,000, for an hourly rate of about $100. This figure is understandably lower for directors of smaller corporations.

For outside directors, tackling the problems and challenges of another corporation may also help to strengthen positions in their own corporations and otherwise accelerate the opportunity to gain marketing insights and high-level experience.

The mere fact that an entrepreneur serves on the board of large corporation is, in and of itself, a marketing strategy. Author Edward

McSweeney says, "Election to the board of a big corporation confers a status unobtainable in ordinary executive and professional life." The professional who is also a director greatly benefits from this association in the marketing sense—his or her small company is viewed in an entirely different light because of the entrepreneur's first-person connection with "big boys."

In hopes of encouraging more corporations to consider women for their boards, the National Women's Economic Alliance published a directory of female directors of the nation's top 1000 corporations. Pat Harrison, who formed the alliance, had the goal of creating an organization for high-powered businesswomen who want to obtain more prestige and power. Helping her members to achieve boardroom appointments is one of the main tenets of her program.

What is the best way to gain board membership? Associate with those who are already directors. Like many things, those who get appointed or elected to a board have inside connections.

MINICASE
WRITING YOUR BOOK

One of the best marketing tips in the world (but one of the most monumental tasks) is to write a book to enhance the promotion of your services. Certainly writing a book is not for the meek or faint of heart—even those thin, 140-page softcover books that you see in B. Dalton's require at least 300 hours of the author's time. Every year 50,000 new books come off the presses, thousands of which were written by entrepreneurs whose primary interest in writing is to use the book as a marketing vehicle.

Carole Jackson, author of *Color Me Beautiful* and founder of the company with the same name, represents a dramatic example of an entrepreneur who used the publication of a book to catapult her business into the big time.

Jackson, who had learned the now-famous color system 20 years ago from a California wardrobe consultant, labored for years as a successful, if unknown, wardrobe consultant. During the development of her book, which remained on *The New York Times* Best Seller List for months and went on to become an international best seller, she inserted a free color analysis coupon.

Something miraculous happened. When the book was published, over 40,000 readers mailed the coupon in to Jackson, who now had an instant customer base, mailing list, and powerful indicators that the market would support rapid expansion. The rest, as they say, is history. Jackson began training other color consultants both here and abroad, established a product line, and hired a full crew to run corporate headquarters. A second book followed, *Color for Men*, and the birth of a new industry took place.

Today, Carole Jackson and *Color Me Beautiful* are synonymous with wardrobe color consultation. Thousands of smaller clonelike competitors have emerged. How does Jackson feel about the time and effort required to write the book and its impact on her company's marketing effectiveness? Without hesitation, she states, "Writing a book is an excellent way to market your company."

MINICASE
CREATING AN ASSOCIATION

The year was 1975. Cavett Robert, a nationally acclaimed speaker and author, was living in Phoenix, Arizona, on the advice of his physician, who felt the climate would be better for Robert's health. After many long months of planning and preparation, the National Speakers Association (NSA) was launched with Cavett Robert as its first president and Bill Johnson as its executive director. Robert's mission was to elevate the status of speaker to that of a profession throughout the United States.

In its first year, a convention was held in Phoenix and was attended by only a score of some of the nation's popular speakers. The atmosphere was casual and informal, but much was accomplished. That year the founding members set in motion what is now one of the most dynamic, effective associations in the world.

Though Robert's objectives were primarily altruistic—for the good of the profession—revenues from sales of his own products and services continued to increase steadily. As more and more speakers joined

NSA, Robert's instructional cassettes and motivational books, and similar products of other founding members, were eagerly purchased.

By 1989, the NSA had more than 2500 members. NSA sponsors a spectacular annual convention, two winter workshops, and a variety of other programs which remain on target with Robert's original mission of upgrading the speaking profession. The beloved Robert, who is held in high esteem by NSA and all its members, has further solidified his position as a renowned speaker, motivator, and mentor.

Would Robert have enjoyed outstanding success had he not formed National Speakers Association? Most assuredly. At the time he formed the association he had already more than proved himself. However, the establishment of the association firmly secured his position as one of the most sought-after speakers. NSA enabled him to achieve even greater success on top of an already successful career.

What association can you start? Determine a need that is not being met. The American Society of Association Executives in Washington, D.C., offers a full complement of seminars and programs for starting, managing, and maintaining a successful association.

Between now and the year 2000, professional service industries will grow between 10 and 20 percent per year. The economy of our nation is already heavily dependent on the service sector. The 1990s may yield an even bigger pot at the end of the rainbow for professional service marketers who position themselves by being known for something, being consistent, appearing to be everywhere, refusing to compromise when it comes to quality, and obtaining professional certification.

10

Becoming a Retail Institution— McDonald's and Other Tales

More than ever before, the entrepreneur of the future will be part of the social fabric.

MARC MORET

The goal of becoming an institution is a lofty one indeed, but a masterstroke of position marketing. Few business entities in our society have achieved the unbounded success of McDonald's. Though competitors have had nearly three decades in which to emulate McDonald's winning ways, in its own industry McDonald's continues to reign supreme. This chapter will take a look at:

☐ How McDonald's positions itself to be perceived as a partner in all communities where a franchise is located

☐ How McDonald's remains at the forefront of the fast-food industry year after year

☐ How retailers are taking advantage of mystery shopper services to ensure that individual branches are operating at the highest standards

☐ How Staples retail office supply dominated a market in a matter of months

☐ Why doing business as usual has become a prescription for failure

---

Does the customer perceive your products or services the way you do? To the customer you are what you project and what you live up to. A key component of effective position marketing is to ensure that the image you wish to project and the image you do project are one and the same.

To illustrate how a business can continually protect market share over several decades, let us look at a fast-food restaurant that is known to virtually all Americans, and is now known throughout the world: McDonald's.

HOW McDONALD'S BECAME AN AMERICAN INSTITUTION

McDonald's has become an American institution because of its acute awareness of its product/service image. McDonald's defines itself in terms of benefits to the consumers that it serves. Its business and marketing definition could mistakenly be thought to be, "We are in the business of selling hamburgers, shakes, and french fries to the general public at affordable prices." While that statement is true, it does not begin to define what McDonald's actually provides, or why it has been so successful.

In the 1960s and throughout the 1970s, McDonald's gained a strong foothold with the American public as a refuge from one's daily trials and turmoil. Starting with garishly colored, tile-covered buildings, McDonald's emerged as not just a refuge, but an ultimate destination.

McDonald's long-term success is best understood in terms of the atmosphere and ambience it provides, rather than its products.

All fast-food franchises essentially offer the same goods. Among franchises the variations in quality of hamburger meat, french fries, shakes, and so forth have relatively little impact on the long-term success of the franchise. What does McDonald's know about the niche it serves and the benefits that the niche values? Plenty. Let us examine what McDonald's offers and how it happens to be exactly what you are looking for.

Fast. All fast-food franchisers serve food quickly, compared to traditional sit-down or take-out restaurants. However, have you noticed that at McDonald's, counter people are trained to ask you for your order before you reach the counter? To some people this is a little irritating, but to the vast majority of McDonald's customers this is meal-ordering heaven. Why such a policy? In a switched-on society the consuming public's expectations are such that even a 5- to 6-second delay of gratification becomes annoying. Television sets today, for example, start in an instant; televisions of the last decade took a minute to warm up. Could a television set that requires a 60-second warm-up time, even if superior in every other category, sell today? No way. The sales clerk on the showroom floor would not be able retain the customer's attention long enough. So with McDonald's ability to greet people as they come in the door, assuming there are not lines such as there are at lunch, instant gratification is met.

Clean. The next time you are in a McDonald's, note the color of the interior decorating: white, light colors. Again, all fast-food restaurants strive to maintain cleanliness, but some with orange paint or wood paneling, or shade or shadows, don't convey the same message of brightness and cleanliness on a subconscious level.

The evaluation form, entitled Manager's "Shop" Report, used by an owner of four McDonald's franchises in the Northeast, follows on the next page.

Convenience. The locations of individual McDonald's franchises, as for most fast-food franchises, are well placed.

Manager's "Shop" Report

	Yes, Pts.	No, 0 Pts.
1. Are the six steps of service being used?		
a. Greet the customer	_____ 1 pt.	_____
b. Take the order	_____ 1 pt.	_____
c. Assemble the order	_____ 1 pt.	_____
d. Present the order	_____ 1 pt.	_____
e. Receive payment	_____ 1 pt.	_____
f. Thank customer—*request repeat business*	_____ 1 pt.	_____
2. Is door-to-door serving time 3 minutes or less?	_____ 2 pt.	_____
3. Is counter time less than 1 minute?	_____ 2 pt.	_____
4. Are window personnel courteous and *smiling*?	_____ 5 pt.	_____
5. Do window personnel help each other?	_____ 3 pt.	_____
6. Are counters clean and organized?	_____ 2 pt.	_____
Total points _____		

Unit # _____   Manager _____

Date _____   Assistant _____

Time _____

Note: There are only points for "yes," none for "no." There are no in-between markings such as sometimes, often, frequently, etc. It is either yes or no.

Established Prices. One of the great fears of the American consuming public, and for that matter the consuming public worldwide, is not knowing how much something is going to cost. In its early days, McDonald's advertised getting a full meal and change for your dollar. The rising cost of goods and inflation quickly debilitated that marketing strategy. What has remained, however, is the lingering perception that the food McDonald's offers, while not necessarily being a well-balanced meal, is attractively priced. Actually, per volume of food that they render, the prices at McDonald's and many other fast-food franchisers are no longer attractive, but simply competitive. Many "sub" shops, Chinese take-out, reemerging diners, and others actually offer a better deal—a greater volume of food—once you clear a threshold of roughly $3.00.

What McDonald's and the other franchisers offer are component parts. You may order just the hamburger, just the shake, or just the fries. The price of each is well known and readily displayed. The benefits to the consumer are full disclosure—no guessing, no worrying. A man with a wife and two children knows in advance exactly what it will cost him to take his family to McDonald's for dinner. He has done it before and he will do it again.

Reduction of Uncertainty. Established prices, along with fast service, clean atmosphere, and conveniently located franchises, deliver to the customer perhaps the single greatest benefit that he or she seeks—the total reduction of uncertainty. In an era in which one might be charged $32.00 or $132.00 for a given auto repair, and where confusion reigns supreme in determining who is delivering local telephone service, the ability to walk into any branch of an establishment across the country and receive the same level of service, the same level of responsiveness, and the same goods at the same price taps deeply into the consumer's psyche.

Atmosphere and Ambience. Sometime within the last 25 years we as a nation began abandoning the front porch, the picnic table, the park, and the public square as the site of impromptu social gatherings. The shopping mall has become one of our three most popular places to spend time outside the home, and McDonald's is well represented within our nation's malls. Even the freestanding franchises have long cultivated their position as acceptable meeting places.

After school, a 12-to-16-year-old group has no problem convening at the nearest McDonald's. Parents with cranky two-year-olds who need to get themselves and their children out of the house know that McDonald's is there, and will always be there, ready, receptive, even uplifting. The child is always glad to receive his or her "Happy Meal." The mother at this stage in the child's development is happy to resort to any technique that will provide her with a few minutes of relative peace and contentment.

Like a stimulating drug, each McDonald's outlet has been designed to serve as an instant party room for today's knee-highs—the next generation of Big Mac consumers. McDonald's has defined itself in terms of meeting mothers' needs so much that all supporting accoutrements, including high chairs and party hats, are at her disposal.

Rest Rooms. With increasing dismay, I find that not all fast-food franchisers maintain rest rooms for the public. McDonald's does in every outlet, and with good reason. Mothers with young children, traveling salespersons, all who take comfort here appreciate having convenient rest-room facilities. Indeed, for a McDonald's to have emerged as a destination required that clean, readily available rest-room facilities be a part of every franchise. In defining their business solely in terms of the benefits to the consumer, one is immediately struck by the thought, "How could they not provide rest rooms?"'

In one celebrated study, a museum in Connecticut tabulated the average number of visitors received each day and the average amount of time that they remained in the museum. During a two-week period when the rest rooms were closed for repairs, the average length of stay dropped by 66 percent. The vast majority of people who patronize McDonald's do not use its rest rooms. Nevertheless, it is an important factor in their overall perception of service.

Parking. Over the years the ratio of parking lot to store size has increased. In numerous franchises throughout the country the parking lot is more than 10 times the square footage of the store itself. More outlets now offer drive-through service. Again, defining parking solely in terms of benefits to the customer, what do you and I as customers want? The ability to get in and out of parking spaces easily. If we are really in a hurry, we appreciate the ability to order and receive our goods without getting out of the car. We want the entrance to be well lit, accessible, and we want the exit to be clearly marked and to provide relative ease in getting back onto the major thoroughfare.

Outside Decor. The baby boom generation, those born between 1946 and 1964, was the first generation of children "brought up on McDonald's." As they matured, so too did the decor, particularly the outside decor of the franchise outlets. Today, earth tones (including browns and greens) with attractive red brick define the typical suburban appearance. Outlets within cities more closely merge with the surrounding urban environment.

Menu. As the baby boomers themselves became parents, McDonald's' menu shifted radically. It never made any pretense at offering well-balanced meals. If you wanted nutrition, there were plenty of other places to go to. McDonald's recognized that throughout the 1960s and 1970s the bulk of the population received their nutrition through other meals. Thus there was no penalty for not introducing anything green into the menu. But the baby boomers were a much more health-conscious group and would not be denied their greens. While McDonald's had experimented with offering roast beef (failed), McNuggets (still here today), and other low-quality, high-profit items such as cookies and soft ice cream, the introduction of salads in the mid-1980s represents its most fundamental change.

To be sure, McDonald's' salads are not high quality, and the pure nutritionist will still not eat them. But keeping true to the concept of defining itself around customer needs, McDonald's salads satisfy a need among many to return to a more balanced diet. In this instance, McDonald's was actually slow to change. Competitors had long offered salad bars and a variety of other items. McDonald's has a history of slowly changing its menu and very carefully introducing new items on a limited basis to see whether they catch hold. But the information reaching the corporate offices and Hamburger University ultimately pointed to the introduction of greens. That having been done, McDonald's was able to reduce the increasing number of attacks on its unbalanced offerings to a great extent.

In addition to these accommodations, McDonald's continues to present what is arguably one of the most successful mass media advertising campaigns in history. Advertisements specifically target ethnic groups, most notably Blacks and Hispanics. McDonald's has entrenched itself as an American institution. The flag flies proudly each day in front of all franchises. There are promotional tie-ins with supermarkets, with community events, even with Steven Spielberg. McDonald's will never be a stranger to the American public because it recognizes that a large measure of its ability to continue to sell to us profitably depends on its ability to keep redefining how it can be a partner in our culture.

Whether it is hospital programs for children, 10K road races, or cosponsoring of community events, the corporation continuously seeks ways to "cut itself in" on that which interests society. Therefore, regardless of whether you like or dislike the food that McDonald's serves, it is likely that you find it difficult to fault it as an organization since it participates so fully in all that is American.

To fully understand the way in which this corporation positions itself, we must also understand what McDonald's does not represent.

Variety. McDonald's is not in the business of providing a wide variety of menu items. With its hamburgers, fish, chicken, and salad, it provides just enough variety so that you could eat there several times before repeating your order. Still, the hamburger is a popular food in the American diet, and since there are many customers who can eat a hamburger several times a week and feel good about it, in serving this niche there is no real reason to provide a vast assortment of menu items.

A Hangout. While teens frequently convene at McDonald's after school or school events, McDonald's is clearly not a hangout. The pressure of relinquishing your table when finished eating so that the next person or group may sit has been built into the system. At least within the American franchises, we are there for the "break we deserve today," but we are not there to linger. You may buy another soft drink or another order of french fries, and frequently you will, but to sit at a table and not be consuming is the fast-food franchise form of sin. It is not as if anyone will come around and ask you to leave, but the pressure is still there. So, too, if you choose to eat in the parking lot, that is your business. But shortly thereafter the expectation is that you will be on your way.

Keeping the Lead

In such a highly competitive arena, and with all the changes taking place in society, to be out of step for just a little while could spell failure. The inroads made by Burger King and Wendy's especially during their famous "Burger Wars" and "Where's the Beef" campaigns, enabled both of those franchise outfits to pick up some gound on the leader. Yet McDonald's continues to prevail as the premier fast-food franchiser. The next time you drive down a strip development with five or six franchises, notice the number of cars in the respective parking lots. Urban or suburban, morning, midday, or evening, on one strip after another, McDonald's consistently has more cars.

Even now, the McDonald's top brass is looking at how it will position itself throughout the 1990s. After carefully studying demographic trends, whom it is serving now and whom it is likely to serve, it will probe important corporate questions. What new changes, if any, should be made internally? What new changes, if any, should be made externally? What are the causes, concerns, interests, and activities of its customers and how can it continue to participate in these arenas? How can it as a corporation participate in American cultural development as manifested at the store level? What moves will its competitors make? What images and advertising themes will appeal to its targets throughout the 1990s?

It is not necessary or practical to change your marketing strategy each time you gain new information about the marketplace or about your role in serving it. Rather, your changes are more likely to be implemented at controlled intervals. A company that keeps changing its message and appeal confuses everyone. Still, the research and positioning that goes on behind the scenes must know no vacation.

SHOP 'N CHEK—HELPING RETAILERS MAINTAIN HIGH STANDARDS

To a large extent, how your products or services are perceived by the target market is influenced by the quality of your sales staff. An alert, attentive, and friendly sales staff enhances the perceived value of any product or service (see Chapter 12). Conversely, an inattentive, uncaring, or unfriendly sales staff will render the highest quality product or the most desirable service less effective and less desirable.

Raising standards to a high level is greatly aided by services such as Shop 'n Chek, which offers the mystery shopper program. With services such as Shop 'n Chek, retailers can readily obtain feedback about how they are being viewed by customers—a real boost for developing and maintaining an effective position.

The use of mystery shoppers uncovers rudeness or alertness among employees, lets management monitor the progress of sales training, and indicates how often customer contact is positive. Carol Cherry, president of Shop 'n Chek, Inc., Georgia, says that to deal with the increased competition for customers, many companies now use mystery shoppers to analyze how the sales staff and individual branches or locations are coming across to customers.[1]

The 14-year-old Shop 'n Chek employs more than 16,000 professional shoppers nationwide to act as the "ears" and "eyes" for marketing executives wanting to know how employees deal with their products and customers. Its national network of specially trained shoppers sips beverages, test-drives automobiles, receives flowers, and samples products from big-name firms to provide clients a snapshot of their business conditions.

"We are a company's eyes and ears in the field," Cherry says. "We encourage clients to use our reports as management measurement tools and to implement changes dictated by our findings." Armed with criteria, objectives, and checklists developed for the client company, these

---

[1] Adapted with permission from *Marketing News*, "Mystery Shoppers Provide Check on Customer-Service Experience," published by the American Marketing Association, June 5, 1987, p. 4.

professional shoppers compare and evaluate retail conditions of business operations, such as product quality, overall appearance, and effectiveness of product sales support.

Cherry said her company's service differs from marketing research in both approach and application. The company deals in fact finding, rather than consumer opinion gathering, and its evaluations are performed on site rather than in a controlled research environment.

Incentive Program

In Shop 'n Chek's mystery shopper incentive program, retailers are alerted that a mystery shopper may visit their store location and award a prize for meeting certain objectives in sales presentations for a particular product. During the visit, prizes are awarded on presentation criteria, such as the inclusion of key product features and benefits during product demonstrations to the consumer. Evaluative reports are submitted to the clients on each presentation witness. Cherry said the Consumer Electronics Division of a large corporation used its mystery shopper program to evaluate sales performance and point-of-purchase assistance at retail outlets carrying its videodiscs.

"The program definitely got the salespeople's attention," said one corporate manager. "We felt it served as a positive motivational tool and made our salespeople rise to the challenge. I read through every evaluation myself," he said. "I then used the favorable comments identified by the shoppers as additional incentives, while the negative comments were passed on to the distributor and then to the dealers. The comments were very specific, from recognizing point-of-purchase to citing a particular salesman's performance."

Shop 'n Chek's system is consistent throughout the United States, Cherry says, "because quality control and scheduling of projects are managed through one office in Atlanta." For clients, this means that it is possible to access the entire 16,000-member network with one phone call.

Evaluating More Than Just the Staff

Because of its organizational structure and design, Shop 'n Chek's service also lends itself to evaluations of operational, marketing, or training issues rather than individual management shortcomings, Cherry observed. Shop 'n Chek can conduct support studies at the retail level, including point-of-purchase merchandise analyses, brand penetration audits, and tracking of client and competitor prices. Results from these presentations help product distributors gain greater perspective about the nature and degree of sales support given their products.

HOW STAPLES DOMINATED A MARKET OVERNIGHT

One day in the life of your business the moment will come when everything is working at optimum capacity. You have apparently positioned yourself well and are profitably serving the needs of your target market. You have allocated your marketing resources wisely, and you have an effective aftermarketing program in place. The very reason you went into business is all but fulfilled. Yet, like snowflakes that melt on your window sill, the golden moment is fleeting. Within the coming year, perhaps the next month, maybe the next week, even this minute some crucial factor in your business environment is likely to change.

In the Bailey's Crossroads section of my home town of Falls Church, Virginia, Southern Office Supply was the premier office supply store throughout the 1980s until the start of 1988. Southern was well located in the L-shaped shopping center at the intersection of Columbia Pike and Leesburg Pike. Both roads were major commercial highways and commuter thoroughfares. There was ample free parking in front of the store. The store itself was appropriately located next to a low- to mid-level-quality department store and a high-volume chain drug store.

The interior of Southern Office Supply was more than adequate, approximately 1000 square feet. As office supply stores go, Southern was doing okay. Over the years they had built up a mailing list and distributed a high-quality four-color, four-page monthly flyer announcing specials and bargain buys. The personnel were helpful if not entirely knowledgeable of the products offered. The atmosphere was one of dedication, seriousness—being low key, perhaps almost somber. You came, you looked around, you made your purchase, and you left. A trip to Southern blended in with the rest of your day and certainly the rest of your errands. It was but one stop along the way, and certainly not an unpleasant stop.

Southern's prices were reasonable. Besides the advertised monthly bargains, one would consider the store's prices to be competitive, definitely not outrageous. Until the beginning of 1988, Southern's major competitors were Miller Office Supply, Ginn's, and Jacobs-Gardner. All three companies had numerous outlets throughout northern Virginia.

Out of Nowhere?

From what must have seemed out of nowhere to Southern's management, Staples arrived in town. Staples took the corner place on the right of the L-shaped shopping strip. The location's previous tenants included Circuit City, which moved to an even larger location, Warehouse Foods, which failed miserably, and Bill's Carpets.

From its first month of operation through the end of the year Staples caught on like wildfire. The store was easily four times the square footage of Southern, as was its inventory. The selection was vast and deep. It is doubtful that any office supply purchasers in the area had ever experienced anything like Staples. It was clean and bright and bustling. The sign said "The Office Super Store," and the outfit lived up to it in every way.

When you first entered, you had the feeling that this was no ordinary office supply store. A large sign indicated that Visa, Master Card, check, Staples credit card, and cash could all be used for payment. Shopping carts, such as those used in supermarkets, were available inside the entrance. All traffic was directed to the right so each shopper would have to walk a minimum of two aisles to get back to the cashier.

Staple's prices were unlike anything the area had experienced. Notebooks, pads, paper, computer supplies: many items sold for as much as 40 percent less than at other office supply stores. If you happened to have a Staples card, and this was encouraged at all checkout counters and by all employees, you could save another 10 percent.

In addition to the traditional items you might expect, Staples also provided accessory office products. Bargains were offered on coffee, juice, business magazines, business literature, reference books—Staples was a one-stop center. Along the left side of the store were placed office copying machines so that you could make your own copies. There were also engraving, laminating, and other related services.

Superior in Every Way

More than just being a physically superior store both inside and out, Staples's employees had a completely different attitude from those of the competitors. They carried a *"we are in business to serve you"* attitude. Perhaps it was because they knew that they were with a winner, or perhaps it was simply a function of good management. The latter is more likely.

Staples was a memorable if not pleasurable experience. Each time you entered the store you felt as if you were in partnership with the store. Many customers commented that the prices were so low that they wanted to stock up as much as possible on the first few trips. They wanted to make sure that these kinds of bargains, whether they lasted or not, were experienced now. There had been nothing like this before.

Along the wall facing customers, just after they finished checking out, was a 6- by 20-foot bulletin board with clear plastic pockets to hold business cards. Across the top were major categories such as real estate, secretarial services, consultants, temporary services, and others. In a few months, hundreds of patrons had put their cards in the plastic sleeves and become part of the Staples family. Southern had actually had a similar technique. Their bulletin board, however, was 3 by 4 feet and cards were held in place by a pin or thumbtack. During its heyday, there were never more than 60 to 70 cards on Southern's bulletin board. By contrast, Staples displayed well over a thousand cards in an organized helpful manner.

Various activity checks throughout the day showed that Staples averaged between 8 and 16 patrons in the store at any given moment, while Southern had fallen off to a little less than two patrons at any given time. By the year's end, other surrounding office supply stores were feeling the impact of Staples's clearly superior methods and distribution of marketing capabilities.

Who Was That Masked Man?

Let us step back now and examine how Staples positioned itself for success in the northern Virginia market, and how Southern Office Supply positioned itself with inevitable results. Staples was already successful throughout the New York metropolitan area, New Jersey, Philadelphia, Boston, and Long Island. Its expansion into the Washington, D.C., area was logical and perhaps even predictable.

Prior to opening in the Bailey's Crossroads area, it visited each of its potential competitors and examined how the shelves were stocked, their prices, ambience, the quality of employees, and many other factors. It determined that there were more than 15,000 workers within a two-mile trade radius and thousands more residents who demographically fit its target niche.

There is no real brand loyalty for office products: a note pad is a note pad and a computer printer ribbon is a computer printer ribbon. Significant price savings were able to separate Staples from its competitors. Staples placed full-page ads in the back of community newspapers and journals which highlighted some of its best bargains. Experience in other store openings showed significant word-of-mouth advertising could be generated.

In every way, then, Staples was more customer oriented. It opened earlier and closed later. It answered its telephone within two rings. It prepared a store layout map and a directory of items for distribution to all customers, which detailed where each item in the store could be found (Figures 11 and 12). An expert directed customers to appropriate aisles. By contrast, Southern and many of its competitors were miserable in orienting themselves to the customer. Clerks were frequently put off, and even acted as if they had been disturbed when asked about the location of specific items.

In leaving Staples, one had a choice of six different cash registers, including an express checkout line. When exiting any of its competitors the shopper was inconvienced by the poor design and lack of counter space. These checkout counters took up everyone's time.

One could go on and on about the superior distribution and marketing techniques employed by Staples. Its ability to move into the market and quickly position itself as an office supply store to be reckoned with is now a matter of record.

While Rome Burned

What of the top management at Southern Office Supply? Though I am not privy to its strategies and activities, based on the fate that befell its stores, here is what it apparently did *not* do:

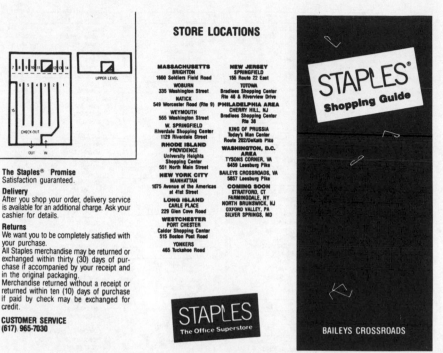

STORE LOCATIONS

MASSACHUSETTS
BRIGHTON
1660 Soldiers Field Road
WOBURN
335 Washington Street
NATICK
549 Worcester Road (Rte 9)
WEYMOUTH
555 Washington Street
W. SPRINGFIELD
Riverdale Shopping Center
1129 Riverdale Street
RHODE ISLAND
PROVIDENCE
University Heights
Shopping Center
551 North Main Street
NEW YORK CITY
MANHATTAN
1075 Avenue of the Americas
at 41st Street
LONG ISLAND
CARLE PLACE
229 Glen Cove Road
WESTCHESTER
PORT CHESTER
Caldor Shopping Center
515 Boston Post Road
YONKERS
465 Tuckahoe Road

NEW JERSEY
SPRINGFIELD
155 Route 22 East
TOTOWA
Bradlees Shopping Center
Rte 46 & Riverview Drive
PHILADELPHIA AREA
CHERRY HILL, NJ
Bradlees Shopping Center
Rte 38
KING OF PRUSSIA
Today's Man Center
Route 202/DeKalb Pike
**WASHINGTON, D.C.
AREA**
TYSONS CORNER, VA
8459 Leesburg Pike
BAILEYS CROSSROADS, VA
5857 Leesburg Pike
COMING SOON
FARMINGDALE, NY
NORTH BRUNSWICK, NJ
OXFORD VALLEY, PA
SILVER SPRINGS, MD

The Staples® Promise
Satisfaction guaranteed.

Delivery
After you shop your order, delivery service
is available for an additional charge. Ask your
cashier for details.

Returns
We want you to be completely satisfied with
your purchase.
All Staples merchandise may be returned or
exchanged within thirty (30) days of purchase if accompanied by your receipt and
in the original packaging.
Merchandise returned without a receipt or
returned within ten (10) days of purchase
if paid by check may be exchanged for
credit.

CUSTOMER SERVICE
(617) 965-7030

STAPLES
The Office Superstore

STAPLES®
Shopping Guide

BAILEYS CROSSROADS

Figure 11. Staples store map. (Reprinted with permission.)

Attend trade shows and conventions and pay attention to the latest developments in the industry. It seems impossible to believe that Southern's top management had not heard of Staples, or had no inkling that the company was in an expansion phase.

Subscribe to and read industry journals, insiders' newsletters, and association reports. An organization as well run and well functioning as Staples does not, and in fact cannot, go unnoticed within its industry. Indication of its existence and progress included its own PR releases, endless reports, and a series of grand openings.

Tour Staples and other competitors' stores. On a regular and ongoing basis, Southern's management should have been visiting the stores and showrooms of all competitors within its own region and beyond. The fact that Staples was not present in the northern Virginia area prior to 1988, but was operating successfully in the New York–New Jersey metropolitan area, should have been cause for alarm for Southern's top management.

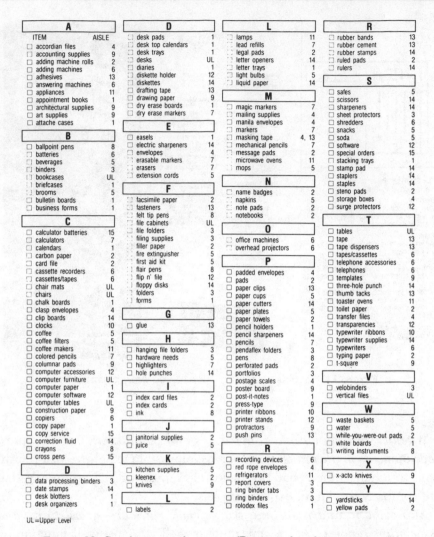

A	
ITEM	AISLE
☐ accordian files	4
☐ accounting supplies	9
☐ adding machine rolls	2
☐ adding machines	6
☐ adhesives	13
☐ answering machines	6
☐ appliances	11
☐ appointment books	1
☐ architectural supplies	9
☐ art supplies	9
☐ attache cases	1

B	
☐ ballpoint pens	8
☐ batteries	6
☐ beverages	5
☐ binders	3
☐ bookcases	UL
☐ briefcases	1
☐ brooms	5
☐ bulletin boards	1
☐ business forms	1

C	
☐ calculator batteries	15
☐ calculators	7
☐ calendars	1
☐ carbon paper	2
☐ card file	2
☐ cassette recorders	6
☐ cassettes/tapes	6
☐ chair mats	UL
☐ chairs	UL
☐ chalk boards	1
☐ clasp envelopes	4
☐ clip boards	14
☐ clocks	10
☐ coffee	5
☐ coffee filters	5
☐ coffee makers	11
☐ colored pencils	7
☐ columnar pads	9
☐ computer accessories	12
☐ computer furniture	UL
☐ computer paper	1
☐ computer software	12
☐ computer tables	UL
☐ construction paper	9
☐ copiers	6
☐ copy paper	1
☐ copy service	15
☐ correction fluid	14
☐ crayons	8
☐ cross pens	15

D	
☐ data processing binders	3
☐ date stamps	14
☐ desk blotters	1
☐ desk organizers	1

D	
☐ desk pads	1
☐ desk top calendars	1
☐ desk trays	1
☐ desks	UL
☐ diaries	1
☐ diskette holder	12
☐ diskettes	14
☐ drafting tape	13
☐ drawing paper	9
☐ dry erase boards	1
☐ dry erase markers	7

E	
☐ easels	1
☐ electric sharpeners	14
☐ envelopes	4
☐ erasable markers	7
☐ erasers	7
☐ extension cords	5

F	
☐ facsimile paper	2
☐ fasteners	13
☐ felt tip pens	8
☐ file cabinets	UL
☐ file folders	3
☐ filing supplies	3
☐ filler paper	2
☐ fire extinguisher	5
☐ first aid kit	5
☐ flair pens	8
☐ flip n' file	12
☐ floppy disks	14
☐ folders	3
☐ forms	1

G	
☐ glue	13

H	
☐ hanging file folders	3
☐ hardware needs	5
☐ highlighters	7
☐ hole punches	14

I	
☐ index card files	2
☐ index cards	2
☐ ink	8

J	
☐ janitorial supplies	2
☐ juice	5

K	
☐ kitchen supplies	5
☐ kleenex	2
☐ knives	9

L	
☐ labels	2

L	
☐ lamps	11
☐ lead refills	7
☐ legal pads	2
☐ letter openers	14
☐ letter trays	1
☐ light bulbs	5
☐ liquid paper	14

M	
☐ magic markers	7
☐ mailing supplies	4
☐ manila envelopes	4
☐ markers	7
☐ masking tape	4, 13
☐ mechanical pencils	7
☐ message pads	2
☐ microwave ovens	11
☐ mops	5

N	
☐ name badges	2
☐ napkins	5
☐ note pads	2
☐ notebooks	2

O	
☐ office machines	6
☐ overhead projectors	6

P	
☐ padded envelopes	4
☐ pads	2
☐ paper clips	13
☐ paper cups	5
☐ paper cutters	14
☐ paper plates	5
☐ paper towels	2
☐ pencil holders	1
☐ pencil sharpeners	14
☐ pencils	7
☐ pendaflex folders	3
☐ pens	8
☐ perforated pads	2
☐ portfolios	3
☐ postage scales	4
☐ poster board	9
☐ post-it-notes	1
☐ press-type	9
☐ printer ribbons	10
☐ printer stands	12
☐ protractors	9
☐ push pins	13

R	
☐ recording devices	6
☐ red rope envelopes	4
☐ refrigerators	11
☐ report covers	3
☐ ring binder tabs	3
☐ ring binders	3
☐ rolodex files	1

R	
☐ rubber bands	13
☐ rubber cement	13
☐ rubber stamps	14
☐ ruled pads	2
☐ rulers	14

S	
☐ safes	5
☐ scissors	14
☐ sharpeners	14
☐ sheet protectors	3
☐ shredders	6
☐ snacks	5
☐ soda	5
☐ software	12
☐ special orders	15
☐ stacking trays	1
☐ stamp pad	14
☐ staplers	14
☐ staples	14
☐ steno pads	2
☐ storage boxes	4
☐ surge protectors	12

T	
☐ tables	UL
☐ tape	13
☐ tape dispensers	13
☐ tapes/cassettes	6
☐ telephone accessories	6
☐ telephones	6
☐ templates	9
☐ three-hole punch	14
☐ thumb tacks	13
☐ toaster ovens	11
☐ toilet paper	2
☐ transfer files	4
☐ transparencies	12
☐ typewriter ribbons	10
☐ typewriter supplies	14
☐ typewriters	6
☐ typing paper	2
☐ t-square	9

V	
☐ velobinders	3
☐ vertical files	UL

W	
☐ waste baskets	5
☐ water	5
☐ while-you-were-out pads	2
☐ white boards	1
☐ writing instruments	8

X	
☐ x-acto knives	9

Y	
☐ yardsticks	14
☐ yellow pads	2

UL=Upper Level

Figure 12. Staples store directory. (Reprinted with permission.)

Today, particularly in retailing, but also in services, an operation that is extremely successful in one part of the country can be counted on to expand.

Communicate with the original equipment manufacturers, wholesalers, and distributors. Many of the items offered in Southern's outlets also appeared in Staples's outlets. In many instances, the two chains were served by the original equipment manufacturers or their distributors. Staples's expansion outside of the New York metropolitan area was known within the industry long before the actual grand opening in northern Virginia. Southern's top management, its business analysts, indeed, all personnel above the clerical level, would have access to this information via the host of distributors and suppliers with whom they may have come in contact.

The Southern Strategy

Suppose for a moment, though one hardly could, that Southern was aware of Staples's expansion and particularly was aware of Staples's expansion to the Bailey's Crossroads area. What could Southern have done in the short term and the long term to try to compete and protect its market share? Stated more clearly, how could Southern have positioned itself to remain a viable force in the market?

On a short-term basis, Southern could have advertised several items at bargain prices and competed head on with Staples, vigorously promoting those items. Through its monthly circular to customers, Southern could have announced a price-slashing campaign and a "we meet the competition head on" message, thus increasing store traffic temporarily. With such a campaign it may have encouraged bulk buying.

It would have also made excellent sense for Southern's managers to visit Staples to determine what the other store was lacking, and to become especially proficient in stocking those items. As a long-term strategy, Southern could have billed itself as provider of "XYZ," the XYZ representing whatever Staples was not offering and that Southern could turn into a draw.

While store renovation is costly, in the short term Southern could have raised its illumination so that it would not appear like a cave when compared to the professional showroom atmosphere that Staples offered. In addition, Southern could have redesigned its storefront displays, changing them from the sleepy, tired array of unexciting products to an eye-catching, customer-drawing, professionally crafted and designed display.

Last, and requiring even less ingenuity, Southern could have made use of in-store shelf talkers, signs that say "bargain," "buy me," "X% off," "sale today," "red tag special," etc.—but it did not.

Crushing the Competition

By midyear, Staples was often ringing up more business an hour than Southern was generating in a day. While Staples was advertising for more help, Southern had cut back its staff. Staples's entire product offering was discounted, while Southern continued to distribute the same monthly flyer and generated less and less response. Even with its neighbor a mere 200 feet away, and more visible marketing clues than one could ask for, Southern went on, set in its ways, not adopting *any* of the high-power marketing techniques Staples had mastered.

What could Southern's market positioning have been? Did it have a large base of commercial accounts that it believed would remain loyal in the face of overwhelming price reductions? Did it believe that customer loyalty transcends outrageous savings? Did it embark on some other failed strategy which was not apparent to observers?

It is easy, after reading what has been described, to regard Southern's management as inept, inflexible, or out of step with the times. Yet, increasingly throughout the 1990s, even those operations that take great pains to be aware of what is happening in the industry may encounter a surprise move by a "Staples."

> **The key to survival and prosperity will be to continuously seek a market position that will set your operation up as different or special, even if it's only for a particular commodity or service.**

Faced with outrageous competition on all sides, there are *always* options to provide products or services profitably in a manner that outflanks the competition.

11

Attaining Key Vendor Status

For many are called but few are chosen.

MATTHEW 22, v. 14

The nature of relationships between large corporations and the key vendors that supply them with crucial products and services is changing rapidly. Increasingly, vendors are called upon to provide a variety of functions that were previously handled by the corporate purchasing department.

In this chapter we will focus on what separates the winning vendors to large corporations from the also-rans and discuss:

☐ The emergence of new partnerships between buyer and vendor

☐ Why buyers count on the vendor for more than ever before

☐ Key elements of favored vendor status

☐ How life-of-the-program contracts offer predictable revenues, smooth cash flows, and greater planning capability

☐ How some corporations help small vendors

☐ Getting the most out of trade shows—corporate America's meeting place

---

The word is out that corporate buyers want and need "a great deal of information" before choosing a company for a prime supplier according to *Purchasing World* magazine. Corporate purchasing agents are expecting more from their suppliers, particularly in the area of quality. *Purchasing World* points out that "some companies estimate that they purchase 70 percent of their quality problems." In other words, the vast majority of end-product quality headaches are shipped into their plants by suppliers in the form of subpar purchase goods and materials. One purchasing agent observed, "there is no way we can improve the quality of what we are doing" without improvements in incoming components.

The vendor who is able to guarantee shipments has a distinct advantage over those who do not or cannot.

FEW ARE CHOSEN

The Xerox Corporation, which is regarded as having one of the premier purchasing programs, undertook a "drastic pruning" of its vendor base, while providing intensive training to key suppliers in such techniques as statistical process control and just-in-time inventory systems. Xerox has also helped suppliers with personnel development programs and longer term contracts that "impel suppliers to become business partners, and build confidence to the point where suppliers share what they have learned."

Among all industrial corporations the average number of suppliers is declining, while single-sourcing is growing in popularity. More than ever, observes one veteran, "relationships are up for grabs." Even long-standing personal relationships are at risk. Purchasers are limiting the number of sales representatives who call on them.

RULES OF THE GAME

Against this backdrop, let us examine the major ways successful vendors position themselves for long-term success in marketing to large corporations.

Vendor Contribution to Value Analysis. Vendors who have been particularly successful in winning long-term contracts with major corporations make key contributions to value analysis. What is value analysis? It is the continual research, refinement, and adaptation of products so that they can be built faster, less expensively, more durably, or be improved in some other significant way.

The vendor who is able to assist the corporate purchasing agent in meeting the agent's buying needs and helping to increase value analysis becomes a valued, if not highly favored, vendor. Corporations seek vendor input because, realistically, who else is in a better position to suggest new and improved approaches to the goods that they supply?

The vendor's success in contributing to value analysis becomes a key marketing tool. Any improvement a vendor is able to suggest or implement suggests to the vendor's customers that the vendor is continuously on the lookout for cost-saving, product-enhancing changes. In addition, the vendor can emphasize his or her role in contributing to value analysis in one corporation when marketing to another corporation. Value analysis becomes a tool for indicating a vendor's innovativeness and extensive concern for the buyer's welfare.

Vendor Supply and Quality Control. In the 1990s, vendors will be called upon more often to provide quality control for the parts and supplies that they produce and deliver to corporate purchasing departments. When the vendor can guarantee an agreed-upon level of quality, major industrial buyers are freed from this function. This reduces the buyer's throughput time in producing the final product. Vendor-supplied quality control also reduces a corporation's labor, inventorying, and return-shipment costs.

> **Vendor-supplied quality control is a natural evolution of the vendor– buyer relationship, and the phenomenon will only continue to grow in popularity throughout the 1990s.**

Once a working relationship is established in which the vendor will supply quality control and this program proves to be successful, the corporate purchasing department gains tremendous confidence and trust in the vendor.

Life-of-the-Program Contracts. Vendors who prove themselves by contributing to value analysis, assuming responsibility for the quality control function, or who indicate superior performance in terms of traditional measures such as price, quality, and delivery, are often invited to participate on long-term contracts. A life-of-the-program contract essentially guarantees that a vendor will be called upon to supply a particular product or service for as long as the customer, generally a major corporation, has a prime contract.

For example, if an aerospace manufacturer wins a multiyear contract with the Department of Defense to design and produce an advanced air surveillance system, then a vendor supplying equipment in support of such a system would retain that status for the duration of the prime contractor's contract.

Vendors who have successfully served in life-of-the-program contracts are also able to leverage such relationships within one corporation when seeking to obtain life-of-the-program contracts in other corporations. The obvious benefits to the vendor—larger longer term contracts with predictable cash flows and predictable revenues—enable the vendor to build a sound business by having fewer but more valuable contracts.

The corporate buyer benefits also. Corporations that know they have a supplier in whom they can rely are able to meet their program goals and timetables with more regularity, and are able to maintain greater project cost control on a long-term basis.

Corporate Sponsored Vendor-Training Programs. After a corporate purchasing department has had a successful encounter or series of encounters with a vendor, or when the vendor has established him- or herself in some unique way, some corporations are willing to pay for vendor training. This training serves many functions. For one, if a vendor is close to being qualified to provide a particular product or service but is not quite there, often the training can help close the gap. Thus the vendor adds to his or her proficiency, while the corporation gains another key source of supply.

In addition, the vendor is able to learn more of the ways of the customer, and hence is better positioned to serve. The corporation assists the vendor in becoming more cost conscious and more efficient, and thus positions itself for long-term cost savings. Both parties establish stronger personal relationships, as most of the vendor training is usually on site at corporate headquarters or key branches.

While vendor contribution to value analysis, vendor-supplied quality control, life-of-the-contract programs, and corporate sponsorship of vendor training programs are looked upon as advanced elements of vendor/ corporate relationships, winning vendors of the 1990s will increasingly seek and nurture these program elements as a normal course of doing business.

In It for the Long Run

What makes for an effective long-term relationship between vendor and buyer? It is a combination of many things. Veteran sales trainer Mack Hanan says that the vendor wants to make the customer comfortable. However, "Comfort without surprise leads to complacency. Surprise without comfort is anarchy."

Both buyers and sellers recognize that the long-term relationship is essential—particularly if the corporation is a significant customer of the supplier. Many buyers ensure that their accounting departments pay in strict accordance with initiated terms so that the smaller vendor is paid promptly. With a healthy cash flow, the vendor can continue to serve the corporate buyer effectively. From nearly all vantage points, the 1990s will see increased cooperation and participation between corporate purchasing departments and key suppliers to ensure their mutual prosperity.

How Else Do Vendors Position Themselves for Success?

Defining a Service Strategy. Successful vendors encapsulate their philosophy of customer service. This need not be more than a 100- or 150-word description of philosophy that conveys a promise to the customer and states how the company will stand by its word. This service statement is often made part of the company's literature, and segments of it may appear on company vehicles, letterheads, and other documents.

Handling Special Requests. Successful vendors regard special requests as opportunities for establishing themselves as companies of distinction.

A late-night delivery or any other type of sudden request is viewed as a challenge rather than a burden.

Serving as Consultants. As we will see in Chapter 13, customers, even large industrial buyers, increasingly look to the vendor or seller as a consultant who can counsel them regarding particular purchase decisions.

Maintenance of Reserve and Replacement Parts. Successful vendors recognize that in addition to meeting contract specifications, they will also be looked upon as the source for spare parts to products or service equipment they are supplying.

Development of Instructions and Spec Sheets. Plain English, easy to follow instructions enhance the vendor's status. These can be supplied for everything from how to properly unpackage delivered goods to properly treating or getting the most use out of them. Even on routine shipments, winning vendors know that the personnel receiving such shipments may be new or unfamiliar with the product or part. Every transaction and every shipment is treated as if it were the first.

Development of Internal Standards. While the customer may only require A, B, and C, the vendor positioned for long-term success often supplies A, B, C, and D, or A, B, C, D, and E. This may not be possible for all products, all deliveries, or all contracts. However, offering the extra touch is a marketing masterstroke when the buyer knows it is being done and acknowledges its value.

Surveying the Corporate Customer. An innovative, powerful tool for ensuring that a contract is being fulfilled correctly is to survey the customer, no matter how large. Successful vendors boldly query corporate receiving dock managers, shipping clerks, engineers, buyers, field representatives, and others to make sure that the vendor, across the board, is serving the needs of the corporation.

Offering Regular, Positive Reports and Updates. Some vendors handling contracts where work is performed over an extended period of time supply weekly or monthly progress reports. These reports can be used as tools for effective position marketing. They are more than a recanting of the performance and effort of the vendor—they are an opportunity to reaffirm the buyer's choice in contracting with the vendor in the first place, and to bolster his or her feelings about using the vendor again.

THE VIEW FROM CORPORATE PURCHASING

Purchasing agents have a great deal more responsibilities than most vendors realize. For example, purchasing agents routinely have the responsibility for:

- Evaluating suppliers
- Identifying, selecting, and developing new suppliers
- Scheduling purchases
- Scheduling deliveries
- Negotiating contracts
- Specifying the mode of inbound shipments
- Controlling inventories
- Managing value analysis activities
- Determining whether to make or buy a component
- Deciding to lease versus purchase
- Visiting plant sites to evaluate suppliers (12 or more visits per year)

Increasingly, corporate representatives are visiting vendors' plants to gain greater understanding of the vendors' operations. The survey form in Figure 13 is representative of that used by larger companies to evaluate potential suppliers.

Criteria by Which Purchasing Agents Judge Vendors

- Reputation
- Dependability
- Reliability
- Price
- Total product line offered
- Inventory assistance
- Materials requirements planning
- Total cost
- Proximity
- Financial stability (see Chapter 8)

Vendor Plant Survey

ORIGINATING PLANT: _____ DATE OF VISIT: _____

REASON FOR VISIT: _____

REPRESENTATIVE: _____

ORGANIZATION AND ADMINISTRATION

VENDOR'S NAME AND ADDRESS: _____

    (INCLUDE PHONE NO.)   _____

PRODUCT LINE: _____

OWNERSHIP: PUBLICLY HELD _____ PRIVATELY HELD _____

GOVERNMENT CLASSIFICATION OF BUSINESS: MINORITY _____ LARGE _____ SMALL _____

NO. OF EMPLOYEES: HOURLY _____ SALARY _____

SALES VOLUME (LAST 3 YEARS): 19 ____ _____ 19 ____ _____ 19 ____ _____

COMPANY OFFICERS, INCLUDING KEY CONTACTS: _____

   _____

   _____

   _____

   _____

PRINCIPAL CUSTOMERS: _____ % OF BUSINESS _____

   _____ "   " _____

   _____ "   " _____

   _____ "   " _____

   _____ "   " _____

   _____ "   " _____

MANUFACTURING

FACTORY AREA (FOOTAGE): _____

BUILDING CONSTRUCTION: _____

ROOM FOR EXPANSION: _____ LAND AVAILABLE: _____

LAYOUT: A = WELL LAID OUT   B = CONGESTED   C = POORLY ORGANIZED   D = UNDERMECHANIZED

        ☐ MANUFACTURING AREA   ☐ ADMINISTRATIVE AREA

DO THEY HAVE LAB FACILITIES? _____

DO THEY HAVE OWN TOOL SHOP: _____ TYPES OF TOOLS _____

TOOLING STORAGE: ADEQUATE _____ INADEQUATE _____

LINE FLOW: VERY GOOD _____ GOOD _____ FAIR _____ POOR _____

PRODUCTION CONTROL SYSTEM: _____

   _____

   _____

   _____

   _____

HOUSEKEEPING: VERY GOOD _____ GOOD _____ FAIR _____ POOR _____

ENERGY POSITION: _____

   _____

   _____

HOW IS MATERIAL STORED? _____

   _____

   _____

LIST OF EQUIPMENT (ATTACHED SEPARATELY) WILL THEY SUPPLY? YES _____ NO _____

WHAT IS CURRENT CAPACITY UTILIZATION? _____ %

WHAT IS CURRENT ORDER FILL RATE (SHIPPED ON SCHEDULE)? _____ %

DO YOU HAVE EXPANSION PLANS? _____ DESCRIBE BRIEFLY _____

   _____

   _____

Figure 13. Vendor plant survey.

Many purchasing agents also have the responsibility for specifying the mode or carrier for outbound shipments, and for managing purchasing activities for other locations. Also, the purchasing agent often has the authority to reverse or change suppliers.

In Their Own Words

Recently *Purchasing World* surveyed its readers to determine the major problems that they face. The chart below encapsulates their findings.

Problems Faced by Corporate Purchasing Agents

"Getting the message across to everyone involved. We are in competition with the world and have to find better ways to get things accomplished."

"Finding new vendors, keeping lead times short, quality high, and unit prices down."

"Need to reduce paperwork and paper shuffling. We are going to MRP driven, on-line purchasing system which will allow more time to negotiate."

"Obtaining favorable long-term price commitments and determining actual costs of freight on common carriers before shipping."

"Balancing or finding the proper balance between price, quality, and the desire for long-term vendor relations."

"Getting quality material at a competitive price when scheduled."

"Timely deliveries by mill and long-term pricing agreements."

"Expediting material to arrive according to our modified JIT system."

"Balancing incoming sales trends against forecast production on long lead items challenges my requirements for a balanced controlled inventory. Coping with seasonal product lines with manufacturing capacity problems also affects inventory levels and creates need for more time in planning to control inventory levels."

"Maintaining good communications with engineering, maintenance, and production personnel, to anticipate needs and have lead times. Reduction of MRO and production parts and operating supplies for minimum inventories consistent with maintenance of operations."

"Too much paper. Prefer direct entry to supplier's computer for stock levels, price, etc."

"Expediting, transportation, lead times, and domestic pricing vs. off-shore pricing."

"Time to do vendor evaluation, time to identify and work with new suppliers/vendors and order expediting."

"JIT vendor orientation."

"Lack of quality suppliers, too much nonstandard material being shipped, and the suppliers do not conform to requirements."

(*Exhibit continues on p. 198.*)

"Maintaining a fully competitive purchasing cycle throughout a product's life cycle. Quality level of purchased parts."

"Time for adequate analysis of vendors, cost, and service."

"Determining actual needs versus initial design estimates."

"Price fluctuations and vendor competition along with long-term contracts."

"Finding the right vendors to provide service as well as competitive pricing."

Source: Reprinted with permission. *Purchasing World,* Publisher's Profile of Readership, verbatim comments, 1985, 1988, Solon, OH.

Do Corporations Help Smaller Vendors?

The question often comes up, "Do corporations help small developing businesses that seek to do business with them?"

About one-third of all Fortune 500 companies help smaller developing businesses in various ways.

Some companies, for example, have a policy specifically for dealing with small developing businesses (SDBs), and some have established small and minority business offices. Some produce directories of vendors and distribute them to their purchasing agents at all corporate branches.

Many large corporations have prepackaged information for would-be vendors on what goods and services are being sought. Some corporations have prepared specialized small-vendor guides to help the first-time or inexperienced vendor.

Increasingly, corporations are providing the names and phone numbers of purchasing agents to anyone who asks. A few highly progressive companies such as Control Data and Conoco provide specialized assistance in the form of management, financial, or technical assistance to small developing businesses. As computers are used more and more in the purchasing function, many corporations also maintain an internal directory of small business supplier capabilities.

Finally, some progressive corporations set goals for utilizing small developing businesses. These are often in the form of dollar goals or a percentage of total purchases.

Figure 14 summarizes the activities of six leading corporations in the use of small developing business vendors.

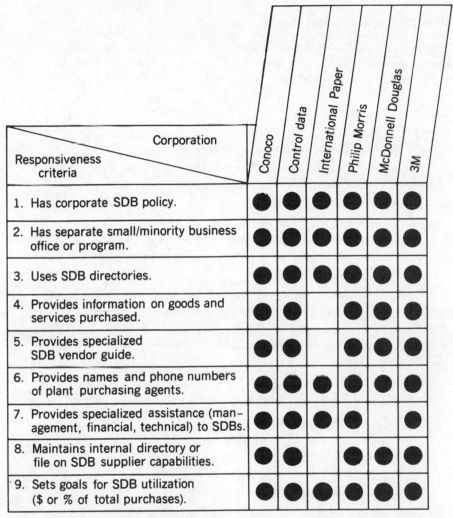

Responsiveness criteria (Corporation)	Conoco	Control data	International Paper	Philip Morris	McDonnell Douglas	3M
1. Has corporate SDB policy.	●	●	●	●	●	●
2. Has separate small/minority business office or program.	●	●	●	●	●	●
3. Uses SDB directories.	●	●	●	●	●	●
4. Provides information on goods and services purchased.	●	●		●	●	●
5. Provides specialized SDB vendor guide.	●	●		●	●	●
6. Provides names and phone numbers of plant purchasing agents.	●	●	●	●	●	●
7. Provides specialized assistance (management, financial, technical) to SDBs.	●	●	●	●		●
8. Maintains internal directory or file on SDB supplier capabilities.	●	●		●	●	●
9. Sets goals for SDB utilization ($ or % of total purchases).	●	●	●	●	●	●

SDB = Small Developing Business.

Figure 14. Characteristics of leading-corporation SDB vendor programs.

Determining Customer Needs

The exhibit that follows delineates the process of determining customer needs, particularly those of large customers from the ranks of major corporations.

Determining Customer Needs

Standards of Quality, Service, and Price

Buyers consider a variety of factors when making purchase decisions. To compete successfully for business, find out what the customer's needs are. Critical needs are:

Determining Customer Needs

Standards of quality

- Can you meet them with current equipment and personnel?
- If your product greatly exceeds the standards, will your price be too high?
- Is your level of quality consistent over time?

Service required

- Do you currently provide service for your customers?
- Is your normal level of service sufficient, or will you need to hire additional employees to provide the expected services to this customer?

Price

- Does this customer consider only price when making a purchase decision?
- Can you offer something more than your competitors for the same price?
- Are the "extras" you offer—higher quality, better service—worth the increased price you charge to each customer?

Communication

Talk with potential buyers or write to corporate procurement offices. Find out:

- What they need to purchase
- What they expect from suppliers
    - Service levels
    - Lead times
    - Delivery schedules
- What help or exceptions they might be willing to give you
    - Technical assistance
    - Financial assistance
    - More frequent payments for a long-term contract
    - Aid in dealing with suppliers for large orders

After you have acquired a customer, communication becomes even more important. Try to:

- Talk with the customer on a regular basis to give him or her progress reports.
- Be available when the customer wants to meet with you.
- Return customers' calls promptly.
- Establish your desire to do a good job and follow it up with *performance*.

- Determine who controls your product or service on a day-to-day basis and *cultivate* him or her.

Cost-Reduction Program

Always strive to reduce costs in your firm without reducing quality. Seek out the advice of your employees for:

- New methods of production
- Improved materials handling
- Streamlining work flow
- New sources of suppliers

Customers will appreciate your passing on any reduced costs to them. This will demonstrate your effectiveness and efficiency in managing your business and will enhance your firm's reputation.

Conformance Standards

You should know what your customers' standards are. It is better to know in advance and determine *if* you can meet them, than to have your product rejected as substandard or unacceptable. This prior knowledge will save you money—for reworking items or purchasing new equipment. Even more important, knowledge of conformance standards and your ability to meet them will preserve your firm's reputation.

Innovation

Always strive for a better way to serve your customers—and *tell* them of the improvements. See below for tips on how to innovate.

Tips on Innovation

- Improve your product.
- Ask your customers if there is a product or service they need or want.
- Improve your service.
- Provide after-hours service.
- Reduce your costs through improved efficiency and pass the savings on to the customer.
- Find new uses for an old product.
- Institute or improve your quality measurement program.
- Develop a new or improved distribution method.
- Develop a new production method.
- Improve your reputation—never be "out of stock."
- Keep a small supply of extra parts on hand for items you currently handle.
- Provide suggestions to maintain your product.

(*Exhibit continues on p. 202.*)

Security

Security involves your plant, documents, and any internal information a customer shares with you—all should be protected. Key security considerations include:

* Plant:
    Installation of a security system
    Use of guards
    Use of watchdogs
    Good illumination of entrances and surrounding areas after dark
* Documents—have a storage facility that will protect them from:
    Unauthorized persons
    Fire
    Other hazards of nature
* Customers' internal information:
    May be related to a new product or service being introduced
    Could be helpful to your customers' competitors
    Will be shared with you if the customer knows you won't "spread it around"

Quality Measurement Program

Certain types of products require close adherence to specifications. Normally these specifications are clearly defined in the contract. A quality measurement program tells the buyer that you have a formal, documented system for evaluating your product according to predetermined standards.

If your contract requires adherence to specifications, the customer may inspect the product at your plant before it is shipped, or at his or her plant after it is received.

A quality measurement program can be a point in your favor when your firm is producing to specifications. If you have this program, *tell* the customer. If you don't have such a program, consider developing one if it suits your type of business product.

Emergency Contingency Plan

If a customer had a fire or flood, could your firm be flexible enough to meet his or her emergency needs? Could you:

* Provide additional inventory ot him or her?
* Provide space for storage?
* Provide a "rush order"?
* Provide special distribution for the customer?

By discussing these needs in advance with the customer, you will demonstrate your concern and provide the "something extra" that will make your firm stand out.

TRADE SHOWS—THE RIGHT TIME TO BE SEEN AND HEARD

Trade shows are the sacred selling turf of corporate America. If something can be shown to prospective buyers or clients—even if only in a picture—there is probably an annual or semiannual trade show related to it. Trade shows are a major and fast-growing method for demonstrating products and services and represent key positioning opportunites for savvy vendors. They may be aimed at the general public, such as home product shows; or at dealers and sales representatives, such as ski resort shows targeted for travel agents.

If you think about the client base for your product or service—from the individual purchaser to the geographic distributor—you are likely to be able to find a trade show attended by people in that client base. More than 9000 trade shows were held in the United States in 1985, double the number held in 1978. *Association Trends* magazine indicated a huge increase in the number of trade shows held in 1988 over 1985, and a concurrent increase in the average size of the trade shows.

Not for the Unprepared

Being part of a trade show is not inexpensive, but when you realize how many interested people you will see face to face in a short time, especially compared to the time it would take to visit each of those personally, the cost becomes a bargain. Because you will get maximum exposure by presenting your business at a trade show, you cannot skimp. You need plenty of trained staff on hand to demonstrate your wares, hand out brochures, and answer questions. You need to pay for registration and space rental, and you need to either rent or ship a booth to set up in your space. You also need healthy amounts of written product or service information as handouts, possibly demonstration models, and maybe even a film or video that visually depicts what you are selling.

In addition to these obvious costs, there are substantial costs in terms of your time and the time of other staff, not just during the trade show itself but also in the planning process and in the follow-up that occurs afterward. "Planning, in terms of setting specific objectives to be achieved by participating in the trade show, is ignored by too many trade show exhibitors," according to Allen Konopacki, a trade show sales trainer.

"Too many companies attend a show and wait for something to happen,"
he maintains. "No objectives have been set. They're not really sure why
they're standing in this mass of people, other than the fact that their
competitors are in the next booth."

Konopacki suggests taking a tough look at the purposes of a trade
show and determining if, in fact, a trade show really does allow your
company to find clients or buyers of its products and services. If it only
provides an opportunity to see people and be seen by them, that probably
isn't enough. Konopacki explains, "Unless you try to generate leads from
a trade show, the medium is inefficient. You spend thousands of dollars
for a one-time exposure to an audience. That's like buying one television
ad and expecting your message to be heard by every person in your
target group."

What You Hope to Achieve

Setting very specific objectives for trade show participation allows you
to accurately direct every effort you make for the show—from training
personnel who will staff the booth to drafting written materials and
determining which potential clients to take out to lunch or dinner. For
example, if your product or service is aimed at the general public, your
objective may be to "take orders for X widgets" or to "generate X solid
leads for follow-up sales approaches." In this case, because you are
looking for high quantity, you need to capture your audience with much
more than an approach that merely says: "look at our booth so you'll
remember us later."

Consider the approach used by many marine insurance agencies when
they exhibit at boat shows. They know most people come to see the
boats, and they also know that an insurance agency does not have a
product to "show." So, they try to make sure their booth is well placed
in a central location and marked by ballons, banners, and possibly even
some interesting boating films or videos. They staff it with plenty of
trained personnel who are ready to smile and offer, "I'd like to tell you
about our outstanding insurance service record," to people who just slow
down as they are walking by. But most important, they are ready to
sign up clients on the spot.

They have stacks of forms to be completed by a boat owner about his
or her boat. Then, on the spot, they use that information to calculate

the cost of insurance and to determine whether someone qualifies for it. If the visitor does, he or she receives a binder number immediately, with a policy and invoice to follow. This is a much more active and successful approach than "here's my card and brochure; give me a call." The more you can do to get a client or customer "hooked" while still at the show, the more likely you are to meet your objectives.

Reaching Distributors Instead of End Users

Because trade shows have grown so rapidly in number, and because you want to get the most for the money it costs to participate, one of the most important questions you will need to answer is, *Which show or shows do I want to attend?* What shows do my targets attend? Then, think of the possibility of reaching those people in a less direct manner such as through agents and distributors (middlemen), who in turn reach your client or customer. It may make much more sense to participate in a trade show attended by agents or distributors than in one attended by end users.

For example, Laura McVain started a business that represents several ski resorts in their nationwide marketing. She participates in trade shows as their representative, but she does not look for shows that would be attended by skiers who might visit the resorts. Instead, she goes to shows that are attended by travel agents who will guide skiers to the resorts she represents. At the trade shows, she runs videos of the resorts, provides brochures about the areas and their amenities, and entertains travel agents in a hospitality suite after trade show hours.

Good Prospecting Opportunities

To come away from the show with a list of blue chip prospects for follow-up (agents who might not actually buy or sign up for anything on the spot, but who are worth your time in terms of follow-up contacts), start by asking the association sponsoring the show for a list of those attending. From that list, begin selecting your potential prospects and send them, ahead of time, some information about your company and an invitation to visit your trade show exhibit.

Follow this up with phone calls, and try to arrange specific times to meet with some of the individuals you have targeted during the show.

The group you have targeted for their high potential will, during the show, slowly narrow down to a smaller group of actual prospects—people you will keep in touch with after the trade show.

Whom to Send to the Show

The best people to send are trained personnel who are informed and enthusiastic about your service or product. This could be you or others on your staff. However, have you noticed how many exhibits are hosted by local temporary personnel whose only prior information is the location of the booth they are handling? It is very tempting to hire "on location," since these people do not need to fly from somewhere to attend. But if you do hire local assistance, you will need to give them plenty of back-up support in terms of knowledgeable individuals from the main office and training prior to the show.

The companies that are most thorough in this regard assemble everybody involved in their exhibit, including company employees, the day before the opening. At that time, they clarify objectives, train local temporary personnel, and prepare a schedule for "working" the booth. Everyone gets the same message about how to handle interested show attendees and how to best represent the company.

One trade show marketing planner suggests informing people who work on the show about the costs involved. When your staff knows the cost of exhibiting, and how important it may be to the company, they will act accordingly.

Follow-Up: As Important as the Show Itself

What will you do to follow up on the contacts you have made during the trade show? Interest can evaporate quickly if it is not nurtured. You will need to stay in touch with contacts you made at the trade show to continue to provide them with information about your products or services. And this is a good way to demonstrate the personal contact you can provide. By doing a good job of follow-up, you maximize your trade show investment.

In Chapter 12 we will discuss how and why every employee in your company must contribute to your marketing efforts.

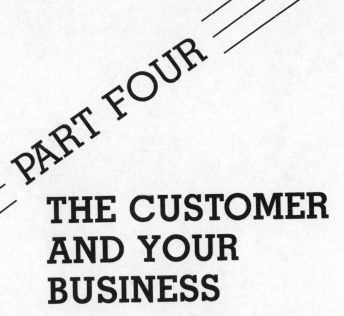

PART FOUR

THE CUSTOMER AND YOUR BUSINESS

12

The Marketing Team

I have failed to take advantage of
many opportunities, but the world
has not failed in offering them.

EDGAR W. HOWE

We have discussed the emerging role of positioning in the long-term success of your overall business efforts as well as various approaches to positioning. This chapter focuses on another facet of effective position marketing—the ability of you and your staff to congeal into a unified marketing team and serve as consultants to your customers. We will explore such issues as:

- [ ] Why everyone in your company must be a part of the marketing team
- [ ] How your receptionist alone can sink your business

☐ How to avoid having any customer feel ignored

☐ The need to support staff marketing efforts from the top

☐ The new selling alliances

Then in Chapter 14 we continue with a more focused look at the skill of successful, professional salespeople.

Marketing is a team responsibility, which includes you, your in-house sales staff, and any network of sales representatives that work for you. Today all must serve as consultants to customers as well as serving as marketers—your better competitors do, or will, and the customers are growing to expect it. The effective business enterprise must be represented by marketers or selling agents who *recognize, accept, and nurture* their role as consultants to the customer. Gone are the days when a sales representative simply made a pitch or displayed a range of options, then pushed for agreement and, ultimately, the close.

> **Successful marketing in the 1990s requires superior sales skills as well as superior consulting skills.**

The effective entrepreneur and effective sales organization in the 1990s will create a climate much like we saw in the Staples example in Chapter 10. This is a climate in which the prospect or customer feels as if the sales staff were there only to help, and as if racking up sales and profits were a distant second to their desire to truly help the customer. This type of atmosphere can only be achieved when the sales staff has been trained to serve as consultants and not simply as order takers or revenue generators.

In addition, today's customer or prospect wants to be sold by knowledgeable representatives who can present options, and who can customize. Today's sales rep must have an in-depth knowledge of competitive products and services, as well as the full range of alternatives in this multioption society. It is simply not enough to have knowledge of the products and services rendered by your traditional competitors.

There may be other products and services in other industries that loom as options for your prospect, but which you may not have considered competitive in any sense. For example, an entrepreneur in the travel agency business is competing not only with other travel agencies but also with sales of motor homes, camping equipment, and sporting equipment. This is because today's multioption consumer may choose to spend four days at one of your favorite resorts, or may choose to spend those four days in a variety of other ways that are also satisfying, fulfilling, and offer the same basic payoff. The options that the consumer faces could be less expensive or more expensive than the traditional resort vacation.

MARKETING, A TEAM EFFORT

Your employees are customer or client contact points in your marketing effort. Drumming up new business may not improve the long-term viability of your firm if your employees are not helpful and informed. We have all been caught in the circle of a telephone receptionist who eludes responsibility or does not know where to refer you. I routinely encounter receptionists who have no idea what the company where he or she is employed does—certainly not a sign that inspires confidence in me about that company.

Your customers and prospects find it frustrating to make calls that lead to delays because employees have no conception of how to answer the phone or to serve as an important component of your marketing team. Conversely, it is gratifying when an employee takes the time to find the right person for you, or takes an extensive message, even if that is not part of his or her job.

The person-to-person contact between employees and customer may outweigh the best advertising, news releases, and promotional campaign to build an organization.

MARKETING ON THE JOB

What are steps you can take to ensure that your staff is helping the marketing effort? First, make your best informed and most personable employees the most accessible to prospective clients or customers. Too often the newest or the least informed person is given the job of handling telephone calls.

Next, recognize that it is important for you and your managers to set an example. If you are impatient, resentful, or disinterested in the questions or suggestions of your staff, then the staff is more likely to treat others in the same manner.

Keep your employees informed. Have they been given a list of departments and do they know what responsibilities are handled by each department? Are they aware of typical questions asked by prospective clients and of the answers to those questions?

Employee morale on the front lines make a strong impact on public perceptions. Frontline employees often take the blame for a poor organization, and thus rudeness and poor morale is not always an employee problem. Yet employees want to be praised and commended for their efforts. "It's vital to maintain open lines of communication between management and staff," advises Lovelock. Acknowledge each employee's importance to the company and the value of his or her contributions.

In the hotel industry, for example, front desk personnel are generally paid less than back office personnel, but are more responsible for the perception of service. They set the image and the mood. The finest room and most delectable food will not bring a customer back who has been treated rudely, or thinks that he or she did not get proper service.

The Marriott chain monitors service through the 5000 guest comment cards received each day. The cards enable the chain to track trends and watch for any deviations. Slow service in a restaurant may not be the waiter's fault, although that is the immediate assumption and the focus of customer complaints. Marriott tracks the difficulties back to the source—which could be the cooks, or maybe even the equipment—and fixes the basic problem.

CALL YOUR OFFICE

Just for fun (but it may not turn out to be such fun) the next time you are away on business or out of the office, call in and notice how you are greeted: If your operation is too small and you will be recognized instantly, have a friend call in. You may want to ask the friend to ask for help with a particular product or service that you offer.

What is the impression that your company is giving? Is it:

- "We are interested in serving you."
- "We would like to do business with you."
- "We appreciate your call"?

Or is it:

- "We are pressed right now."
- "We are glad you called, but we have many callers."
- "We have a lot of calls, you are no more important than the next caller.

Or, worst of all:

- "Why exactly are you calling?"

How you sound to your various publics is an important element in winning them over. Traditionally, government agencies tend to be the poorest at answering the phone. A particularly aggravating response when answering the phone is to name only the division and not the company itself.

> **Your phones must be answered in a manner that is convenient for callers, not for your staff.**

For example, the customer calls in and for whatever reason is connected to shipping. How does shipping answer the phone? "Shipping"? The customer must then endure the ritual of determining that it is the shipping department of the company he originally intended to call.

If your telephone system is designed to route callers to the various departments, each department still must answer with the name of your organization and its particular division. For example, when calling your local Ford dealer to try to reach the parts and supplies department, the proper response of that department would, "ABC Ford, Parts and Supplies."

SERVICE!

The refrain "service just ain't what it used to be" has been shouted by customers at most service retailers, observes Murray Forseter, publisher and editor of *Chain Store Age*, so often that the industry runs the risk of falling into indifference on the issue.[1] A great deal has been written

[1] Quoted with permission. Murray Forester, editorial, "Service Ain't What It Used to Be," *Chain Store Age*, General Merchandise Trends. Published by Lebhar-Friedman Inc., New York, NY, January 1987, p. 5.

on America's service economy, but if your sales staff is not fully adept at providing service to the customer in the way that the customer wants to be served, that is, serving as a consultant and helping in the decision-making process, then customer service is not truly being rendered.

How many times have you walked into a store, office, or sales branch and needed help, did not know where to get started, and wanted to speak to someone who knew what he or she was talking about? How many times did you leave, not because the product or service could not be provided by that enterprise, but because you could not be accommodated in a way in which you felt comfortable? The customers and clients you will be attempting to attract have been through that experience. If your sales staff or sales representatives cannot or, worse, do not serve in the critical role of consultants, you could be losing a fortune in revenue every day.

Your goal is to have no one feel ignored—zero tolerance! If all of your sales help are currently tied up with customers, *have you instructed them to greet an incoming customer while continuing to serve the present one*?

The proper technique is to tell the present customer, "Excuse me for a second, would you mind if I take a moment to tell this person I will be with him shortly?" You will get almost 100 percent agreement from the present customer and alleviate the anxiety and concerns of the customer who might otherwise feel that he or she is being ignored.

EDUCATION AND ITS BENEFITS

Educating your employees with up-to-date information about your services and offering them courses on handling people will improve perceptions of your outfit. Role play is an effective method for instructing your staff. One employee may play an irate caller while someone else responds in a helpful, positive manner. The rest of the group can observe and suggest alternate courses of action. This type of training can sensitize employees to customer needs.

Recognizing the importance of training, one company initiated a one-month program to remind employees of the importance of providing fast, effective service and eliminating "bureaucratic runaround." Employees sported buttons that read, "It IS my job." They were coached, through departmental meetings, on solving problems themselves when possible, directing inquiries to the right source, and maintaining a good rapport with callers. Each department submitted a list of questions most commonly asked by customers, along with a suggested response.

As part of the marketing effort in another organization, a research program was undertaken to discover what the company's training needs were. A program was developed to meet those needs. The needs analysis included an internal organizational audit, which identified the staff's strengths, talents, and capabilities, and an external audit, which evaluated a variety of trends in their environment.

The staff went through values-clarification activities. It concluded that methods were not as important as service. In addition, values clarification revealed that the organization operated in a competitive environment, and that employees are in fact involved in "marketing" and "selling," even though such activities may be labeled differently.

ARM YOUR STAFF

Increasingly, your sales staff will have to be armed with educational tools. These educational tools will support their ability to serve as consultants. Particularly for businesses in an emerging industry, or in an established industry that is now offering emerging products or services, the ability to serve as an educational source takes on paramount importance. This is because you are faced with a dual function of both educating and selling the prospect. The time between a product being developed and actually marketed successfully can be considerable.

There are legions of stories of entrepreneurial companies that attempted to penetrate a marketplace before training the appropriate staff and developing the educational materials that were necessary to succeed. These companies, and the staffs that served them, were in the marketplace too early, and were faced with the monumental task of both educating the target market that the new product or service existed and explaining why it was needed.

SUPPORT FROM THE TOP

If employees feel supported by management, they will go through fire and brimstone for an organization. When the leaders have a sense of excitement about the work, it transfers to staff members. "Employees must be made part of the marketing effort. Share your customer information with them," advises a Philadelphia executive. "Develop your team first and the (marketing) plan second. Create ownership."

A manager in a leading defense contracting firm recognized the importance of maintaining the professional edge among his employees and the problems inherent in doing so. "Because we had an enormous multiyear contract, employees often became lax," he said. "It is important that the employees on the phone or on site with the contracting agency recognize that every contact they make adds—or subtracts—from our marketing efforts. Also, at all times, they need to feel like they are being supported from the top."

TEAM SPIRIT THROUGH COMPANY NEWSLETTER

A newsletter for employees serves many useful purposes. It can provide information about different departments or it can be used as a vehicle for support from the president and enhance a feeling of unity among employees. A newsletter can also provide educational tips. Even if your staff numbers 25 people or less, a newsletter can be a worthwhile vehicle for maintaining cohesion.

Employee newsletters most definitely have helped motivate employees, and increased internal communication and the flow of ideas about an organization's goals. Have you ever noticed the pride on the face of a clerk sporting an "Employee of the Month" button? People of all walks of life appreciate recognition for a job well done. Management books have long advised "catch someone doing something right" and then offer immediate praise. Praise is even more effective when given publicly. Ask the local reporters to write feature stories about recognized employees and spotlight them in your newsletter.

Some nonmonetary incentives used to spark enthusiasm include giving outstanding employees training and special educational opportunities, greater access to upper management, and more freedom to manage themselves. In the end, everyone just wants a little recognition.

MINICASE
THE MARKETING TEAM APPROACH
IN BANKING

Thomas A. Bracken, an executive vice president of New Jersey National Bank in Pennington, New Jersey, found that a group approach to building a relationship with a customer helped the bank create a structure that prevented sales opportunities from falling through the cracks, and positioned the bank as one seeking healthy, long-term customer relationships.

At a time when competition among financial services is at an all-time high, Bracken says that the answer to the following question could make or break a bank's ability to survive and succeed in its market:

How do you maximize sales without sacrificing top quality customer service?

New Jersey National Bank has begun to answer that question with the introduction of its Banking Group. The Banking Group is a pioneer approach to commercial and retail banking which eliminates any overlap of effort among salespeople, and positions the bank to saturate its market for financial services.

The structure of the group is unusual, but simple: the primary selling forces of the bank, the commercial and retail divisions, maintain individual responsibilities within their given areas, but the lines between them are continuous, rather than exclusive. Together, they form the Banking Group. From a strategic standpoint, the structure allows the bank to tap into the diversified financial needs of the entire market on every level.

Initial contacts by the commercial division, for example, are complemented and expanded through lateral referrals to the appropriate trust and retail banking people. This builds a cross-selling momentum that ties the customer to the bank more closely than ever before.

In approaching the market with a united front, the Banking Group projects to customers a team image that is powerful and consistent. In tying together the bank's primary sales areas, the group promotes ongoing interaction and creates a single image of a service-oriented institution whose staff is in tune with each other and with its customers.

A bank sales manager, working closely with the trust officer in her region, succeeded in pulling in more than $1 million in new trust business from a single customer. Teamwork, careful planning, and an attractive proposal to the customer paid off handsomely. Ideally, the Banking Group eliminates a customer's primary reason for leaving a bank: "No one there knows me anymore."

Interaction and business referrals among group members ensure that more than one person knows a customer and his or her background, and can respond to a customer's individual financial needs. This provides important continuity for the customer, and a level of personalized service that leaves the customer feeling catered to.

Sometimes it is a personal touch that makes the difference between a little new business and a lot of new money. At New Jersey National, a senior account manager went out of his way to hand deliver a credit application to a business customer instead of just dropping it in the mail. In delivering the application, the senior account manager and the customer began talking about the customer's family. Their conversation led to a one-on-one meeting with the manager of the bank's personal trust group and culminated in a new $300,000 investment advisory account.

In summary, the Banking Group uses a team marketing approach to facilitate cross selling and relationship banking, and supports the theory that the more products a customer has with a bank, the less likely the customer is to take his or her business elsewhere.[2]

THE RISE OF ALLIANCE SELLING

Now let us turn the corner, and as an entrée to the next chapter on professional selling, further explore the notion of the marketer as consultant. Veteran sales trainer Jack Cohen, based in Baltimore, Maryland, calls this phenomenon the creating of "selling alliances." Cohen sees them forming in markets everywhere today. "This trend is in tune, because people simply don't buy based on product or price consideration

---

[2] Printed with permission. Interview with Thomas A. Bracken, executive vice-president, CoreStates, New Jersey National Bank, Pennington, NJ.

alone. The emotional factor is an integral part of the buying decision," say Cohen. Buyers, even industrial buyers, now readily admit that, in addition to the key vendor criteria outlined in Chapter 11, trust, pride, and excitement are important factors which influence their buying choice.

"Such emotional demands are entirely real and quite appropriate in our ever-changing, vibrant marketplace and must be served with style and care," says Cohen, who is director of the Sales Dynamics Institute and has more than 34 years of experience in sales as a trainer, manager, and marketing and sales consultant. To create sales alliances and to position your marketing staff as consultants to the customer, there must first be "attitude coordination." Cohen defines this as having everyone in the organization pledge to be customer driven.

Once this commitment takes hold, there must be "operational coordination," where all departments and services are working together as a team to produce, sell, or deliver, and serve the customer in such a manner that he or she gets complete satisfaction. As such, recruiting, selecting, training, motivating, and directing new sales staff becomes a real challenge, especially since these individuals will be interacting with the prospect's emotional psyche.

Prior to the advent of consumerism in the early 1960s, when there was just product and price to consider, the tasks of sales managers and salespeople were accomplished with simpler skills, generally learned through apprenticeship-style training. "Now," says Cohen, "since emotional factors are more fully recognized and accepted by the more sophisticated professional as a legitimate and worthy component of the buying equation, today's salespeople must become more highly skilled, more empathic, warm, friendly, and trustworthy.

Cohen is a believer in and teacher of the sales reps as consultants because this approach to selling effectively serves both the buyer and the seller. It also gives rise to and nourishes a selling alliance: sales reps must continue to shape the marketing culture and aggressively seek out friendship and trust with their customers. In the process, sales reps serve the prospects as consultants, guiding and helping them to identify their needs, select their product, and determine the level of personal service they desire.

The "dominant" salesperson has difficulty with the listening skill. A selling alliance can only be achieved by "listening and questioning more and talking less, ". . . thereby maximizing the customer's participation during the sales process. Cohen finds that customers want to participate in the "sales communications" to the fullest. The "dominant" salesperson is the star of the show and, therefore, discourages prospect participation, whereas the "consultant seller" makes the customer the star.

"Two major forces exist in every selling situation: the needs and demand of the buyer and the skills and services of the seller," says Cohen. In earlier times, the buyer was seen as an adversary or an opponent, while the seller was considered to be a pirate or a warrior, who used warlike "strategies" and "tactics" to surround, outmaneuver, and defeat the buyer. Cohen notes, "Selling was perceived as a hostile act of business war (in both attitude and operations)."[3]

Today sophisticated, enlightened managers and sales performers realize that prospects buy when needs are fulfilled or problems solved. "It then behooves both the buyer and the seller to dedicate themselves to the development of that marketing culture which will set the mood for selling alliances," says Cohen.

A caring, well-trained sales professional, believes Cohen, "will settle for nothing less than complete customer satisfaction. A reasonable, understanding consumer will want his salesperson's company to earn a fair profit for the product and level of service it has provided and will need to provide for back-up support." Thus, more selling alliances take place, a greater portion of the customer's purchasing dollar will go to selected companies, thereby gaining in return more personal favor, higher quality products, better service remedies, and more competitive pricing for the buyer in the future.

"Selling alliances must be the goal of all traders in products and services," says Cohen, "simply because it's good business. *Buyers need and want trusted salespeople, and sellers need and want repeat business. Every customer has relatives, friends, and associates who are also wanting and seeking trusted salespeople.* They would all be delighted to join a selling alliance, given a meaningful invitation."

[3] Printed with permission. Interview with Jack Cohen, president, Sales Dynamic Institute, Baltimore, MD.

13

Selling—The Newest Profession

Everything in nature is a cause from which there flows some effect.

BENEDICT SPINOZA

Selling is a dynamic art, ever-changing as humanity changes. We continue our exploration of this lucrative art by tapping the wisdom of veteran sales trainers, psychologists, and researchers. With all the developments in the field of professional selling, in many ways, it has become the newest profession. In this chapter, we will examine the following:

☐ New techniques for getting to "yes"

☐ Why many customers want you to make the decision for them

☐ How appealing to the right brain eases the sales toward completion

☐ How to unlock the "restricted" buyer

☐ Why storytelling wins customers

☐ How to evaluate your sales staff

As a marketing and sales consultant, Jack Cohen is always surprised to see large amounts of money and personnel assigned to the prospecting function. If more of that prospecting dollar were committed to intensifying customer focus, and aimed toward building the selling alliances described earlier, the rewards of more repeat business and referral endorsements would generate a larger share of sales, and in an easier, profitable fashion.

Many firms, committed to such philosophy, earn 80 to 90 percent of new and repeat business each year from their satisfied clients and the leverage of their referrals. In today's business climate Cohen sees a continuing movement toward greater enlightment between buyer and seller and a higher level of respect for each other, in both the content and the ambience of the buyer–seller communications.

PRIMED TO SAY YES

To determine the underlying principles that cause us to say yes when confronted with an effective presentation, Arizona State University psychologist Robert Cialdini attended several sales training sessions. He found that the avalanche of choices confronting most individuals combined with the information overload they experience in their daily lives has forced many people to take shortcuts or quicker routes to decision making.

In his book *Influence: The New Psychology of Modern Persuasion* Cialdini says that "we respond to trigger features such as friendship, commitment, consensus, authority and obligation." These trigger features "tell us almost automatically when we can correctly say yes to a request." Cialdini found that the most effective salespeople today and the most effective sales training incorporate such trigger features into their sales presentations.

TAPPING INTO THE RIGHT BRAIN

Sales trainer and nationally known speaker Dave Yoho of Fairfax, Virginia, comments that the most effective selling is done by appealing to the right brain of the prospect. The "right brain" (a metaphor, not exactly the real thing) is that hemisphere which enables us to enjoy the arts, practice our intuition, and see beyond the merely immediate or logical. Poets, artists, writers, greater chefs, and creative geniuses seem to have developed an ability to tap into their right brains with the result of having a wider range of artistic impressions.

Yoho says that when you tap into the right brain of the prospect, you can appeal to him or her in ways that break through layers and layers of resistance that the left brain, nuts and bolts, "show me," purely rational thinking often display.

Sales trainer and author Steven Salerno estimates that about 50 percent of the 11 million salespeople in the country today use some of these new subtle yet sophisticated techniques, although only between about 25 and 30 percent are fully indoctrinated in their correct use. Donald Moine, a Rodondo Beach, California, based psychologist and president of the Association for Human Achievement studied the approaches of salespeople earning between $500,000 and $1 million a year in personal income.

Amazingly, Moine found that the majority of them used a form of story telling. Moine observes that an expert salesperson uses parables or anecdotes, some as short as three to five sentences in length. He found that these can be virtually hypnotic to the listener and have such a strong impact that the prospect cannot dislodge the image of the product from his own mind. He thinks about it that night, and wakes up the next morning thinking about it. Moine terms this technique "conversational hypnosis."

Upon reading of these techniques, you may regard this as manipulative or as somehow undermining the traditional sales–customer relationship. Yet these salespeople are doing nothing more than creating an environment in which the customer feels safe and responsive. Moine stresses that by painting a visual picture of what a product or service can do for a prospect, rather than simply listing its specifications, the customer is literally able to envision the use of the product or service in a pleasurable, compelling way.

HELPING THE RESTRICTED BUYER

Jonathan Evetts, president of Evetts Sales Seminars in Rhinebeck, New York, specializes in sale-success presentations for associations and corporations. "For many people," says Evetts, "the most frustrating part of selling is when the customer agrees with everything that you say, admits that your product is exactly what is needed, promises to buy, and even outlines the size of the proposed purchase, but the order still fails to materialize."

When this happens, and it seems that nothing more can be done, try looking beneath the surface to understand what is preventing the customer from acting in his or her own, and your, best interest.

> **Someone who simply cannot seem to implement a decision is often at the pull of opposing forces that gradually restrict his or her freedom of movement, until the ability to act is neutralized.**

For instance, the buyer who is instructed to stock at levels high enough to fill 90 percent of orders from the shelves, but at the same time to reduce overall inventory size, may also be told to "pioneer" little known products not carried by his competitors and still make sure that every line carried "turns" at least five times a year. Factor in a few costly buying errors (with the underlying fear of being fired), and these conflicting orders may be enough to reduce a usually decisive person to a condition that could be described as a "decision lock."

As an entrepreneur with marketing responsibilities you may sympathize, but you can never accept the excuses offered by someone suffering from this complaint. "Instead, by taking the initiative in making the decision for the customer," says Evetts, "you can often produce rewarding results for both parties."

MINICASE
UNLOCKING THE RESTRICTED BUYER

Evetts's own company had been only surviving when he took over. Sales were flat or falling. Having tried all the basic methods for reactivating the territory (improved sales support and product training, working closely with key existing distributors, and opening carefully selected new ones), it became clear that while his company was selling more of its older products to the shrinking heavy industrial market, its new high-tech items were not moving as they should. The company was mortgaging any future growth by not selling to meet a changing economy.

"If something didn't happen very soon, we were about to receive a sharp lesson in the law of diminishing returns," tells Evetts.

"The problem was most acute at our largest established distributor, who insisted on buying just the older products, and on working the same old markets that he always had, while refusing to consider anything different.

"At this point, our salvation appeared in the form of a new industrial manager that the distributer hired. He had the foresight and experience to see what needed doing. He recognized the need for change, and promised to handle our whole, broad line, while penetrating new markets in the emerging service economy. Plans were laid for large semiannual stocking orders, for sales meetings and fieldwork, and for setting up subdistribution throughout the territory.

"My partner and I, feeling that our major problems were well on the way to being solved, parted at the airport and went home to await the promised order.

"Weeks passed, with phone call after phone call to the new manager, who always expressed enthusiasm for our products and promised the order for the very next week. Months went by as the project grew colder and colder, and it gradually became evident that he was under increasingly conflicting pressures from within his company. One day, having grown tired of making excuses to our head office, I called for a meeting with the manager.

"My partner and I met with him in his office at 10 A.M. and were were still there at noon. By prearrangement with my partner, our conversation throughout the meeting was deliberately kept as light and upbeat and as far from serious topics as possible, with no pressure at all to write the big order.

"Lunch was not at the manager's usual restaurant since we wanted him to eat well but not feel too much at home. Again, the conversation was mainly about hockey and skiing, with only the most general references to business. It was not until he had finished his dessert and was murmuring vaguely about 'getting back to the office' that we saw that the time had come to ask for the order.

"To make quite sure that I had my full say, we had seated the sales manager at the window end of the booth, with my partner next to him and me directly opposite. To leave before we were ready, he would literally have had to jump over the table.

"I waited for a lull in the conversation and decided on a verbal blitzkrieg. Looking him straight in the eye, and using the same hard tone learned in overcoming objections in telephone selling, I said, 'Jim, we've guaranteed you everything you've asked for to get this line going and we're all agreed about what needs to be done. We've had meetings and endless phone calls, and again this morning we danced all around that big order you promised us months ago. So, why don't we just go and write the order right now?'

"The effect of these few words on him was quite astonishing. The hand holding his cup shook enough to spill liquid on the tablecloth, while he went quite pale and swallowed air for several seconds.

"Just as suddenly, the look of acute distress faded from his face and the color returned. He straightened up in his seat, drank his coffee in one gulp, placed his cup firmly in the saucer, and replied, 'Yes, let's do it.'

"During the walk back to the office, he was like a different man. All the doubt and indecision dropped away as he visibly regained the positive attitude that had at first so impressed everyone.

"Fortunately, there were no further hitches, and the whole program worked out very much as planned. With such a large inventory on their shelves, both the owner and the manager committed themselves to offering our complete line.

"Three years after we had received that first order, the manager began talking about how successful the program with our line had become, and how this success had benefited his career. His good judgment in taking a risk, and ordering as he did, had resulted in a new freedom to make decisions that had, in turn, moved his group to the forefront of the company, and he was soon to be promoted.

"I had always wondered how he viewed my abrupt demand that he live up to his original commitment, and whether he bore a secret grudge for the jolt it had given him. As discreetly as possible, I asked about his feelings at the actual 'moment of impact,' and said I hoped I had not been too forceful.

"To my considerable surprise, he had no recollection of the incident, but insisted heatedly that he had initiated the entire program. He did, however, recognize that the writing of the first big order had been instrumental in bringing to a close an unhappy and indecisive period, and had signaled the start of the success to which he had already referred.

"I still encounter 'waverers,' only now, having once determined where our joint interests lie, there is no hesitation about helping them make up their minds, knowing as I do that the right purchasing decision will make them look good and may help their careers."[1]

Many lessons can be drawn from this actual case history. The customers and clients you serve face an ever-increasing array of responsibilities, time pressure, and information overload and are no better at making choices today, and indeed may be worse than their counterparts of years past.

> **When the right man or woman walks in the door with a product or service that can save them money, save them time, increase their efficiency, and in general make them look good, they are going to be far more inclined to listen to that person than ever before.**

If you and your staff become more adept at serving as consultants and marketers rolled into one, and the terms are not mutually exclusive, you will be positioning your firm for success.

TRENDS IN SALES TRAINING

Ira Westreich, a professional sales trainer and president of Ira Westreich Associates, offers a consensus among a variety of top sales trainers from across the country regarding the nature and focus of sales training in the 1990s. Westreich found that:

1. Many smaller companies are moving in the direction of training their sales staff with "out of house" services. Companies are looking for more than a quick-fix solution. They are seeking follow-up and support sales management programs.

[1] Printed with permission. Interview with Jonathon Evetts, president, Evetts Sales Seminars, Rhinebeck, NY.

2. The word "selling" is becoming more widely accepted in professional terminology. Sales training is on the increase within the areas of professional groups such as accountants, architects, dentists, advertising agencies, television and radio stations, newspaper and magazines, and financial institutions. (For selling in the professions see next page.)

3. The entry of women into the selling profession has leveled off somewhat, with the exception of the real estate industry.

4. The more progressive and aggressive companies are continually searching to upgrade the quality of people representing them.

5. The older, more seasoned salespeople (not necessarily the most productive) are still displaying a reluctance to accept change.

6. Newer salespeople, who are steadily increasing their levels of productivity, are constantly staying tuned to opportunities of growth where they are currently employed, as well as to the growth potential in other organizations. Few are staying forever.

7. Younger people entering the sales field are anxious to acquire training and guidance.

8. Many companies talk a great deal about telemarketing skills and are engaged in the activity, but not as efficiently as they could be.

9. Too many sales managers are allowing paperwork, computer printouts, and lack of priorities to reduce their coaching time in the field with their sales teams. Behind-the-desk guidance is not enough.

10. Despite breakthroughs in the process of selling, as discussed previously, the greatest obstacle in the development of salespeople is to remove from their thinking the concept of being a "pitchman."

11. Repeat and refresher sales and management training is becoming increasingly evident, once the companies get a taste of people development.[2]

---

[2] Printed with permission. Information compiled by Ira Westreich, president, Westreich Associates, Baltimore, MD.

OTHER EMERGING TRENDS IN SELLING

Here are other findings that indicate the nature and scope of the changes in professional selling:

The cost of a sales call is now $229.20, according to a report by McGraw-Hill Research.[3] The study surveyed 1714 vice presidents of sales and sales managers in industrial companies. The cost of a sales call has gone up 11.8% since 1983. Also, based on the survey, the cost of a sales call decreases as the size of the sales force increases.

A study in the *Small Business Report* noted that in many professional and technical companies, salespeople primarily act as consultants, and incentive pay simply does not apply. The same report also found that commission is prevalent at newer, smaller companies without big sales staffs.

Only about 6 to 7 percent of companies pay entirely by commission. Only 19 to 20 percent pay on a salary-only basis. Most companies today offer various salary/commission-incentive mixtures.

Starting with salary compensation makes sense in some situations. When sales is a stepping stone to a management position, there may be no need to use commissions to "entice" people to stay. Also, when the sales managers have set realistic goals, they can often motivate their people without using commissions.

SELLING IN THE PROFESSIONS

Selling in the professions requires many of the same skills as selling an industrial product. For example, you must transfer credibility and establish rapport. One very successful professional sales marketer advises to figure out "the bit size that the prospect will pay." Bring up fees halfway through the initial scoping and then deliver a line such as, "It is too early to really tell, but this looks like about a $35,000 job." Of course

---

[3] As reported in *Sales and Marketing Management*, Bill Publications, New York, August 1987.

it is really only a $30,000 one, but you have to anticipate being knocked down a bit.

This successful consultant advises asking the question, "On what basis will you be making a decision regarding my services?" He advises trying to close on the spot, then sending a confirmation letter which, simply boiled down, says "all we need is a starting date." It is important in the professional service market (or in any market, for that matter) to remember that any time that two people meet, one is selling the other something, even if it is simply an idea.

You can reduce fee anxiety by mentioning that you are aware of the prospect's concerns, but also recognize that "the least expensive solution is to get the job done professionally, quickly, and completely."

KEEPING UP WITH THE COMPETITION

Keeping up with the competition in your own industry is no secret. In his comprehensive book, *Competitor Intelligence*, Leonard M. Fuld, president of Information Data Search in Cambridge, Massachusetts, outlines 18 basic strategies for keeping up with what the other guys are doing.

To get beyond the stage in which you are observing and reading about what your competitors have to offer, you consider buying some of their products so that your sales staff can become fully knowledgeable in what is good and bad about the competitors' products. Don't worry, as some misdirected sales managers believe, that letting your sales staff in on what another company is offering will discourage them. All products generally have specific features which are superior to the competition, and all products have features which are, in some cases, not as good as the competition.

What will be the effectiveness of your sales staff when, being asked by a prospect, "How does this measure up to the XYZ product?" your staffer is able to reply in precise terms rather than in generalizations? Do General Motors executives test-drive Fords? Does their sales staff? One would hope so, but in the dinosaur-like U.S. auto industry, I would not place any bets.

You and your sales staff need to know precisely what your competitors are and are not offering in order to enjoy superior sales encounters. The 1970s and, unfortunately, the 1980s strategies aimed at keeping the sales staff ignorant of the products of others, while revved up about their own, represent an antiquated approach to selling. Moreover, how can your staff serve as *consultants* without a full understanding of the products and services available to the consumer?

COMPETITION FROM TANGENTIAL COMPETITORS

In the 1990s it will be necessary to maintain up-to-date knowledge on those developments in other industries which may impact and hamper the sales of your products or services. Let's return to the example of a travel agency. Sales of recreational vehicles may be limiting the vacation packages that the agency has traditionally been able to sell.

Without data or information about RVs, the individual sales agent is hampered in his or her ability to be effective with prospects. It may just be that the physical depreciation of RVs after a few years renders them a bad purchase. Similarly, the high consumption of gasoline, motor oil, auto parts, and the need for costly repairs may not be known by that prospect who is vacillating between taking the plunge and buying a wildly expensive RV or staying with convenient, well-planned, restful vacations for now and in the years to follow.

The easiest way, and perhaps the most effective, to obtain information about how other industries may be impacting your sales is to rely on your industry associations, many of whom are forever compiling data on trends affecting their members (see Chapter 4). As we will see in Chapter 14, many of the techniques for staying in the forefront of your customers' minds yield additional information on how to sell and serve them more effectively.

14

Staying in
the Forefront

Too much of a good thing is
wonderful.

MAE WEST

Studies indicated that it is nine times more
difficult to attract new customers and clients than to retain existing ones,
and that in the course of 10 years 81 out of 100 cutomers drift away.
Yet, the high art of marketing after the sale—which helps retain customers—is known by too few.

In this chapter we will look at techniques for developing and maintaining
a successful marketing program that will enable you to take full advantage
of the customer and client relationships that you are developing. Specifically, this chapter will answer the following questions:

☐ Why is it unnecessary to stay in the forefront of all customers'
  minds?

☐ What is your QOR—quality of relationship with your customers and with whom should it be improved?

☐ What are some effective techniques to stay in the forefront?

☐ What is aftermarketing and how does it aid in overall marketing and positioning?

☐ What is positive stroking?

A plethora of articles and books exist today that stress "making the customer king," "staying close to the customer," and upgrading the service component of your business. These *are* important steps in building long-term business in any industry or profession. However, *to accomplish them often requires innovative if not outlandish approaches* (as judged by your more staid competitors). So let's get innovative, if not a bit outlandish.

NOT FOR ALL CUSTOMERS

Based on the Pareto principle, 80 percent of your customers will account for only 20 percent of your revenues, while 20 percent of your customers will account for 80 percent of your revenues.

> **Staying in the forefront of all customers' minds is not always mandatory; you need to prioritize your forefronting efforts.**

This may seem contradictory to advice given earlier; it is not. Marginal customers and clients who patronize your business on an infrequent basis must always be handled in a highly professional, helpful manner. The key is that your concerted expenditure of human resources and marketing effort is made on those customers and clients that will remain so for the long haul. You cannot easily predict at the outset who will turn into a long-term customers, yet as we saw earlier you can identify the profile of those who tend to become long-term customers.

ORIENTING YOUR MARKETING STRATEGY FOR THE LONG HAUL

Besides the simple fact that the customer is inclined to keep ordering from you, there are at least 10 reasons why the customer is worth keeping and why it is important to stay in the forefront:

1. A good customer tends to talk about your products or services with other potentially good customers. Word of mouth advertising is always the most effective form of advertising.

2. Good customers actually help you run a more profitable operation. They make key suggestions and offer input and advice that the infrequent customer is not likely to offer.

3. Your advertising and promotional vehicles are more readily noticed by those customers and clients who buy from you frequently. They also tend to react more readily to any product or service that you introduce—often the established customer will be surprised and perhaps among the first to purchase.

4. The long-term customer or client is more receptive to your suggestions about other products and services. One of the reasons why the customer may keep buying from you is that he or she sees you as a creditable source and representative of the products and services in your industry.

5. Your incidence of bad checks or fee-collection problems is lower when you are doing business with long-term customers.

6. The profile you draw of those who use your products or services regularly enables you to pinpoint other potential long-term customers. If you are popular among one group, chances are you can capture other members of that group.

7. Selling to the same people is more rewarding and less difficult. The converse is to continually be doing business with strangers.

8. Steady customers tend to order faster and with more ease than first timers. The net result for you is greater sales per customer with less time and effort.

9. It is easier to solicit the opinions of long-standing customers, even if they stop patronizing your business or if the relationship is upset in some other way.

10. As the needs of your good customers shift, so, too, may the needs of other less frequent customers. Your long-standing customers can serve as a source of mini-marketing research.

REVISING THE MARKETING STRATEGY TO INCLUDE AFTERMARKETING

I define aftermarketing as "the final part of the marketing process, which involves ensuring complete customer or client satisfaction and undertaking those activities that keep one's business, products, or services in the forefront of the minds of those served."

Some entrepreneurs regard an effective aftermarketing program as too costly, or contrary to a healthy bottom line. Yet just the reverse is true. A variety of businesses and institutions are finding that an effective aftermarketing program does much more than help to stay in the forefront of customers' minds. It helps to build sales.

You have worked hard at developing your position in the marketplace. You have built a strong customer or client base. Now is not the time to relax. Effective position marketing requires that you develop an aftermarketing plan that will enable you to stay in the forefront of the customer's or client's mind.

> Revising marketing strategy to include aftermarketing can be a difficult process if you attempt to "tack on" some aftermarketing techniques to partially conceive a marketing program.

Instituted in a proper and timely manner, aftermarketing will enable you to remain continuously at the forefront of those to whom you sell. There are numerous steps for making sure that your aftermarketing is as strong as your marketing. Here are some of the most popular:

Placing Greater Emphasis on Support Staff. The people who follow up the sale should be trained to represent the company as well as the people who made the initial sale. All buyers want confirmation that their purchase decision was a good one. All customers apreciate knowing that you care about them as much after the sale as you did before.

Generous Distribution of Customer Survey Forms. Do not be afraid to continually solicit the input and advice of your customers through various report forms. Virtually any business or professional service can benefit from the input of the people it serves. Reply cards can take many forms, including postage-paid cards, in-store suggestion boxes, personal follow-up letters from the chief executive, or a preprinted form about the condition of the company's shipments. Examples from 7-Eleven and the United Savings Bank are given in Figures 15 and 16. Do not discount the value of the cards. They let the customer know that his or her opinion is important and that you use the input to better refine your service delivery.

Maintaining Your Word. An old maxim in the consulting profession goes, "Only promise what you can deliver and always deliver more than you promise." Your sales staff and staff assistants must treat what they say to the customer as if it were written on parchment. Nothing will keep you in the forefront of the customer's mind more efficiently than meeting promised shipping dates, responding to requests for information, and acting as if "your word is your bond." The Skyline Clubs (see Figure 17) pledge to respond to all member communications within 48 hours, *with a solution*.

Budgeting for the Placement of "Thank-You" Advertising. The most successful companies and professional service firms recognize that advertisements and formal messages that say, "Thanks, we appreciate your business," are just as important as the ads and messages that first brought the customer in. In *Marketing Your Consulting and Professional Services* we discuss how public thank-you messages, which are really nothing more than printed advertisements, can be used in local newspapers to both thank existing customers and encourage new ones to call.

> *J.W. Harris and Company, Industrial Lighting Supply, wishes to thank its 1500 customers for their long-term support. May your next year be the brightest ever.*

Anticipating Customer Needs. What is the life cycle of the product you sell or the service you render? After customers buy once, what else is necessary for their continued satisfaction? What additional products or services will enhance the value of their original purchase? What follow-up information or maintenance suggestions or instructions can be sent periodically to provide a valuable service and keep you in the forefront of the customers' minds?

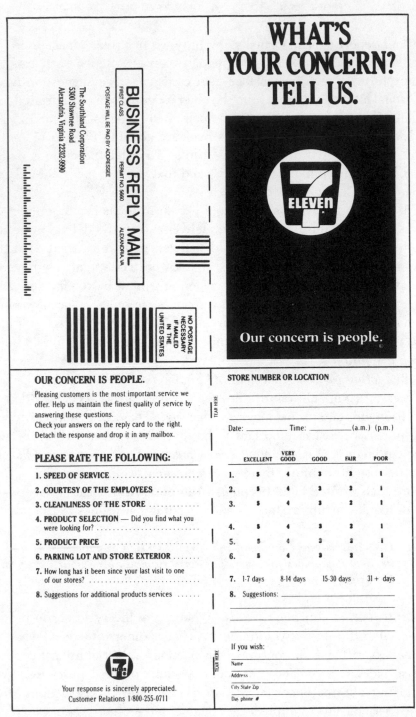

Figure 15. 7-Eleven customer reply card. (Reprinted with permission.)

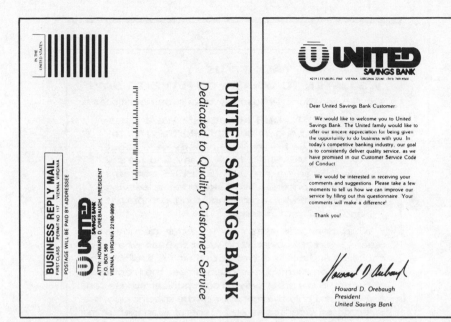

Figure 16. United Savings Bank customer service response survey. (Reprinted with permission.)

What Else Does the Customer Need?

[ ] Service call
[ ] Follow-up instructions
[ ] Extra set of instructions
[ ] New supporting product
[ ] New supporting services
[ ] 60/90/120-day maintenance reminder
[ ] Personal letter from CEO
[ ] Newsletter telling how others use it
[ ] 3-month follow-up survey
[ ] Flier on new applications
[ ] Upgrades, enhancements
[ ] Important notices, warnings
[ ] Trends, new developments
[ ] Other

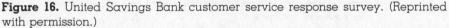

From the Managers

TALK TO US . . .
WE LISTEN TO WHAT YOU HAVE TO SAY!

The Skyline Clubs' Philosophy to our members reads:

> **SERVICE TO OUR MEMBERS:** We are passionate in caring for our MEMBERS and for the business we are in. <u>We honestly care about what our MEMBERS have to say, and we say "yes" when we can</u>. Our MEMBERS' concerns are our concerns. We take pride in serving them in a timely, accommodating, competent and consistent manner.

What does this mean to you, our members? It means we really do care and want to hear what your concerns and needs are about the clubs. Utilizing the Member Comment Boxes located near the front desk at each club is a great way to communicate these concerns, to not only the manager of the specific club, the Director of Operations and General Manager of all three clubs, but also to the entire staff through which your needs are met.

Your member communications are not taken lightly. Once received, a manager must respond within 48 hours with a solution to the concern, what action was or will be taken, what the status is concerning a situation or what is planned in the future for a specific area.

We need your comments; you are our eyes to the club and we value your opinion. As a result of previous member comments, exercise classes have been added, Fitness Center equipment has been purchased, amenities have been enhanced, music has been adjusted and monitored, coffee provided and waiting lists for cardiovascular equipment have been reformated. These changes could not have been fully realized without your help.

Thank you for your feedback. We appreciate your honesty and genuine concern for your clubs. Only with your help will The Skyline Clubs continue to be on the leading edge of excellence.

In health,

Dan Campbell	Lauren Polo	Nancy Hummers
Skyline City	Crystal Gateway	Crystal Park
Manager	Manager	Manager

Figure 17. The Skyline Clubs—From the Managers. Smith Club Management, Inc., August 1988. (Reprinted with permission.)

Any one of these items makes for an excellent reason to get in touch with a customer again. This serves a twofold purpose, (1) to truly serve the customers and (2) to stay in the forefront of their minds.

DETERMINING THE QUALITY OF RELATIONSHIPS WITH KEY CUSTOMERS

Quality of relationships (QOR) is a concept introduced in *Marketing Your Consulting and Professional Services*, which is of great importance for effective aftermarketing. Here is how to determine the QOR with all of your customers and clients, and to upgrade and improve the QOR in those areas where it is needed.

Identify the 20 percent of your clients or customers that account for 80 percent of your business. Since these are the most important customers, your QOR analysis focuses only on them. (While it is useful to have a high QOR with the 80 percent of your customer base that accounts for only 20 percent of your revenues, it is not practical and profitable.) In identifying your better customers or clients consider such items as:

- Volume of business in the last 12 months
- Volume of business in the month
- Potential volume in the next 12 months
- Their familiarity with you or your staff
- Your familiarity with the buyer or the business he or she represents.
- Your sense of the relationship
- Other appropriate criteria

Then list all of your key clients. If the list is longer than 50, you may stop at 50. This list can be prepared using any of the commonly available software programs, or it can be produced manually, using the QOR analysis on the next page.

For each criterion other than specific sales data (A and B) fill in a number between 1 and 10 for each customer, 10 being the highest. If

Quality of Relationship Analysis

A. Date of first purchase

B. Size of first purchase

C. Volume of business last 12 months

D. Anticipated business, next 12 months

E. Makes referrals

F. Pays on time, or no collection or fee problems

G. Ease of transaction, that is, no long distances, shipping charges, delays

H. Familiarity with all of our products and services

I. Their familiarity with you or your staff

J. Your familiarity with the buyer or the business he or she represents

K. Your sense of the relationship

L. Other . . . You may need to produce other columns particular to your business or industry.

	A	B	C	D	I	E	F	G...
Customer 1								
Customer 2								
Customer 3								
Customer 4								
Customer 5								
Customer 6								
.								
.								
Customer 50								

a customer is one of your biggest buyers, but the QOR is not all that it could be, then you must actively take steps to improve it. Conversely, if you have a high QOR (E to K) with a customer or client who is not otherwise a big buyer (A and B), here is an opportunity to exploit the relationship profitably for increased sales.

STEPS FOR ASSESSING YOUR AFTERMARKETING PROGRAM

If you are able to answer the following questions affirmatively, then your aftermarketing program is sound. If you answer no to any question, consider it an area for improvement.

[Y] or [N] *Is what happens to customers or clients after they exit your business as important to you as their purchase?* This question is not designed to test your altruism. It is simply good business. If the customer has a favorable experience after buying your product or service, then you may have a favorable experience thereafter. If he or she has a slightly less than favorable experience, this is likely to impact your business over the long run. When you are not aware of a customer's unfavorable experience, you are losing valuable information that is essential to your overall marketing program.

[Y] or [N] *Are all of your resources expended on marketing your product or service, with nothing left to support aftermarketing?* This is easy to determine. What is your aftermarketing budget? Effective aftermarketers allocate as much as 20 percent of the overall marketing budget to maintain communications with the customer, and ensure that the customer feels good about the purchase and is getting his or her money's worth.

[Y] or [N] *Are competent, trained staff in charge of aftermarketing responsibilities?* Aftermarketing cannot be left to customer service representatives on their first job unless they have been trained effectively and imbued with the company's policy on service after the sale.

[Y] or [N] *Do you personally maintain active interest in customer feedback systems?* Staying in the forefront means responding to needs. You cannot respond to needs unless you are getting feedback. Second-hand feedback is okay, but periodically you need to get first-hand feedback through direct interaction with responsive customers.

[Y] or [N] *As a consumer yourself, are you cognizant and appreciative of other businesses' aftermarketing courtesies?* For example, my auto repair service routinely sends a postcard when it is time for my quarterly maintenance check. It is just a small gesture, but every 90 days without my having to think about it, I know it is time to bring my car in for preventive maintenance. The system works. Although my car has traveled 55,000 miles, it still looks brand new. In the last three years I have averaged less than $300 per year for repairs and maintenance.

[Y] or [N] *Can you incorporate the winning aftermarketing strategies employed by others into your business?* Frequently, the answer is yes.

[Y] or [N] *Have you computed the cost of capturing a new customer versus the cost of retaining an existing one?* Often companies that throw hundreds if not thousands of dollars into advertising to generate new business do not know the answer to the question posed above. Aftermarketing techniques tend to be far less costly than first-encounter marketing techniques, just as staying in the forefront of customers' minds is less costly in the long run than making the initial sale.

THE RISE OF THE CUSTOMER RELATIONS FUNCTION

In the 1990s we are likely to see a rise in "dedicated" customer relations functions. This involves setting up a full-time staff or department that only handles customer relations. This development is a departure from the traditional technique of divvying up customer relations responsibility among staff that are primarily responsible for other areas of the business.

While the cost of establishing a dedicated customer relations function may appear inordinate at first, there are actually many advantages from the standponts of both cost and effectiveness.

1. In smaller enterprises, customer relations need not be more than one person. Large or small, customer relations representatives relieve others in your company from handling tasks they may not be suited for, however well intentioned. Many companies find that a full-time customer relations staff is able to yield a quality of aftermarketing that could not be achieved otherwise.

2. Customer relations can be assigned many of the aftermarketing responsibilities and techniques discussed throughout the chapter. The customer relations department can be proactive in orientation rather than merely reactive. A proactive staff effectively enables you to "cut problems off at the base," while continuing to build a loyal customer base. A customer relations staff that is well versed in the operations of the business and maintains liaison with all the departments provides a clear message to your customers and clients that they made a good decision in doing business with you.

3. A dedicated customer relations staff can provide effective management information such as:

- The number of callers per day, week, month
- The number of service questions, complaints
- Use by product, service, division, line
- Customer calling cycles following purchase
- Demographics of callers
- Effective methods of resolution
- Additional information via conversational surveys
- Additional information via follow-up letter surveys
- Possible improvements in operating instructions, boilerplates, spec sheets, and customer guides
- Geographic distribution of problems, complaints, suggestions, praise
- Reports of opportunities for additional sales

Turning Complaints into Opportunities

"We view a customer who is complaining as a real blessing in disguise. He or she is someone we can resell," says Lewis Carbone, vice president of marketing communications, National Car Rental.

> **Effective handling of complaints can vault you from the doghouse to the forefront of the customer's mind.**

The American Automobile Association and General Electric were two of 22 companies, government agencies, and voluntary agencies cited for exceptional complaint handling in *Update*, a follow-up to the mid-1970s study *Consumer Complaint Handling in America*. "Companies are taking the lessons of the original study to heart and using proactive complaint handling as a competitive tool," observes Virginia Knauer, director of the U.S. Office of Consumer Affairs, which produced both publications.

"Corporations which actively solicit complaints and resolve them to the consumer's satisfaction—some of the nation's largest companies have adopted this policy—are amply rewarded through repeat business from customers they would have otherwise lost," Knauer says. "More complaints are being handled with greater efficiency by fewer people at less cost."

General Motors, the New York State Public Service Commission, the California Attorney General's Office, and the Major Appliance Consumer Action Panel were cited as innovators in complaint handling.

800 Numbers Offer "Keep in Touch" Power

Many recent developments have accelerated the value of the 800 number as an effective aftermarketing techique. Since 800 numbers were introduced, they have helped change the way many firms do business. Direct marketing is growing at a rapid pace, with thousands of businesses nationwide providing 800 numbers for the convenience of their customers. 800 service is used in many ways, from checking the availability of products and placing orders to comparing prices and locating new sources of supply, all done simply by using your telephone.

There are now more than a half million toll-free telephone numbers throughout the United States, with the number rising every year. Direct toll-free numbers are regarded as helpful ways to:

- Give operational instructions directly to consumers
- Gather information on quality control
- Direct consumers to the appropriate service centers
- Honor warranties
- Handle grievances
- Encourage new orders or repeat orders

The Pillsbury Company reports receiving some 750 calls a day on their 800 number. Many of the calls represent questions or compliments, although there are also a fair number of complaints. Regardless of the nature of the calls, Pillsbury operators are trained to ask additional questions about users' experiences with products. Following the conversation, all callers are sent a questionnaire as a method of ensuring satisfaction.

Seven-Up recently printed the company's 800 number on the label. Thereafter the company experienced a huge increase in direct customer contact. One spokesperson said, "we are tapping into customers that we had not reached before." In addition, Seven-Up's mail response also picked up following installation of the 800 line.

POSITIVE STROKING AND HOW IT WORKS

An effective method for staying at the forefront of key customer's minds is to practice the art of positive stroking.

> **Positive stroking involves making extended efforts to let the customer or client know that he or she is important to you.**

Positive stroking can help to build additional sales volume, generate excellent word of mouth, and get customers talking about you so they serve as ambassadors for your business to others.

Some techniques of positive stroking are simple and obvious, but would require an inordinate amount of time or resources to maintain. For example, if you run a retail store, you could personally greet all customers, send everyone thank-you notes, or take other measures to have direct or indirect contact with a minority of your customers. Sticking with the 80/20 rule, independent of the line of business, it is best to focus positive stroking efforts on the "upper 20 percent." If you have the time or resources, or if your business is more conducive to it, then positive stroking techniques can be undertaken for more than just the "upper 20 percent."

The key to effective positive stroking is taking novel approaches for maximum advantage. Many companies have initiated a policy of having the president or other appropriate officials send a personal letter to customers or clients who have made a purchase above a certain size. This is a nice positive stroke and keeps down the number of letters that have to be sent out.

Saying Thanks All the Time

Jack Lorms, an Oregon-based realtor, believes it is important to say thanks anytime you have the opportunity to do so. Writing in *Real Estate*

Today, Lorms says, "In addition to expressing your feelings and strengthening your lines of communication, thank-you notes can create a favorable impression that will last. A few real estate people send notes because they are looking only for short-term gain. Those who are patient and don't bother to write leave the field wide open." He notes that the thank-you note is not a trick of the trade or the means to an end. The proper way to approach a thank-you note, says Lorms, is to send it "simply as an expression of appreciation. Any other benefits are extra."[1]

In your business, the note is a strategic element of position marketing. Your goal is to use every weapon at your disposal to make sure that your company is positioned properly in the minds of those you wish to serve. Therefore, the thank-you note is important.

How long should the note be? Lorms says, "People often get discouraged when the message they write looks lost on a full-size sheet of business stationery. They give up and toss the note in the wastebasket. Busy as they are, they forget the whole thing." The note therefore need only be brief and to the point. It is advisable to prepare stationery simply for this purpose. Any printer can provide inexpensive 4½″ × 5½″ sheets folded once. With this size, there is room only for two or three sentences, which is all you wish to send anyway.

There is no harm in having a key staff assistant take charge of the note-sending responsibility, even signing for you. The customer is not collecting signatures, nor is the note likely to be saved for any reason. What matters is that you send it; and it is likely that you are the only company president or manager that they have heard from in the last month, last year, or in their consumer lifetime.

Your staff should be writing letters, too. Your salespeople and all others who come into direct contact with customers and clients further your positive stroking quest by sending their own letters. Why? Targeted action letters have proven to be excellent means of generating good will, enhancing good customer relations, and, in the long run, increasing sales. You must build staff letter writing into the system—make it a regular and ongoing part of your staff's overall job responsibility.

What kind of letter should your staff be writing? A thank-you letter to follow up an order, sale, or contract is most important. Also important are letters to provide follow-up information, even when they were not

---

[1] Excerpts reprinted from *Real Estate Today*® June 1986, by permission of the National Association of Realtors.® Copyright © 1986. All rights reserved.

asked for or expected by the customer, brief notes introducing new products or services, and simple "keep in touch letters" that need say nothing more than "we are thinking about you" or "hope all is well."

In using letters as a proactive positive stroking technique, here are several tips:

- Have a second party (in house) review the letter before it is mailed. This will ensure that a wrong message is not conveyed inadvertently, and that spelling, punctuation, and grammar are correct.

- Produce a set of standard letters your staff can use. Standard letters can cause problems as the letter may appear stilted, the same customer may get the same letter twice, and it is difficult to keep on top of which customer received what.

- Provide a brief amount of staff training time for writing effective notes. This requires no more than one hour per person, and can be done en masse. Have your most effective note writer lead or have significant participation in the session.

- If conducive to your line of business, establish daily, weekly, or monthly goal figures. These can be mandatory or not, depending on your aims, so that your staff knows what is expected of them in this area.

- Encourage staff to circulate any customer or client replies. Make a cause célèbre out of any particularly flattering reply.

- If you are so moved, provide reprints of some notes you have written, of which you are particularly proud.

Here are some traps to avoid in letter and note sending:

- Not all staff will be comfortable writing notes. It may be necessary to assign a designated letter/note writer, depending on how you are set up.

- An unexpected or occasional personal note is certainly a nice touch. If repeated too frequently, however, among some customers, it may have a diminishing effect. Generally speaking, a note per customer every three months is reasonable, although depending on the situation, more frequent intervals can be established.

- If you or your staff are writing formal, impersonal notes, the strategy will backfire; you will defeat the very purpose of sending notes. Be sure that everyone understands that these notes are to represent a personal touch, not a corporate tactic or obligation.

- Note writing is not without its cost. If each staff person were to write only 10 letters per week, with a staff of 10 the cost would exceed $1500.00 a year—not a large sum, but one that should nevertheless be budgeted.

- Avoid note-sending campaigns only when trying to drum up more sales or following sales. Long-standing customers will appreciate receiving notes that apparently are not connected to "selling."

Do not underestimate the power and value of note writing. Especially when a hand stamp is used, your company's letter or note can easily stand out among a stack of 2 inches of highly impersonal, third-class direct mail.

Here are some samples of appreciation letters and notes you can offer:

Sample Appreciation Notes

Thanks for your recent order of _____ . You are a valued customer and we truly appreciate your business.

I (we) hope that you get maximum enjoyment out of your new _____ . I will give you a call in a few weeks to make sure everything is working well.

Although you made your purchase just recently, I don't think it is too early to say congratulations. We stand by our products 100 percent and believe that you have made a sound purchase.

You are our kind of customer, and we are glad that we are your kind of store. (Or, we hope we are your kind of store.)

Serving customers (or clients) like you is the reason why we are in business. I hope to see you again soon.

Thanks for stopping in today and taking the time to learn more about XYZ. Here is the additional information I mentioned. I will give you a call next Tuesday to see whether you have any questions.

It was a pleasure meeting you last week. I know that your time is valuable and I appreciate your spending the time you did with me.

As president of DEF, I know that I speak on behalf of our 350 employees when I say we truly appreciate your business.

The High-Level Phone Call

The phone can be used in the same way as letters and notes. Here are the advantages and disadvantages of using the phone over the note and letter writing approach:

Advantages

- The phone provides two-way feedback, can stimulate sales or help identify problems that may be converted to additional opportunities for your company.
- Phone calls *can* be less time consuming and less expensive. However, we all can think of many instances in which this is not true.
- Many members of your staff may prefer phone calls to notes, and may be more effective in conversation than in writing.

Disadvantages

- Some customers may see the call as an intrusion. This rarely happens when they receive a note in the mail.
- The call could be forgotten more quickly than a letter or note.
- Lots of busy signals, people not home, and incorrect dialing may render calling somewhat tedious.

For superpowerful stroking some owners and managers make direct calls themselves. Once again, this technique is not for everybody, and should not to be used with every customer, unless perhaps you are in some form of contracting or services where a limited number of customers provide your entire revenue base.

Getting to Know You

By all means get to know as many customers on a name basis as possible. If you serve other businesses or large corporations, learn the names of those people beyond your immediate contact. For example, if you sell tool and dye products to a local manufacturer, learn the names of people in billing, shipping, quality control, and administration, not just in purchasing.

One of my positive stroking techniques as an author working with publishing houses is to learn the names of the marketing manager and the regional sales staff, the publicity manager, the foreign rights representative, various production editors and staff assistants, mail order representatives, and trade show and convention representatives. Following the completion of a book, I always write a letter to the publisher and the chief executive officer thanking them for the opportunity to work with their fine staff. On a frequent basis I send notes to all the above individuals, offering praise, recommendations, or information and tips that may help the sale of our mutual product, the book. As we discussed in Chapter 4, getting the names of the appropriate department managers and other people is becoming less difficult all the time.

Follow-Up and Appreciation Strategies

Additional follow-up and appreciation strategies are helpful for staying in the forefront of the minds of those whom you wish to reach and influence continuously. Many techniques, such as sending select invitations to open houses, presale announcements, and discounts to long-standing customers, may already be familiar to you. These strategies have been covered in many other books.

> **Letting customers and clients know that you appreciate their business will never go out of style.**

There is no need to get gushy, but much like telling your spouse on a regular basis that you love him or her, you really cannot go wrong by letting customers and clients know on a regular basis how much you appreciate their business. Some businesses state on their letterheads: "We appreciate your business." Other businesses include the message on invoices and other correspondence. Do not dismiss such a simple message either printed, typed, or conveyed orally.

Everybody wants to feel special, even if in the tiniest ways. McDonald's campaign of years ago, "You deserve a break today," was an excellent example of indicating that the customer is important. Really, who would not agree with the statement that they deserve a break today?

Giving the Gift or Novelty

In many customers' minds gifts equal appreciation. Here are 15 ways to give gifts and novelty items for maximum advantage:

- Give a gift to the spouse of your customer instead of the customer. This will get the two of them talking about you, and you will be remembered.

- Give a gift to the customer's children. They will be eternally grateful—the customer, not just the child.

- Send a brief letter suggesting one of several gifts you are thinking of offering and have each customer check off the gift that he or she wishes to receive. This serves several functions: (1) It closely ensures the match between items sent and desire of receiver. (2) This strategy builds anticipation. (3) The novelty of the approach will make you stand out.

- Send two gifts rather than one. The price of the two can equal what one would have cost. One of the gifts can clearly be more expensive than the other. Again, you will stand out, as few do this.

- Give a gift certificate that is for a show, restaurant, or resort stay. Anytime the customer has to travel, that is, make a vacation out of it, you raise the probability of being remembered.

- Give a gift based on your inside connection or privileged status. For example, one former Capitol Hill staffer bought folders with notepads from the Congressional Supply Store at the standard price of $5.00 each. The folders looked good, but what was even more thrilling to the people who received them was that they included the official seal of the U.S. Senate. Nowhere else in the United States or around the world could one buy such a folder.

- Give a gift that you can add to, that is, the customer starts off with the base unit and then is encouraged to add additional units. The encyclopedia companies practice a variation of this by selling volume "A" at bargain prices.

- Monogram standard items such as pens or pencils for your customers in their names. This can be done inexpensively and offers a nice touch. Most customers appreciate seeing their names on items, especially when they did not pay for it.

- Create your own reason for giving a gift, such as your company's anniversary.

- Do send Christmas cards, the more colorful, large, and elaborate the better. Many people silently note who sends them cards. Others count the number of cards that they receive. If it is a good customer, it makes sense to be on his or her mantle during the holidays.

- Give timely gifts based on the season or world events. For example, during the drought of 1988, small fans made an excellent gift. Following Secretary Gorbachev's visit to the United States, vodka worked well. Every even year there are elections; every fourth year, Olympics; and a host of other preplanned activities in between.

- Give the receiver the original box, warranties, and so forth. You may even consider including the invoice and sales slip should the customer wishes to return the gift. This is no negative reflection on you. If the customer returns it, for cash or for something else, you still get "credit" for having given the gift in the first place and initiated the process of exchange.

Recognize that like anything, gift giving has a cost. The key question with every strategy is: Is this enabling my company to stay at the forefront of those we wish to continue to serve?

Asking Favors of Your Customers and Clients

Dale Carnegie knew it 50 years ago. One of the simplest and most effective ways of getting people to notice and remember you, if not like you, is to ask a favor of them. The psychological dynamics of asking a favor of someone are more complex than you might at first imagine. Consider that in order to ask a favor of someone, you have to get the person's attention. The act of asking instantaneously makes you somewhat beholden to them. As generous in spirit as many of your customers or clients may be, they do not see it quite that way. They feel flattered that you think enough of them to make a request.

If you are asking for their feedback, you convey the message that you value their opinion. If you ask for a few moments of their time, you value their participation. Here are several effective ways to ask favors of your customers:

- On site and on the spot, ask customers about their preferences regarding package sizes, shelf arrangements, store displays, and other store features.
- Ask how to overcome a problem you face.
- Design brief and formal surveys that quickly capture the input of customers.
- Ask for customer particiption in a brief demonstration or experiment. If you desire and if appropriate, offer a five dollar gift certificate or some other incentive. This is usually not necessary—people are generally pleased to participate.
- Set up a well-marked customer suggestion box, "Please do us a favor, give us your suggestion."

When incorporated into your overall marketing and positioning strategy, techniques for staying in the forefront can quickly set you apart from the rest, and in the not too long run, make a healthy contribution to revenues.

15

Self-Assessment: Customers Won and Customers Lost

Ten years from now we'll wonder how we ever were satisfied to give no better service than we do today.

GEORGE M. PULLMAN

Assessing why you both win customers and lose customers is an essential, but often overlooked element of effective position marketing. If you do not know or understand all of the reasons why you are winning customers, how can you effectively duplicate what works best? And if you are losing customers, what can you do to address the situation? In this chapter we will look at how to assess the critical success factors of your business and answer the following questions:

□ Why is accessibility so important to your business?

□ Do you know how each of your customers heard about you?

□ Whom among your customers and when should you solicit for advice?

□ What are some simple methods for evaluating lost business?

□ How do professional service firms lose clients?

□ Can you win back a lost customer and, if so, how?

The exercise of assessing customers won and lost enables you to reflect upon past and current marketing effectiveness, while also helping to identify current and future areas of opportunity or need for attention. Are you offering the winning combination of goods and services in a profitable, effective manner? Is your staff sensitive and responsive to customer or client needs? Do you periodically review your marketing strategy in the face of shifting markets? Do you regularly monitor the activities of competitors?

Many entrepreneurs do a good job in assessing the effectiveness of individual components of the overall marketing program, such as the quality of products or services offered, skills of the selling staff, advertising and promotion, and aftermarketing. Often these components are examined independent of each other. However, a balanced assessment of marketing effectiveness must be broad based.

ASSESSING YOUR CUSTOMER GAINED/ RETAINED POTENTIAL

Are You Accessible?

As Holland Cooke says in his book *How to Keep Your Press Release Out of the Wastebasket*, "The difference between a successful and an un-sucessful expert is that the expert made himself or herself accessible." So, too, the art of effective positioning often hinges on the ease with which the customer or client *is able* to patronize your goods or services.

If a customer can reach you the first time that he or she attempts to do so, often, that may be the single greatest reason why he or she becomes your customer.

Arnold Sanow, a business consultant and lecturer, includes his office phone number, his home phone number, and his car phone number on his business card (Figure 18). Sanow wants you to get in touch with him and he lets you know it by providing phone numbers of where he can be reached virtually throughout the day. He reports that he often does receive calls from new potential clients while he is in his car. The callers tell him that rather than speak with an answering machine or a reception service, they appreciate the ability to get in touch with him immediately.

How important is accessibility in business services, in manufacturing, or in construction? Acknowledging that ours is a society of time-pressed people, if a customer can reach you easily, this may be the reason why he or she becomes your customer. In a time-pressed society instant accessibility translates into more customers won, independent of the value of your products or services.

Acknowledging Our Referral Sources

Doctors and dentists have long recognized the importance of asking new patients a particular question. Usually somewhere at the bottom of the patient history form there is a question that says, "How did you hear

Office: (703) 849-8114
Car: (202) 374-9133
Res: (703) 849-8627

THE BUSINESS SOURCE
BUSINESS DEVELOPMENT SPECIALISTS

ARNOLD SANOW   2859 COORS PARK COURT
                      FALLS CHURCH, VIRGINIA 22043

Figure 18. Arnold Sanow's business card. (Reprinted with permission.)

of us?" Most patients will dutifully write in "recommended by a friend" or "doctors' referral service," "saw your advertisement," "saw your offices while I was driving by," or any one of a number of reasons.

Capturing Vital Data

How often do those of us in nonmedical fields fail to capture these vital data? Recognizing the source of new business should be the burning quest of all entrepreneurs. You need to know:

- Was it the *Yellow Pages* ad?
- Was it our brochure?
- Was it a recommendation from a satisfied customer?
- Did you see our booth at the convention?
- Do you work nearby?
- Do you live nearby?
- Are you dissatisfied with your former service?

There seems to be an inverse law regarding the quest of businesses to determine how customers heard of them. The bigger the business, the less likely it is to be interested in how you heard of them. Yet, that is precisely the type of input necessary to keep successful businesses successful.

Recently I became disgruntled with the hand-held dictation equipment that I had been using for years. The tapes started jamming up, words in the sentences were truncated, and I was losing all confidence in the equipment. Determined to find a new dealer/distributer, I started calling around town. I finally settled on a small dealer way across town who seemed to know what he was speaking about.

After purchasing a new model and coming home, I realized that the dealer had not once asked, and I did not think to offer, why I was seeking him and his products in the first place. He never asked:

- If I had previously used dictation equipment
- Whose equipment I used
- How I liked or did not like that equipment

- What features I was particularly interested in having
- What kinds of work I would be doing with the dictator
- How many hours per day or week I anticipated using it
- Then: how I had gotten his telephone number
- Why I had decided to call him
- Why I ended up making a 25-minute trip when there were other dealers closer by

To be sure, this gentleman was able to make a sale and to serve me successfully. Should anyone ask, I will certainly recommend his business. Yet, he is missing vital data from me, a single customer, that could enable him to attract others with similar experiences and needs.

It Is Not Always Location

Many retailers make the mistake of believing that the customers they attract are largely a function of location. This type of parochial thinking can actually limit revenues in the long run. Three drugstores are equally distant from a large condominium project in Fort Worth. The drugstores vary somewhat in size and products offered but are similar in most other respects, including hours open, accessibility, and general quality of merchandise offered.

One drugstore consistently captures more business from the condominium project than the other two, though there is no particular locational advantage. The reason? The manager of the winning drug store is in the habit of asking customers where they are from in the area. Over many weeks, when he realized that he was capturing a significant portion of the condominium business, he began to cater to their needs. He started stocking $25 \times 12 \times 1$-inch filters for heat pumps because that was what the condo residents needed. And, to his benefit, each resident needed one each month.

Similarly, he began stocking bathroom filters, reflector light bulbs, microwave popcorn, and a variety of other items that directly addressed the needs of this large body of customers.

The other two stores did a healthy volume of business, but never having assessed why customers came to them, went about business as usual—they offered seasonal sales, special discounts, and two-for-ones.

Over time, the drugstore in tune with the needs of the condominium (and I might add, in tune with the needs of other nearby groups) enjoyed a healthier volume of business. The sales per square foot was higher, the profitability was higher, the average cash register ring-up was higher. The other stores had little chance of matching the revenues of the winning drugstore.

Integrity Pays

The 1980s unfortunately saw widespread graft and corruption in our highest levels of government, in industry, on Wall Street, and elsewhere throughout our society. Many polls now indicate that the American people are eager to return to a more ethical society where right and wrong count. They are less attracted by flash and promise, but are retained with interest, substance, and follow-through.

More than at any time perhaps in the last 15 years, simply operating a reputable establishment helps win customers. How is this achieved? By telling it like it is. The vendor who honestly states that the delay will be closer to two hours rather than 30 minutes has a higher potential for retaining long-term customers when in fact the delay will be about two hours. The shopkeeper who explains why the $10.00 higher priced item is not necessarily better than the less expensive equivalent retains customers. The auto mechanic who finds one small thing wrong with your car, fixes it in six minutes at an appropriate charge, and sends you on your way is the one you will come back to.

Customers have "had it" with being manipulated. Your ability to play it straight and charge appropriately is one of your most valuable assets.

MINICASE
VANGUARD COMPANIES

James O'Toole is a professor of management at the University of Southern California. To prove to his students that corporations could be run with the "same high moral standards with which many people choose to lead their private lives, he conducted research to find examples of companies that produced high-quality goods, behaved morally and ethically, and invested in the people they employed. In short, O'Toole found companies that made money *not despite having high ethical standards but because of them.*

In *Vanguard Management: Redesigning the Corporate Future* O'Toole found that eight large companies, including Atlantic Richfield, Control Data Corporation, Dayton-Hudson Corporation, Deere and Company, Honeywell, Levi Strauss and Company, Motorola, and Weyerhaeuser Company served as excellenet role models. He also found several small- to medium-sized companies that measured up, including Peter Burwash International, Chaparral Steel Company, Felt Products Manufacturing Company, W. L. Gore and Associates, Herman Miller Incorporated, Koll Morgen Corporation, Lincoln Electric Company, Lord Corporation, and the Olga Company.

All of these companies make high-quality products and have excellent reputations for customer service. Many other management experts regard these companies as "models of business excellence" according to O'Toole. These companies offer job security for employees and attractive employee stock option plans. They are led by "farsighted, risk-taking chief executive officers," who are able to articulate high moral standards and a social purpose for the companies they lead.

Most important, observed O'Toole, they are "very profitable." While these are not "perfect" companies, their eagerness to identify and honestly address their shortcomings have resulted in long-term profits. The customers and clients of these companies have a well-developed sense of what these companies stand for. In short, these companies are well positioned.[1]

Solicit Your Customers and Clients

Your existing customers and your former customers represent a highly valuable source of information that you simply cannot duplicate or obtain elsewhere. The people who buy from you can tell you how you do or do not serve their needs. Thus it behooves you to install or upgrade methods of obtaining customer and client feedback. You might think that a franchise as successful as 7-Eleven would not have a need to offer

---

[1] Interview with James O'Toole, author, *Vangard Management: Redesigning the Corporate Future*. New York: Doubleday, 1985.

customer evaluation cards. However, the Southland Corporation knows that remaining successful means not coasting, not taking the customer for granted, not guessing what is right and what is wrong.

In *In Search of Excellence* Peters and Waterman pointed out that up until just before the time of his death, J. W. Marriott personally read all the guest evaluation cards turned in at the Marriotts throughout the country. Mr. Marriott knew that these cards were worth their weight in gold in enabling his hotel chain to remain successful.

ASSESSING LOST BUSINESS

Many of the reasons why businesses lose customers did not exist before. Today clients in the professional services are much more apt to change counsel than ever before. Among business services and retail stores customers will flock to the "new kid" on the block if the store is bigger or newer, the prices are better, the selection is deeper, or, hardest of all to combat, "everyone shops there."

In many lines of business today customer loyalty lasts only as long as they do not discover a faster, easier, cheaper, closer, more enjoyable way of fulfilling their needs. Product manufacturers, vendors, and contractors to other businesses or particularly large corporations may have long-term contracts in hand, but nevertheless can also lose customers due to a variety of internal or external factors.

No one really likes to assess lost business; it is painful. Realizing what we did wrong, where we botched it, how we messed up is no one's idea of fun. Yet it is a necessary and useful exercise to help close the gap through which customers slip away.

There are many reasons why we lose customers and clients, and considering each of them in detail would fill an encyclopedia. Nevertheless, your ability to identify the four or five major reasons why you have lost customers and clients is an important step in retaining your existing customers, attracting new ones, and possibily winning back former customers.

Lost Business in Professional and Business Services

Some of the reasons why clients are lost include the following:

Not Explaining the Billing Rate or Service Charge. You know the scenario, you have felt it yourself as a consumer. You retain a professional to do a job for you, you get back the bill, and you are ready to scream. People are more willing to pay a high price than most of us realize—what they want and need is to be able to understand why the charges were necessary. Detailed billing combined with an early, personal explanation will go far here. Explaining at the outset what a particular job is likely to cost may scare away some customers, but will result in a net gain.

Not Treating the Customer's or the Client's Problem as Important. It seems so simple: the customer comes in looking for some empathy and some help. But the entrepreneurs in professional and business services are too caught up in their own problems to be able to convey to the customers, "Yes, Mr. or Mrs. customer, your problem is important to me." One accountant put it to me this way: "It got so that I was simply looking at a set of figures and I forgot that these data strongly impacted the lives of the clients that had retained me."

Overpromising. This usually results from weak selling capability rather than poor scheduling. In an effort to win a client or customer that we believe might otherwise be lost, there is a tendency to overpromise to win this customer, believing that we will be able to "catch up" later and deliver on the promise. This seldom happens. In the long run, businesses in the habit of overpromising develop a reputation for underdelivering. This being so, these businesses struggle harder for clients and customers, and thus *tend to continue to overpromise*. Once it starts, it is a terrible cycle to break out of.

Failing to Keep in Touch. Many clients and customers simply change patronage because they come to believe that you no longer care about doing business with them. With our information overload, in our time-pressed society even your most enthusiastic customers may not call back as expected. Today this does not necessarily mean that they are not interested in doing business with you. More often, what it means is that they are very busy. The solution is to extend yourself all the way, rather than meeting them halfway. You must call to schedule the periodic checkup, the annual review, update, renewal, and so on.

Devaluing the Customer. How many times have you been eager to land a new account or client, then with the passage of time you convey to that client that winning other new accounts is more important to you? No one likes to feel like yesterday's news, yet all too often we lose the enthusiasm and vigor we displayed when we first sought somebody's business.

Lost Business Analysis: Professional and Business Services

How many customers or clients did we lose in the past 12 months due to the following?:

[   ] Not explaining the billing rate or service charge

[   ] Not treating the customer's or the client's problem as important

[   ] Overpromising

[   ] Failing to keep in touch

[   ] Devaluing the customer

Lost Business in Retailing

We have already seen how location dramatically impacts your ability to attract a strong customer base. Independent of location, however, let us explore some of the factors why you lose the business of people who were once regular customers.

Ineffectiveness of Sales Help. When your sales help finds other things to do besides serving customers, customers will find other places to do business.

Pressuring Customers. This usually occurs when your sales staff gives the impression that it is more important to them to get on to the next customer than to adequately and patiently serve the one before them.

The customer only has to feel pressured *once* before deciding never to return.

Serving customers involves straddling a thin line. On the one hand you cannot ignore them, and on the other hand if you are serving them, you cannot rush them.

Inconvenient Hours Open. Remember the example on page 261 about the three drugstores in Fort Worth? The winning drugstore strived to meet the needs of the market. Do your opening hours reflect customer needs? Banks have traditionally been faulty in this area. Banks that still maintain the 9 A.M. to 3 P.M. shift are losing a considerable amount of business to banks open as late as 5, 6, and 7 P.M. Are your hours open convenient for you and your employees *or* for your customers?

Atmospherics. Does your store deliver the message: "We are glad you are here?" Do the people convey this message? Or do you convey the message: "Sure, we're in business, but we don't see any reason why we have to be cheerful about it"? Long Island, New York based veteran sales trainer and motivator Alan Cimberg says that he would rather be greeted by someone who was trying to smile or trying to be friendly than someone who was a sincere grouch or stone-faced. Management consultant and sought-after speaker Dave Yoho says, "Each of us, throughout the course of our lives, never gets enough of one thing, and that is love." Translated into your business that equates to a friendly, cheerful sales staff.

Lack of Clear-Cut Policies. Are your purchasing policies clearly stated? For example, under what conditions do you accept a personal check? credit cards? credit accounts? People feel uneasy when they are not sure how they may pay for their goods. Do you have a return policy? Is it clearly posted? You do not have to duplicate the policy of Nordstrom's—100 percent return on all items, no questions asked—but whatever the policy, let it be widely known. If it is not, you are likely to turn off customers and experience some conflicts that need not have happened.

Failure to Keep Pace with Industry Trends. When is the last time you visited a competitor's store? It need not be someone in the local area, although that it advisable. As we saw in Chapter 10 on Staples, you and your management staff must get into the habit of visiting stores, showrooms, outlets, and locations of competitors. The service, benefit, or feature that you do not offer could very well be causing the loss of customers.

Receptionist Capability. Your business's inability to answer the phone effectively can be the greatest single cause of lost business.

One very effective retailer in Wilmette, Illinois, outside of Chicago, used to assess how his store benefited different customer types by assuming their roles. He sold stereo appliances and related items. Frequently he would walk outside the store, pretend he was a college senior, a housewife

Lost Business Analysis: Retail Operations

How many customers did we lose in the past 12 months due to the following?:

[   ] Inattentiveness of sales help

[   ] Pressuring customers

[   ] Inconvenient store hours

[   ] Poor atmospherics

[   ] Lack of clear-cut policies

[   ] Failure to keep pace with industry trends

[   ] Poor receptionist capabilities

---

with three children, a retired executive, or any one of a number of other people. Then he entered his own store and approached it as if he were one of those customer types. This gave him a totally new perspective as he walked through the aisles, looked at various display cases, and posed questions to his own sales staff.

As a result of these exercises, he frequently rearranged displays, changed the heights of some products, advertised to attract particular niches, and oriented his sales staff in a manner that could accommodate different customer types. When you think about it, this is a pretty good exercise for anyone in business to practice.

Lost Business as a Vendor or Contractor

Assessing lost business in vending and contracting entails many more factors than in other lines of business. When calling on a potential buyer, there are many reasons for not getting the job or the contract, including:

- Lack of adequate preparation
- Lack of knowledge of the customer's needs

- Inability to present your own products or services effectively
- Not dealing with the right person
- Failure to convey your ability to complete the task at hand successfully

Here are some of the reasons why you can lose a formerly good customer:

Telephone Accessibility. It is as important here as in any other line of business. Sometimes, however, the purchasing agent or buyer needs to make a change on short notice and thus his or her need to get in touch with you is paramount.

Inadequate Progress Reporting. It is not just the product or service that you make and deliver that is important to buyers, as discussed previously; it is also important to keep the buyer informed. In addition, no one likes surprises unless the surprises are favorable in nature. A vendor or contractor who does not accurately and swiftly convey problems of which the buyer should be informed is setting himself or herself up for lost business in the future.

Inability to Meet Contractual Obligations. This speaks for itself, quality and delivery being the most crucial elements.

Failing to Pass On-Site Inspection. If buyers visit your plant or office and it is not up to par visually, you may also be losing potential business. Is your location clean? Are supplies stored conveniently, yet out of the way? Have your employees been briefed, and do they conduct themselves as professionals? What do the outside and the inside of your place of business say about you as a contractor? Would you do business with yourself based on appearance? If the answer is no, then you will probably get the same answer from buyers.

Poor Quality Control Resulting in Too Many Defects. This is a major cause of lost business. Does any of the following characterize your operations?

- Defects due to machine or human error
- Ineffective quality control program
- Inadequately trained staff
- Underskilled staff
- Improper equipment

- Operating beyond optimal capacity
- Accepting unreachable time frames, resulting in errors

Lost Business Analysis: Manufacturing

How many customers did we lose in the past 12 months due to the following?:

[ ] Poor telephone accessibility

[ ] Inadequate progress reporting

[ ] Inability to meet contractual obligations

[ ] Failure to pass on-site inspection

[ ] Poor quality control resulting in too many defects

Lost Business in Other Industries

If you are a tour operator, provide transportation, offer some form of instruction, equipment installation, or any other variety of business or service, you too need to assess the reasons why a customer is lost. The common denominators for such an assessment include:

- Continuously gaining feedback from present and former customers
- Keeping abreast of changes within the industry
- Assessing the quality and price of your products and services versus those of competitors
- Examining the effectiveness of your advertising
- Living up to the position that you have in the minds of those you are interested in serving

WINNING BACK CUSTOMERS AFTER LOSING THEM

When assessing customers lost, consider that a significant portion of those customers and clients need not be lost forever. You may find, as many business have, that regaining a lost customer is no more difficult and may be easier than winning a new customer.

In the professional services and in some business services you can usually sense when a customer or client has withdrawn. When you sense that something is wrong, more often than not there is. In retailing it is possible to review a customer's history of purchases by credit card or check (or by receipt if you capture such information on each cash transaction) to observe breaks in consumption or shopping patterns.

In manufacturing, serving as a vendor to other manufacturers, or in contracting or construction, when something is wrong between you and the customer, he or she will often let you know and as soon as possible.

Many entrepreneurs, fearing criticism or ill will, are fearful of calling the former customer to determine what went wrong, and what if anything could be done to regain his or her business. However, there is no better way than to go directly to the source. Often a former customer or client who is willing to take the time to talk with you is giving you a signal that he or she can be won back.

Whom do you need to get in touch with today? The answer is apparent and represents the person or account you have been avoiding while hoping that somehow everything would work out. What are the possible reasons that a customer might stop doing business with you? He could have found a better price or better service, her needs could have changed, he could have had an unvoiced grievance, or she may have simply gotten out of the habit of doing business with you. Luther A. Brock, Ph.D., direct marketing specialist, writing in *Direct Marketing*, recommends the following tips if you choose to devise a "customer-retrieving letter."

1. Recognize in the first part of your letter that the customer has not done business with you for awhile. Open with:

   > "We miss you."
   > Or
   > "Losing a customer is like losing a friend. This is why I want you to know how much we . . ."
   > Or
   > "The enclosed Savings Coupon is our way of saying 'We'd like you as a customer again.'"

   Notice how each gets right to the point.

2. Put more emphasis on how the reader will again benefit from your product than on something having gone wrong with your relationship.

Once you have acknowledged that you would like the customer back, go on to something more upbeat and persuasive.

3. Make the reader feel like part of your business family. Even though you may sell to millions, individual ex-customers are concerned only with themselves. And if you make them feel important to you, as though business really matters, they are far more apt to return.

4. Don't wait long before getting out customer-retrieving letters. Look at customers' buying records. If they have normally ordered every three months, say, and you have not heard from them in six months, start writing. And keep right on sending letter after letter until you are convinced that they are gone for good.

5. After you do retrieve lost customers, get out a regular monthly mailing to them. Never take them for granted. People love personal attention. And the more attention you pay them, the more they will buy from you.[2]

Calling Instead of Writing

If you decide to call, slowly and calmly introduce yourself, state your position with the company. Then instead of referring to your observation that the customer no longer patronizes your business, pose the question: "You have been a good customer of ours in the past, and I would like to know personally how we can continue to serve you. After that let the customer do all the talking. He or she will either give you the specific things you can do, or tell you why he or she has chosen not to return.

In either case it will be a valuable call because you will either regain a lost customer or gather information that will enable you to help retain existing customers or clients.

The next three chapters offer summaries of consulting reports and analyses of actual cases—only the names are disguised to avoid disclosure.

[2] Reprinted with permission. Luther A. Brock, "Customer-Retrieving Letters Need an 'I Miss You' Tone," *Direct Marketing*, April 1985, p. 22.

PART FIVE
CASES

16

The Accounting Firm That Wanted to Be Exciting

Fortune and fame is a curious game.

JAMES TAYLOR

In this chapter we look at how one of the largest accounting firms in the nation wanted to change its image to that of something outside the bounds of its industry. LMV wanted to be regarded as "exciting." The article reprinted below reveals part of LMV's attempt to position itself outside of what clients and prospective clients expected or wanted from an accounting firm. (The names and a few disclosing items in the article have been disguised.) First read through the article. Then we will tear it apart to show why effective postioning could not occur.

Polishing the Professional Image

1   William Misler would have enjoyed being commissioner of baseball. Instead, he's the provocative managing partner of a large accounting firm. Says Misler, 53, of his would-be management of baseball:

"They didn't like my policies. I wanted all-flannel uniforms, no night games, nothing played west of the Mississippi, and travel only by train. Baseball was fantastic for 60 years—until they decided to move it to California."

Since he can't take the baseball commissioner's place, Misler has decided to go to bat for accounting, the occupation he has pursued since 1962 when he was graduated with a bachelor's degree in accounting. He thinks it's time to make the numbers game more "romantic."

2   Misler is the chief executive officer of "LMV," an accounting and consulting organization with some 160 offices in more than 70 countries (including 33 in the United States). He says:

"We're trained to find fault, find the big mistake. I spent the first part of my career trying to find fault, playing corporate watchdog, laboring under the idea that all corporate management is fraudulent."

Having audited thousands of financial statements, he concludes that "most of corporate America is pretty straitlaced" when it comes to presenting the bottom line. He continues:

"Of course, the press focuses on the problems, tells us that corporate America has no values. But for every 'war story' you find, there are thousands of ethical businesspeople out there whose finances don't make the press."

Finding corporate thieves doesn't take a lot of skill, Misler says. He adds:

"It's usually a case of spotting either an employee scam or corporate-management fraud. Generally, dishonest employees have something simple going and could steal forever with dummy invoices or the like—unless they get greedy and careless. They usually get greedy and careless."

Management fraud usually turns out to be playing with income. Misler explains:

"You can usually spot it because the same people who are handling the cash are handling the invoices. So as an accountant, you look for segregation of responsibility to support that the company has reasonable internal control."

"Rounding" is one of the new money mismanagement games. Explains Misler:

"Let's say you're rounding off hourly wages by a half cent. If you round it off the wrong way 100,000 times, then write yourself a check for that amount, you'll still balance out."

3   Hoping that the statute of limitations has expired, Misler confesses that he once stole a gallon of martinis using the same system that modern hoodlums employ to steal corporate funds. The incident occurred in the 1950s at a hotel on Long Island. The host of a cocktail party was serving martinis and Manhattans from 12 gallon-size olive jugs. He intended to use the jugs as his audit. If he got back a dozen jugs, either empty or full, he figured he hadn't lost any liquor to thieves. Says Misler:

"How hard is it to find a gallon olive jug? We found an extra one, and we returned 12 jugs, but we also walked away with a gallon of martinis."

When a profession does little more than look for the schemes of others, it soon can become boring. Accountants, justifiably, can blame some of their "rotten" image on newspapers and other media, says Misler, and on their own communication techniques. He explains:

"A writer once did an article in a well-known newspaper which claimed accountants were dull. The article itself wasn't dull, however, and that's why it left many believing the profession is boring. The writer told the story of a man in a hot-air balloon who got lost and landed in a field. Eventually he saw a fellow passing by and asked where he was. The passer-by replied, "In a basket in a field," to which the fellow in the balloon said, "Your information is precisely accurate but useless; you must be an accountant." In reality, however, accountants have some of the sharpest minds in the business or economic community. But I don't know how exciting numbers are.

"The *Financial Times of London* also contributed to the professional image of dullness. It once said that bureaucrats in business, unions, and government are dinosaurs—and 'about as imaginative as the average company accountant.'"

Accountants don't fight back. In fact, says Misler, they perpetuate the image of dullness with dull communication. He explains:

"I think it was *Forbes* that said we write double talk, use too many 'therefores' and 'whereases.' We make our writings appear dull, so we appear dull. Have you ever found anything exciting about the footnotes in a financial statement? They're like reading a phone book—a great cast of characters, but no plot."

As a result, LMV has an entire division for communications. Says Misler:

4 { "Communicating is our way of trying to bring humanity into a very dull subject. Take the subject of estate planning. Anybody coming up through the executive ranks should plan early on for his or her estate. That's a touchy area nobody wants to discuss. It sounds deadly. But in the last issue of *Viewpoint*, our quarterly magazine . . . , we talked about estate planning. We had a real catchy cartoon cover—a family in a castle surrounded by a moat that was keeping two IRS agents at bay—and a clever headline, 'Up the drawbridge! Planning your estate. Tips on keeping the IRS out of your back yard and back pocket!'"

The firm's articles are "serious, meaningful, and informative," maintains Misler. He continues:

"The way we introduce [the article] is not. If it's plain vanilla, people aren't going to get as excited about it as they are about a hot-fudge sundae. We have
5 to do things that entice readers. But the bottom line is that the substance has to be there."

6 Misler is attempting to perk up—and stir up—the profession in other ways. Last year, for instance, he launched an advertising campaign to solicit mergers. The ad took up a full page in a prestigious journal and openly invited firms to
7 { discuss teaming up with LMV. There was nothing illegal or unethical about the ad; it simply never had been done before. Says Misler:

"It's true that the trade paper had occasionally accepted and published ads from other firms seeking merger partners. The big difference was that such previous ads were couched in discreet terms, directing inquiries to a post-office box number."
In contrast, his ad asked, "What's the big secret?" The message avoided what Misler calls "verbal ballet steps" and spelled out the kind of merger partner in which his firm was interested.

(Exhibit continues on p. 278.)

8   More than wanting a merger partner, Misler wanted to keep the firm's name before the profession. He says, "I would like to see it as one of the most recognizable names in the profession."

Misler predicts that the entire accounting field will be different by the year 2001, and he mentions several specific changes.

9   For one thing, he says, its leaders will become more outspoken.

10 For another, the office as it exists today, for all practical purposes, will fade from existence. It will shrink to a small group of people, perhaps only one person, who will set objectives and assign tasks to workers using computer terminals in their homes to develop, analyze, and transmit accounting data.

Finally, accounting will be a "value-added service." Instead of finding fault, accountants will come up with constructive, beneficial ideas and work with their associates in developing tax-saving concepts and business plans. Misler says, "It's

11 better to help a company prevent an irregularity than to let it go for two or three years and then come back and report how much someone stole or what went out the back door."

Misler says he believes "we have to package accountants and accounting services like we package other things." He adds:

"The image of accountants has improved quite a bit in the past 10 years. I hope it's because of people like us out there marketing the profession that has improved its image."

Among those who find Misler's professional style refreshing are Bill Hillson, managing partner of Colton and Company, and Kurt J. Ramis, executive director of the Society of Certified Public Accountants.

"Misler is kind of a controversial guy in the profession," says Hillson. Having known Misler through professional committee work "and having played golf together," Hillson says:

12 "[Misler is] quite a force in [the] public-accounting world. He sort of comes out of left field and is not the best-loved managing partner in his group because he's so aggressive. He's a maverick. But you have to listen to him because he's got good ideas, and he's more innovative than others. He's a good force in the accounting field and bears listening to."

13 Public accounting is not dull, says Hillson. He adds:

"Whether it's dull for an accountant at [a] tractor company, I don't know. But there's nothing dull about Misler's style of accounting, about communicating with people with problems. There's nothing dull about that."

Hillson confirms that the image of accounting is changing, but he says he doesn't think Misler "should take credit or blame for changing it entirely." Hillson continues:

"The image has changed for some time, but people don't recognize that. People think we're in [the] tax business, but we're in the business of helping clients solve their problems, whatever they might be. We're talking about financing, personnel, new product markets, relocation possibilities, client mergers. Auditing, a major part of accounting, is less and less an important function.

*   "I hope the profession can be encouraged by Misler. It's our view that the CPA should be projecting an image that is reflective of his work to allow the public to understand the breadth of services. It's important to let Misler's personality shine through.

"There are many services beyond those of traditional accounting and auditing, which—don't get me wrong—remain important. We have more of a consulting nature. The CPA basically assists his clients in making important business decisions." Ramis adds:

"Accounting is perceived as dull. It's not uncommon for the general public to view the daily content of our jobs as less exciting than those of authors, artists, attorneys, plumbers, physicians—even delicatessen owners. The CPA has to make some special effort to show that perception is not fact."

To show that accountants pursue as many interests as other people and are not confined to a desk "with a green eyeshade and quill pen," the Society of Certified Public Accountants, among other things, publishes *Windows*, a quarterly journal that features CPAs doing interesting work—such as an accountant bringing out a new wine in a winery. Says Ramis:

"We're designing an article on art as a financial subject. Part of the viability of an art gallery is that it makes money."

Further, he recalls a young auditor who had to become a specialist in both cattle and photography:

"His task was to verify how many head of cattle were on a particularly large range. There were so many in the herd, they couldn't just be counted like so many widgets on the shelf. The auditor got on a horse and painted them red so that he could find them from the air. He then used aerial photography to count them." Adds Ramis:

14 { "[It's] not dullness but a consciousness in discharging responsibilities to a client. [An accountant's] affairs are not a laughing matter. It's appropriate that a CPA have the capacity to take seriously many financial matters, not clown around with that subject. If we were at lunch, we'd have an easier time getting [him] to talk

15 { about anything, even his sex life, before he'd speak of his financial personal affairs. They're taken very seriously."

With the possible exception of the brief mention of LMV's communication division capability, for which no anecdotes were provided, are you enthusiastic about calling this company? The following outlines why the article fails to benefit LMV and what could have been done to derive more benefit from the article.

How the Article Hurts the Company's Position or Fails to Convey a Positive Message

1. Useless, but can't be extracted.
2. How many offices in how many countries?
3. Makes reference to Misler's theft.

4. Supports thesis article is supposed to refute.

5. Never use this word in print.

6. Pure fluff.

7. Poor word choice.

8. This paragraph deflates the strength and purpose of the merger ad and this reveals the core mission—self-promotion.

9. Needs elaboration.

10. Does not tie into the article's central theme "polishing the image . . ."

11. Gem is buried deep.

12. Ugh!

13. Me thinks the lady doth protest too much. In general, you can't have an article saying we're changing the image. You have to convey action, show Misler in the field, doing, being.

14. Not useful or relevant.

15. Weak close.

What Should Have Been Done Using This Positioning Vehicle

A. Accent engagements—"in action," here's what we do, here's what our clients say.

B. Refer to statistical/industry trends, that is, turnover of firms. What clients are seeking and so on.

C. LMV to conduct its own survey and refer to results in articles and PR.

D. Insist on copy review before publication.

E. Offer positive anecdotes, not tales of college pranks.

F. Use in the field pictures, no executive at desk, no poster on the wall. Demonstrate interaction.

* Gem of the article—should have been the lead.

G. Have several action photos ready.

H. Have fact sheets and prefaced statements nearby.

General Leveraging Strategies—What Still Could Be Done

1. Send reprint to all parties mentioned in article.
2. Eliminate nonproductive article passage from reprint.
3. Display in front reception area of all offices.
4. Use in corporate mailings.
5. Resell second rights to article.
6. Send to all accounting industry publications for possible reprint.
7. Send to industry magazines for possible reprint.
8. Use reprint when submitting authorized manuscripts to editors.
9. Have marketers in each office use reprint to stress a point, that is, "communications."
10. Use portions of article for speech emphasizing the changing image/ role of the accountant.
11. Use extraction in corporate promotion literature, that is, LMV is headed by JM, a man described in _____ as "worth listening to."
12. Add to logbook of other LMV promotional literature, to serve as guide for national and individual office effort.
13. Use in college recruitment.
14. Use in mergers and acquisitions.
15. Use in proposals.
16. Rework into smaller article, minicolumns.
17. Send to all accounting societies, both state and national, for their libraries, for "anthologies" on the changing image.
18. Send to book authors in the accounting profession.
19. Use as part of portfolio to get a TV/radio talk show, that is, position Misler as leading accountants into new era.
20. Send copies to smaller newsletter for reprint as is or excerpting.
21. Issue news release that LMV's CEO was recently featured.
22. Send letter to the editor expressing thanks for in-depth treatment of an important issue.

Extraction of Statements for Use in Corporate Literature

- "A good force in the public accounting field"
- "Aggressive"
- "You have to listen to him . . . he's got good ideas and he's more innovative than others."
- "Bears listening to"

Other Uses

- Run an edited version with an explanatory preface in the LMV company magazine.
- Have associates throughout the country write to the original magazine saying it was a super article.
- Include as chapter/passage on larger LMV work (that is, book) on the changing image of the accountant.
- Solicit other industry shakers for material, and position LMV/Misler as the headquarters or leader for the change.
- Get mailing list of original magazine.

17

Custom Builders— A Position in Search of New Markets

A wise man does not trust all his eggs to one basket.

MIGUEL DE CERVANTES

Custom Builders, Inc., of Manassas, Virginia, has been in business since 1982. The firm specializes in custom building, restoration, and renovations, particularly for eighteenth-century homes, within a 50- to 60-mile radius of Manassas. The principals have developed a unique capability in custom design for the specialty housing market, including fireplace design and construction as well as general interior work. CBI employs nine tradespeople, and additional labor can be added easily.

CBI has a sterling reputation for quality custom craftmanship among the customers it has served. What it does not have is perspective on identifying new targets.

To aid this firm in more firmly establishing its position as a high-quality custom builder, we examined the client's present customers, suppliers, and methods for obtaining new business, and specifically gathered information in the following areas:

☐ Preservation and historical societies

☐ Federal government and private-sector contract announcements

☐ Subcontracting opportunities

☐ Construction associations

☐ Advertising techniques in this industry

☐ Sources of supply

Here is the plan mapped out for CBI.

Preservation and Historical Societies

There are a large number of organizations in the greater Washington metro area whose purpose is to facilitate the preservation of historic homes, buildings, forts, and other "Americana." CBI should contact the groups listed below to obtain information on planned as well as ongoing restoration and preservation projects.

Advisory Council on Historic Preservation. The Council is active throughout the United States as well as internationally. Since the enactment of the National Historic Preservation Act in 1966, the preservation program has become increasingly effective. Funding and a degree of protection extend to thousands of historic sites. While not entirely halting the destruction and disfiguration of valuable landmarks, these benefits have made a dramatic contribution to the preservation and restoration of hundreds of these properties throughout the nation.

In more recent years an added dimension to the traditional historic preservation movement has emerged: the idea of historic preservation as an isolated activity limited to showplace restorations or museums has been superseded by a view of preservation as a facet of broader environmental concerns. Attention is still paid to monumental sites and structures, but preservationists now emphasize the need to *protect a wide variety of properties that reflect all aspects of the American heritage.* Entire neighborhoods, where architectural unity or strong cultural patterns may give an area special character, are now receiving greater attention. The relationships of sites and structures of the man-made environment, their aesthetic harmony, or the way they complment one another in some general function are now seen as important contributions to the quality of life in a community.

National Trust for Historic Preservation. The National Trust for Historic Preservation is a private nonprofit organization chartered by Congress with the responsibility to facilitate public participation in the preservation of sites, buildings, and objects significant in American history. Under the Trust's Consultant Service Grants programs, institutions contemplating redevelopment may be awarded funds to hire specialists for feasibility studies. CBI, by maintaining information on grant recipients, can develop a list of potential customers.

The following books may be ordered through the Trust's bookshop:

- *Revolving Funds for Historic Preservation* by Ziegler, Adler, and Kidney (business guide for the preservationist)
- *A Guide to Federal Programs: Programs and Activities Related to Historic Preservation* (summary information on 200 programs and activities)

Other Groups. The following organizations [contact names, streets, and phone numbers have been deleted here and throughout] offer further information on restoration projects:

- National Association of Housing and Redevelopment Officials (Areas of interest: urban renewal, housing codes, and other aspects of community development.)
- American Institute of Planners (AIP is the national professional society of city planners in America. Areas of interest: critical issues of urban growth and change, as well as environmental and social balance, community development, land use, and housing.)

- American Institute of Architects (AIA)
- Society for American Archaeology
- International Council of Monuments and Sites
- National Endowment for the Arts
- U.S. Historical Society

Contracts and Bidding

Commerce Business Daily. The U.S. Department of Commerce publishes the *Commerce Business Daily*, which provides subscribers a daily list of U.S. government procurement invitations, contract awards, subcontracting leads, sales of surplus property, and foreign business opportunities.

Under *service* category z, "Maintenance Repair and Alteration of Real Property" and *supplies equipment and material* category #55, CBI may find invitations to bid on contracts that are well within the firm's capabilities. To order, write to Superintendent of Documents, G.P.O., Washington, DC 20402.

General Services Administration. The client's services and capabilities are among those sought by the General Services Administration. The GSA divides contracting work into two areas, depending roughly on whether a contract exceeds a certain dollar amount. It was recommended that CBI contact GSA to discuss how CBI may get on the GSA bidder list, and how CBI can best take advantage of the administration's programs for small contractors.

Dodge Reports. The Dodge Division of the McGraw-Hill Information Systems Company issues a report listing all currently planned construction projects in a given area. The Dodge Reports are recognized within the construction industry as leading sources of contract information. Contact the Dodge Division of McGraw-Hill Information Systems Company to discuss how the reports may be of benefit to CBI.

Subcontracting

Identifying Prime Contractors. By contacting prime contractors involved in private dwelling construction, CBI may obtain work as a subcontractor. Even in modern homes and developments, in certain sections or rooms, specific designs or carpentry may be requested that CBI is *better capable of handling than the prime contractor*. Sources for identifying prime contractors include the following:

- *Blue Book of Major Homebuilders*
- *Guide to Construction Products*, Producers Council
- *Sweet's Light Construction Market List*, Sweet's Division, McGraw-Hill Information Systems Company (This list represents approximately 80 percent of all businesses and organizations involved in the construction of one- and two-family homes and townhouses.)
- *Mid Atlantic Trade Directory*
- Metropolitan Washington and Adjacent Counties Carpentry Contractors (Examples: 3 of 50: Addition Builders, Inc., Vienna, VA; Amac Construction Company, Springfield, VA; Blanker Builders, Silver Spring, MD.)

Association Memberships. By joining a reputable, well-established builders' or contractors' association, CBI can meet prime contractors *directly* at association functions.

The Associated Builders and Contractors, Inc. (ABC) Northern Virginia Chapter meets on a frequent basis to discuss, or hear speakers on, topics of concern to the members. ABC offers its members opportunities for business contracts through meetings, seminars, and social events. There is a common bond among hundreds of member contractors, subcontractors, and suppliers. Through its annual membership directory, the association will also put member companies' names in front of hundreds of others in the construction industry. For further information, contact Associated Builders and Contractors of Northern Virginia, Springfield, VA 22150.

Sources of Supply

The *Blue Book of Major Homebuilders*, the *Guide to Construction Products*, and the membership list of the Associated Builders and Contractors (all previously mentioned) also serve as excellent sources of supply. In addition, the following major wood manufacturers maintain regional outlets that serve the northern Virginia area:

- Automated Building Components, York, PA
- Koppers Company, Inc. (treated wood), Baltimore, MD
- Georgia Pacific, Landover, MD

Over 50 industry magazines, which are also excellent for identifying suppliers, are available in fields that would benefit CBI. A list has been provided to CBI.

Advertising and Promotion

Personal Contact. The best method for promoting the firm is through personal contact. The client should strive to attend association meetings, seminars, dinners, and so on, and spread the word about CBI's past accomplishments and present capabilities. A continuing effort should be made to promote the business whenever the opportunity presents itself—to other builders, neighbors, townspeople, interested passersby, and so on.

Before and after Brochure. A convenient marketing tool for CBI is a "before and after" brochure or notebook that clearly illustrates the company's recent accomplishments. It is difficult to describe how an older home looked before services were performed by CBI.

The photography and quality of the brochure should be first rate, so that the image and a sense of the highly specialized work of the company can be conveyed. Also, reference letters from previous contracts should be obtained and shown to interested parties.

Directory Listings. Trade directories are good sources of advertising. Based on the cost, frequency, and circulation of the publications (which the publishers will readily supply), CBI may wish to be listed in at least one of these sources. This form of promotion, however, generally does not yield immediate impact, nor will it be as effective as *personal contact* with prime contractors and potential customers.

Other Suggestions. Other traditional methods of advertising and promotion that CBI should continue or begin to use include the following:

- Placement of an informative, legible sign facing traffic on all construction sites, including name of company, principals, mailing address, and phone number. Also, similar information should be printed on all company vehicles.

- *Yellow Pages* listing in phone books distributed within the trade radius, and at least one *Yellow Pages* display ad (preferably in the northern Virginia *Yellow Pages* directory).

Recommendations

The following recommendations will help increase CBI's market base, promote the business in several key areas, and enable the client to identify multiple sources of supply:

- Contact preservation and historical societies for information regarding restoration projects.
- Seek invitations to bid through the *Commerce Business Daily*.
- Write to the Dodge Division of McGraw-Hill to learn of planned construction activity in the metro area.
- Call the GSA to take full advantage of opportunities.
- Order the directories suggested to identify prime contractors for possible subcontracting.
- Join active construction associations to meet members and promote the firm.
- Use the directories, named suppliers, and industry magazines to identify multiple sources of building supplies, especially lumber.
- Engage in personal contact to promote the business at every opportunity.
- Design a "before and after brochure" for distribution to "passersby" as well as to targeted groups.
- Place an advertisement in a trade directory for long-term promotion.
- Place information sign on job site.
- Place at least one *Yellow Pages* display ad.

18

A Small Shopping Center Competing with Giants

Identifying the problem is 90 percent of the solution.

CHARLES KETTERING

The Alpine Shopping Center faced a variety of problems, including outrageous competition from several larger, better designed shopping centers. This report, a summary of what was actually presented to the merchants, explains the problems the merchants faced and how they could reposition themselves to remain viable. It includes recommendations offered to increase customer traffic.

As a result of the engagement, the merchants' chief task was to initiate those actions immediately, which would better position them among the giants. These recommendations are listed at the end of this chapter.

Alpine's ability to install all directories, maintain sectional compatibility, attract a fast-food franchiser, coordinate mallwide sales, install public restrooms, and have many stores open earlier to attract early risers enabled it to greatly increase its traffic over a six-month period. Thereafter, Alpine positioned itself, through group advertising, as "the quick stop shopping center" and was able to enjoy sustained success over several years before the center was razed for mixed-use development.

The Alpine Business Association comprised the majority of current owner/managers within the Alpine Shopping Center who had watched the drawing power, attractiveness, and total sales volume of the shopping center decline steadily over the past several years. The Association met once per month to discuss a variety of topics, including seasonal promotions, potential mall inhabitants, membership dues and collections, security, and competition. The Alpine Business Association was headed by Mr. Ray Pulero, who allocated a generous portion of his time, considering his other primary responsibilities as a retail manager and businessman.

The town of Windsor has undergone rapid change since the Alpine Shopping Center first opened in 1964. Next, Windsor Plaza was built. In 1970 and 1971 Hilltop Plaza and the Freestate Mall opened for business. The Whitehall Shopping Center next to Windsor Plaza, and the Pointer Ridge and Collington Shopping Centers to the south on Route 301, were added thereafter. Plans were drawn and proposals submitted for the Windsor New Town Center, which should have potentially added hundreds of thousands of square feet of additional retail shopping space.

Statement of the Problem

The Association's basic problem was that it was only marginally effective in maintaining and promoting the shopping center. Observed maintenance and operational problems included the following:

Within the Association:

- Late or nonpayment of dues by member stores
- Ineffective collection policy
- Nonmembership of some shopping center stores

- Lack of formal financial statements, particularly sources and uses of funds statements
- Disproportionate burden of responsibility on some association members
- Clarification needed between short- and long-term goals

Within the Shopping Center Complex:

- More than 90 percent of storefronts and displays faced inward only
- Low overall retail compatibility between shopping center tenants
- Inconsistent merchandise displays
- Low visibility within mall
- Restroom facilities not readily available
- Multiple vacant stores
- Low morale of employees

Within the town of Windsor, as stated in the introduction, significant competition existed. Problems faced by the Alpine merchants included the following:

- Newer, more accessible shopping center competition
- Near market saturation of Alpine's trade area

Methodology

The specific methodology employed includes the following:

- Determination of the Alpine Shopping Center trade radius, retail market (including median family incomes times retail expenditure factors), market share of competitor shopping centers and market share of the Alpine Center
- Comparison of shopping centers in trade area
- Comparison of grades of merchandise offered in trade area (visual)
- Analysis of retail compatibility with shopping center, by section and aggregate

- Discussion of Association communication and interaction, including strengths and weaknesses

Analysis

1. *Trade Radius Determination.* The Alpine Shopping Center is located on Route 450 and bounded by Superior Lane to the east, Scarlett Lane to the west, and Stoney Lane to the south. The expected trade radius of a community shopping center of 150,000 leasable square feet with shoppers' goods stores (jewelry, clothing, appliances) and services (shoe repair, dance instruction, laundry) can range from 5 to 15 miles, depending on:

- Availability of major access roads
- Natural and artificial barriers
- Amount of advertising
- Competition
- Longevity

The trade radius for the Alpine Shopping Center extended north on Route 3, approximately 3 miles from the intersection of Route 450 and Route 2, westward to Windsor State College and bisecting Route 50 near the airport freeway. From that point the boundary extended southward to the intersection of Routes 214 and 301, eastward approximately 3 miles north on Route 3

This radius had been established by examination of maps depicting major roadways and natural and artificial barriers, observation of traffic patterns, discussion with merchants, and limited discussion with shoppers.

2. *Retail Market Size.* The population of Windsor was approximately 40,000. There were 9700 dwelling units. The City Planning Committee estimated the median family income to be somewhat over $20,000 per year. The additional population within the Windsor vicinity and Alpine Shopping Center trade radius was approximately 8900. The total number of dwelling units in the trade area was approximately 11,870.

Multiplying the median family income by dwelling units yields $237,400,000 total gross income. It is estimated that 34 percent of the total gross income was spent on a mix of retail goods and services similar to those offered by Alpine, including such major categories as food expenditures (home and away); tobacco; alcoholic beverages; household operations, furnishing, and equipment; clothing; personal care; reading; automotive supply; and other similar expenditures.

Total retail dollars available in the trade area equaled $80,900,000:

$$\$237,400,000 \times 0.3407 = \$80,900,000$$

(total gross income $\times$ expenditure factor = retail dollars available)

3. *Market Share.* The combined retail square footage of the shopping center competitors of Alpine totaled 658,200. Conservative estimates of the average sales are given in Table 2.

Thus the sales volume of the competitors was approximately 70.6 million dollars. Alpine's market volume was estimated to range from $9.4 million to $10.3 million. In terms of market share, Alpine captured 11.6 to 12.7 percent, with the midpoint equaling 12.15 percent:

$$\frac{9.4}{80.9} = 11.6\% \qquad \frac{10.3}{80.9} = 12.7\%$$

Alpine's market capture is significantly lower than its physical size would indicate:

$$\frac{150,000 \text{ ft}^2 \text{ Alpine}}{808,200 \text{ ft}^2 \text{ total competitors + Alpine}} = 18.6 \text{ \% of retail space}$$

Table 2. Estimates of Average Sales

Name	Square Footage	Sales Volume
Hilltop	111,000	$11,544,000
Freestate	280,000	31,360,000
Windsor Plaza	96,000	9,312,000
Whitehall	10,000	950,000
Collington	60,000	6,000,000
Pointer Ridge	100,000	10,400,000
Other	1,200	1,080,000
		$70,646,000

While Alpine comprised approximately 18.3 percent of the total retail space, its market capture was only approximately 12 percent. The vacancy of several stores within the mall accounted for only 1.1 percent of the lost market opportunity:

$$\frac{150,000 \text{ ft}^2 - \approx 10,000 \text{ ft}^2 \text{ vacant, Alpine}}{808,200 \text{ ft}^2 - 10,000 \text{ ft}^2} = 17.5\%$$

The estimated average sale per square foot of the occupied stores was approximately $70, which appears to be significantly lower than that of the competition, who collectively averaged over $90 per square foot.

4. *Shopping Center Comparison.* As an aid to the client, a comparison of appearances of the Windsor Shopping Centers was provided. The Alpine Shopping Center ranks lowest in four categories and tied for lowest in two other categories. Alpine was the most attractive internally.

Short-Term Action

It was recommended that the Association immediately address itself to the following items of a short-term nature:

- Install three mall directories at entrances, preferably mall layouts drawn to scale and labeled.
- Repair parking lot bumps and potholes.
- Accentuate entrances and exits to and from the mall.
- Persuade Dunnigan's management to open the currently locked door facing the mall.
- Block the planned skateboard shop's move to the shoppers' goods section of the shopping center.
- Slightly trim internal shrubbery, which acts as a visual barrier to consumers moving about the mall.
- Discourage children from loitering and riding skateboards anywhere within the mall.

Merchandise

Discussion with Windsor town residents who had shopped at multiple locations revealed that there was some dissatisfaction with the items or display in the major department and food stores. Moreover, it was found that direct competitors from department and food stores operating in other Windsor shopping centers were *perceived* to be superior in variety, style, and display. It was recommended that the Alpine merchants employ the merchandising checklist presented earlier to monitor all the stores in the shopping center.

Alpine Retail Compatibility

1. Sectional Compatibility. The section of the Alpine Shopping Center from the jewelry store to the restaurant was composed primarily of shoppers' goods stores. These are generally stores which offer goods that are purchased on an infrequent basis, often require extended deliberation on the part of the consumer, and for which consumers will drive extended distances for specific styles, brands, and prices. The shoppers' goods section of Alpine was observed to be well laid out, and the stores were highly compatible with one another. Each store helped generate traffic for its neighbors.

A mixed section of stores was found starting with the jewelry store and moving to the hardware store across the sidewalk to the large variety store, over to the men's clothing store. These stores were moderately compatible with one another, except for the auto accessories shop.

From the health food store down to the shoe repair and laundry was the services section of the shopping center. Retail compatibility here was moderate to low. The following pairs of retail neighbors are *not* conducive to generating traffic for their neighbors:

- Health foods + dog grooming
- Dog grooming + music shop
- Skateboard + dance instruction

The convenience goods section of Alpine extended from the hair salon to the supermarket with moderate to high retail compatibility throughout. The placement of the supermarket, liquor store, and drugstore yields high retail compatibility.

It was recommended that the Association exert as much influence as possible on the leasing agents to at least maintain sectional compatibility.

2. *Aggregate Compatibility.* A grid of the retail compatibility between all stores within the Alpine Shopping Center was tabulated and presented. It was significant to note that the average compatibility for the entire center was 1.8. This was, in the consultant's opinion, sufficiently low to warrant extended study of the arrangement of, and future leases issued to, merchants in the Alpine Shopping Center.

Specific recommendations concerning present tenants and their optimum placement included the following:

- Place health food store in or near the convenience goods section.
- Place chicken take-out closer to the convenience goods section, but clearly away from the barber shop and the jewelry store.
- Do not allow the skateboard shop to move into the shoppers' goods section.
- Separate auto accessory and men's clothing stores.

3. *New Store Opportunities.* By estimating the aggregate retail square footage per store type within all the shopping centers in town, the Alpine merchants gained a clear picture of which stores had significant competition, which stores had little competition, and which new stores should have been sought to complement the existing tenant mix at Alpine.

Based on the observation of all shopping centers, the addition of the following stores would have yielded a positive contribution to Alpine:

- One fast-food restaurant or pizza franchise
- One high-quality sporting goods and apparel shop
- One floor covering store whose stock included floor tiles and rugs
- One small furniture store offering contemporary furniture, lamps, and outdoor furniture

The following stores would also have added favorably to the overall retail mix:

- One florist/plant store
- One high-quality bakery/delicatessen
- One coin, stamp, and hobby shop
- One bookstore

Alpine Business Association Administration and Procedure

Prior to generating increased shopping center traffic on a long- and short-term basis, the Alpine Business Association needed to undergo several changes in order that more could be accomplished at meetings. The following recommendations were made:

1. Meetings should be conducted on the same day of the week, every two weeks. An agenda should be established and distributed *prior* to the meeting. All members should be allowed to contribute to the formation of the agenda by submitting a brief, written note to the Association's president at least three days before the meeting. In addition to the agenda, a one-page *summary* of the last meeting should be included, followed by the names of the attendees. A time limit for the meeting, perhaps 45 minutes to an hour, should be voted on and adhered to. At the start of each meeting a review of previous agenda items and action taken should precede all other business.

Hereafter agenda items requiring action should be assigned to various individuals of the Association on a volunteer basis or, if needed, by equitable appointment. At subsequent meetings, individuals should report on these assigned agenda items. The burden of responsibility must constantly be rotated. Officers of the Association must delegate responsibility to a high degree, and ideally work no longer on Association business than anyone else. The situation facing the Alpine merchants demanded full Association participation. There could be no more silent, passive attendees.

2. The Association would continually exert pressure upon nonparticipating merchants within the shopping center to join the Association.

Nothing short of picketing their stores would be too strong. Without full membership, the shopping center could not take full advantage of the "economies of scale" regarding co-op advertising, secretarial and administrative aid, security, service, and so on. The Association would visit each nonparticipating merchant.

3. A balance sheet and a sources and uses of fund flow statement must be prepared and made available for any merchant's examination. Without such a statement it is highly unlikely that an uncooperative merchant would suddenly begin to pay dues to the Association. The consultant would, upon request, instruct the Association's treasurer, bookkeeper, or administrative secretary on how to construct such statements.

4. An arrangement may have to be made to allow currently nonparticipating merchants into the Association without paying the total sum of past charges. This must be done by group consensus, with personal and nonproductive squabbles laid to rest.

5. The responsibilities of the secretary/administrative aid to be hired should include the following:

- Collecting dues and follow-up
- Creating and placing co-op advertising
- Developing an Alpine logo
- Recording Association meeting minutes, compiling a one-page summary, attendance lists, and, in coordination with the president, developing a meeting agenda
- Acting as receptionist and liaison with regard to visitors, phone calls, mail and other correspondence, cosigning the Association's checks, and supervising the security guard to be hired

6. Time must be taken every fourth or fifth meeting to establish and discuss progress toward long-term goals.

Traffic Generators

The recommendations below were made to increase mall traffic following the Christmas season, during the traditionally slow retail months of January and February:

- Coordinate an advertising red-tag sale in all stores, thereby inducing customers to visit several stores per visit to see "what's on sale in this store."
- Set up a free health clinic in a vacant store, including blood tests, blood pressure tests, or other useful medical services.
- Set up a vacant store with a children's minilibrary. Show cartoons and kids' films on selected days, and advertise accordingly.
- Schedule one store per day to open early to accommodate "early birds."

Long-Term Consideration

It did not appear as though Alpine would be able to compete on a long-term basis with present or proposed shopping centers in and around Windsor unless drastic actions were taken. Negotiations with the landlord needed to be made to change the "package" offered to potential lessees to make it more attractive.

The Association's members must attend zoning commission and town meetings en masse, as the shopping center needed many improvements, including mall directories and more clearly defined entrances and exits, to increase consumer accessibility. An entrance directly opposite the Freestate Mall entrance, adjacent to the traffic light, would have given motorists who were stopped at the light time to decide to enter the Alpine Mall.

The shopping center was in desperate need of more visible store frontage. At the very least, external signs should have indicated which store a consumer is driving behind. Construction of highly visible, well-kept restrooms would increase the average time spent by the average shopper inside the mall area.

Recommendations

The following general management recommendations were developed for use by the Alpine Business Association:

- Installation of mall directories, repair of parking lot, and trimming of excess shrubbery
- Blocking the skateboard shop move, discouraging loitering

- Use of a merchandising checklist so that stores could make objective evaluations
- That the Association fight to maintain "sectional" compatibility
- That the Association primarily attempt to attract one fast-food restaurant, one high-quality sporting goods and apparel shop, one floor-covering store, and one furniture store
- That efforts be made to attract one florist/plant store, a high-quality bakery and delicatessen, one coin, stamp, and hobby shop, and one bookstore.

For the Association to be more effective, the following recommendations were made:

- Meet for a shorter time every two weeks. Solicit agenda items prior to meetings.
- Follow agenda, initiate delegation of responsibility for action, and make progress reports at next meeting.
- Induce all retail merchants to join the Association.
- Prepare formal financial statements.
- Hire a secretary and prepare outline of his or her duties.
- Reserve time in the meeting for discussion of long-term goals and objectives.

To generate more immediate mall traffic these recommendations were made:

- Coordinate mallwide red-tag sales.
- Offer free health clinics in vacant stores, also attractions for children.
- Open some stores early for "early birds."

In the long run, the Association must consider undertaking these recommendations:

- Develop a promotional package.
- Exert strong influence on zoning commission for favorable rulings.
- Renovate mall so that more store frontage is visible to motorists.
- Construct public restrooms.

Roster of New Terms and Concepts Introduced

Ace-in-the-hole theory. Assumption that as a product or service vendor, you can anticipate a future want or need of the target niche, one that you can profitably provide. The trick is when to play your ace in the hole—too soon and you lose a fortune, too late and you are swamped by competition.

Advertising. Any paid form of nonpersonal presentation of ideas, goods, or services by an identified sponsor. Advertising is the main form of mass selling.

Aftermarketing. The process of planning and executing the steps necessary to retain key clients and customers for the long run; part of the overall marketing process, although as yet not widely adopted.

Anticipatory marketing. Application of "the right place before the right time" approach to serving a targeted niche. It requires calculated risks, resulting in potentially higher payoffs. Unfortunately this practice will be a necessity.

Bidding. Process of formally indicating interest in contracting with another party to perform a specific task or set of tasks. It generally includes an itemized cost and fee schedule.

Brainstorming. Concentrated effort, usually among a group, to generate suggestions, ideas, or solutions quickly and without needless qualifications, to be examined and evaluated afterward.

Business cycle. Definable pattern of changes in business activity which is periodically repeated. Particular cycles do not correspond to any accounting period.

Business name. Registered business name, usually on a "doing business as . . ." (D.B.A.) form filed with the local government. Part of the business licensing process, it prevents any other business from using that same name for a similar business in the same locality.

Business plan. Strategy or game plan of a business. It includes a review of all its components and their contribution toward company objectives.

Buyer. Individual charged with the responsibility for identifying, analyzing, and selecting goods and services.

Calculated buy-ins. Amount of resources allocated to a market opportunity in advance of the known return, that is, in the advertising business, a firm might spend several thousand dollars to woo a potential client; pursuit of large revenues should the potential client be won.

Capability statement. Written description of a business's background experience and current activities that demonstrate effectiveness in offering specified goods or services.

Centralized commodity management (CCM). Purchasing program whereby a commodity manager buys specified items for all plants and divisions.

Certification. Obtaining acknowledgment of professionalism and competence from an accredited association, society, or certifying body.

Certified purchasing manager (CPM). Accreditation awarded by the National Association of Purchasing Management to individuals who have satisfied certain minimum requirements and who have demonstrated a high level of professional competence and integrity.

Client-centered marketing. Continuing process of developing and enhancing advocate-oriented relationships with receptive people who are or can be useful to you in using, retaining, and referring you and your services.

Clipping bureau. Business whose chief function is to supply article reprints or information on a selected topic.

Communication. Transmitting a message from a sender or source to a receiver.

Consumer market. All individuals and dwelling units who buy or acquire goods and services for personal consumption.

Consumerism. Organized movement of citizens and government to enhance the rights and power of buyers in relation to sellers.

Corporation. Legal form of business granted a charter, recognized as a separate entity having its own rights, privileges, and liabilities distinct from those of its members.

Credentials. Awards, achievements, certification, and experience signifying one's professional standing in a chosen field of endeavor.

Customer. Only element crucial to the existence of a business; person or group with potentially unmet needs.

Customer charting. Maintaining complete, individualized data on every transaction and encounter with every customer.

Customer service. Satisfying and assisting consumers by various means, including offering technical assistance, handling grievances, providing information, and making substitutions.

Data base. Focused information compiled and arranged for easy access and flexible use.

Direct mail. Form of advertising in which a message is sent to preselected targets.

Distribution channel. Set of parties assisting in transferring particular goods or services from producer to consumer.

Distributor. Element or party in the channel of distribution who transfers items of value to other parties in the channel.

Documentation. Written materials which support claims as to specific or general capabilities; may include proofs, photos, testimonials, references, and other supporting evidence.

Entrepreneur. Individual who actively conceives of or invents products or services in an attempt to create a profitable opportunity.

Exposure. Gaining visibility, insights, and experience beyond one's immediate working environment, that is, throughout the entire organization, the community, or the industry.

Fishbowling. Operating a plant or office with the understanding tht clients or visitors base purchase decisions on many factors, including the cosmetic appearance of your premises.

Franchising. Form of licensing by which the owner (the franchisor) distributes or markets a product, method, or service identified by a brand name through affiliated dealers (the franchisees) who are given exclusive access to a defined geographic area.

Geographic segmentation. Subdividing a market into units such as continents, nations, states, regions, counties, cities, or neighborhoods.

Good faith. Acting with a sincere belief that the accomplishment intended is not unlawful or harmful to another.

Goodwill. Intangible assets of a firm, established by the amount paid for the going concern above and beyond book value.

Hit-by-a-truck positioning. Being so well known or established by the product or service you offer, or by some other feature, that you have to be literally hit by a truck before being moved from that position.

Image. Sum total of all perceptions others have about you and your capabilities.

Implied warranty. Guarantee arising from contract law, which implies that goods for sale are reasonably fit for their ordinary and intended, or particular, purpose.

Just-in-time (JIT). Program for eliminating waste by assembling the minimum resources required to add value to a product. It is often typified by low inventories or stockless production, but is not an inventory program per se.

Leveraging. Process of identifying and capitalizing on the smallest number of actions that produce the largest number or amount of results.

Life-of-the program. Working arrangement whereby one vendor is used exclusively to supply a product for as long as a corporation produces a certain end product.

Maintenance repair and overhaul (MRO). Purchasing category for goods or services that preserve or enhance capital assets and resources.

Market. Set of existing and prospective users of a product or service.

Marketing. Process of planning and executing the conception, pricing, promotion, and distribution of ideas, goods, and services to create exchanges that satisfy individuals and organizational objectives.

Marketing information system. Network of people, equipment, and procedures to collect, organize, analyze, evaluate, and distribute timely, relevant, and accurate information used by marketing decision makers.

Marketing management. Analysis, planning, implementation, and control of programs designed to create, build, and maintain mutually beneficial exchanges with target buyers for the purpose of achieving organizational objectives.

Marketing plan. "Hard-copy" end product of the marketing planning process.

Marketing planning. Continuing process of auditing the company and its markets to identify opportunities and problems, establishing priority, setting goals, allocating and organizing resources required to accomplish the goals, and scheduling, doing, and monitoring results.

Marketing research. Systematic collection, analysis, and reporting of data to provide information for marketing decision making.

Marketing segmentation. Marketing strategy conceived to produce a product or service that embodies characteristics preferred by a small part of the total market for the product or service.

Marketing strategy. Marketing logic by which a business seeks to achieve its marketing objectives.

Market penetration. Systematic campaign to increase sales in current markets of an existing product or service.

Market segment. Distinct or definable subset of a target market.

Material requirements planing (MRP). Systematic approach to purchasing which involves forecasting needs, identifying sources, establishing delivery schedules, and monitoring programs.

Microresearch. Ability to draw upon marketing information that pinpoints the history of transactions that you have had with individual customers or buyers, their likely purchasing patterns, and other salient data.

Mind styles. Thought processes manifested by visible life-styles.

Motivation. Factors within each individual causing him or her to act.

The new partnerships. High-quality relationship between buyer and vendor, characterized by life-of-the-program contracts, buyer-sponsored vendor training, vendor-assured quality control, and other contract elements.

News release. Announcement of community, state, national, or international interest distributed to print media by the organization for and about whom the release is written.

Niche (or marketing niche). Identifiable market or market segment which can be perpetrated readily and prosperously.

Objectives. Established goals or desired end results, often quantified.

Organizational chart. Linear depiction of responsibility and authority within a company or institution.

Patent. Licensing of property rights to an individual or a corporation for exclusive use and protection of a product or process.

Payback period. Length of time required for the net revenues of an investment to return the cost of the investment.

Personal selling. Professional marketing effort involving face-to-face communication and feedback, with the goal of making a sale or inducing a favorable attitude toward a company and its product or services.

Physical distribution. Tasks involved in planning, implementing, and controlling the physical flows of materials and final goods from points of origin to points of use to meet the needs of customers at a profit.

Procurement. Contract award that secures the delivery of specific goods or the performance of specified services.

Product. Product or services that can be offered to a market for acquisition, use, consumption, or adoption, satisfying a want or need.

Product differentiation. Presenting a product such that it is perceived by customers as unique or somewhat unique as compared to other products available.

Product line. Group of products that are closely related because they satisfy a class of needs, are used together, are sold to the same customer groups, are marketed through the same type of outlet, or fall within given price ranges; also full range of products marketed by a company.

Product mix. Set of all products and items that a particular seller offers for sale to buyers.

Promotion. Act of furthering the growth and development of a business by generating exposure of goods or services to a target market.

Proposal. Document designed to describe a firm's ability to perform a specific task or tasks by indicating that the firm has the facilities, human resources, management experience, and track record to ensure successful project performance and completion.

Prospecting. Seeking potential buyers or customers; identifying and contacting likely candidates for the purchase of your goods or services.

Purchasing agent (as used here). General term connoting any employed individual whose job responsibility involves in some way the buying of goods or services.

Purchasing department. That portion of a company charged with the task of buying goods and services, supplies and commodities, and maintenance, repair, and overhaul.

Purchasing manager. Person who supervises, trains, and develops buyers and assistant purchasing managers while maintaining some direct buying responsibilities.

Qualifiable vendor. Supplier of goods or service who may be able to fulfill corporate needs competently.

Qualified vendor. Supplier of goods or service who is able to fulfill corporate needs competently.

Reputation. Perception of value and integrity that you have demonstrated in serving your customers.

Running without the ball. Preparation and planning necessary before launching a new product or service, entering a new market, or undertaking any innovative marketing strategy, before actually earning revenues in this area.

Sacred turf. Arenas in which a vendor can appropriately position himself to attract potential buyers, such as conventions, trade shows, on-site installations, and other orchestrated encounters.

Sales management. Operations and activities involved in the planning, directing, and controlling of sales activities.

Sales territories. Market allocations based on geography, line of business, or other criteria which facilitate the sales management function.

Scanning. Reading technique used with large-volume materials, which involves reviewing table of contents, index, lists of charts and exhibits, and occasional paragraph leads.

Security clearance. Certification or other form of inspection which signifies that measures have been taken to ensure that an individual or company does not pose an identifiable risk, particularly espionage or sabotage.

Selling. Exchange of goods, services, or ideas between two parties.

Skimming. Reading technique that involves perusing the first few sentences and paragraphs within an article or chapter to see whether the information is pertinent to your immediate quest.

Social responsibility. Concept of a corporate conduct which demonstrates concern for and participation in the surrounding community and society in general.

Sole source. Soliciting and using only one vendor to supply predetermined products or services.

Sourcing. As in "identifying new services." Can be for goods or services, or for the vendors that supply them.

Standard. Basic limits or grade ranges in the form of uniform specifications to which particular manufactured goods may conform, and uniform classes into which the products may or must be sorted or assigned.

Standard industrial classification (SIC). U.S. Bureau of the Census classification of industries based on the product produced or operation performed by the industry.

Standardization. Process whereby uniformity and conformity is sought.

Statistical process control. Quantitative tool for enhancing quality control, which relies on probability, theory, and random sampling techniques.

Supplier. One who fulfills product or service needs.

Supplier certified. Working arrangement between buyers and vendors in which responsibility for inspection rests solely with the vendor.

Target market. Portion of the total market that a company has selected to serve.

Target marketing. Focusing marketing efforts on one or more segments within a total market.

Test marketing. Selecting one or more markets in which to introduce a new product or service, and marketing program to observe and assess performance and what revisions, if any, are needed.

Trade association. Organization established to benefit members of the same trade by informing them of issues and developments within the organization and about how changes outside the organization will affect them.

Trade credit. Interfirm debt arising through credit sales and recorded as an account receivable by the seller and as an account payable by the buyer.

Trade show. Commercial or industrial formal gathering in which sellers at preassigned stations present goods and services for possible sale to prospective buyers over a concentrated time period.

Value analysis. Approach to cost reduction in which components are studied carefully to determine whether they can be redesigned, standardized, or made by cheaper methods of production.

Vendor. As used here, synonymous with supplier; one who fulfills product or service needs.

Wheeling. Examining all other departments or divisions within a company to whom you can sell any of your products and services.

Further Reading

Brandnames: (Revised) Who Owns What, by George and Diane Frankenstein; Facts on File, Inc., 460 Park Avenue South, New York, NY 10016. 457 pp., $65. Comprehensive guide to consumer brand-name products and their North American manufacturers.

Business Organizations, Agencies, and Publications Directory, edited by Kay Gill and Donald P. Boyden; Gale Research Co., Book Tower, Detroit, MI 48226. 2031 pp. (2 vols.), $265/set. Directory of 22,500 business information sources grouped into five different categories: national and international organizations, government agencies and programs, facilities and services, research and education, and publications and information services. Entries include name, address, statement of purpose, and contact information when available. Master index includes names and selected key words.

Encyclopedia of Business Information Sources, 6th edition, edited by James Woy; Gale Research Co., Book Tower, Detroit, MI 48226. 878 pp., $188. Lists "live" and print sources for over 1100 business topics, including marketing and market research. Includes a 40-page listing of subjects.

Getting Your Public Relations Story on TV and Radio, by Tracy St. John; Pilot Books, 103 Cooper St., Babylon, NY 11702. 30 pp., $4.95. Tailoring press releases to editors' and producers' requirements.

How to Keep Your Press Release Out of the Wastebasket, by Holland Cooke; Holland Cooke Publishing, 3220 N St., N.W. Suite 1215, Washington, DC 20007. 126 pp.,

$14.50 paperback. An insider's guide to getting your message aired on radio or television, or in print. Anecdotal, witty, and insightful.

Marketing for Nonprofit Cultural Organizations, by Nancy J. Church; Clinton-Essex-Franklin Library System, 17 Oak St., Plattsburgh, NY 12901. 136 pp., $5 paperback. For fine arts and humanities groups with small marketing budgets.

Marketing without Advertising, by Michael Phillips and Salli Rasberry; Nolo Press, 950 Parker St., Berkeley, CA 94710. 224 pp., $14 paperback. Practical, how-to marketing strategy for small business based on customer loyalty and recommendations.

1987/88 Adweek Agency Directory, $9.95. Puts information on more than 4500 agencies, 1500 PR firms, and 300 media-buying services at your fingertips. Thousands of contacts, billing information, addresses, phone numbers. Six editions available separately or as a boxed set.

1987–88 Consultants & Consulting Organizations Directory, 7th edition, edited by Janice McLean; Gale Research Co., Book Tower, Detroit, MI 48226. 1750 pp., $344/set. More than 10,000 listings of U.S. consultants and consulting firms with contact information, principal executives, and purpose and activities.

The Perfect Sales Presentation, by Robert L. Shook. $16.95. Five of America's most talented and distinguished sales experts provide lessons in effective selling: Mary Kay Ash, founder/chairman of Mary Kay Cosmetics, Inc.; Joe Gandolfo, America's No. 1 life insurance salesman; and three other No. 1 salespeople cover selling from personal appearance to overcoming client resistance.

Prescription for Advertising, by Edmond A. Bruneau; Boston Books, P.O. Box 9909, Spokane, WA 99209-9909. 163 pp., $20.45. Easy-to-read guide to all aspects of advertising.

A President's Guide to Developing Sales Strategies, by Robert B. Thomas, Thomas Partner/Adv., Suite 1034, 3255 Wilshire Blvd., Los Angeles, CA 90010. 50 pp., $9.95. Practical advice for CEOs. Also has follow-up worksheets.

Appendix C

Bibliography

Articles

Battenfield, Bob. "Finding an Agency." *Journal of Applied Management*, May 1980, p. 16.

Baum, Herb. "Most New Products Start with a Bang, End Up as a Bomb." *Marketing News*, March 27, 1987, p. 27.

Blum, Jonathan D. "Astute PR Transforms Ollie North's Image." *Marketing News*, Sept. 11, 1987.

Bracken, Thomas A. "Group Approach to Building Relationships." *Bank Marketing*, Sept. 1986, p. 22.

Brock, Luther. "Customer-Retrieving Letters Need an 'I Miss You' Tone." *Direct Marketing*, Apr. 1985, p. 122.

Foley, Kevin. "A Good Photo Is Worth 1,000 Bad Ones." *Marketing News*, Dec. 5, 1986, p. 12.

Fox, James. "Advertisers Jump on News Events." *USA Today*, Feb. 14, 1988, p. 6B.

Garvey, L. Kim. "Public Relations for Small Business." *Small Marketers Aids*, vol. 163, Dec. 1977, p. 2.

Greenberg, Eric Rolfe. "Staying Close to the Customer." *Management Review*, Apr. 1986.

Haber, George. "PR, the Cornerstone of Your Business Image." *Connektions 50*, July 1983, p. 24.

Juilland, Marie-Jeanne. "Alternatives to a Rich Uncle." *Venture*, May 1988, p. 62.

Kichen, Steve, and Mathew Schifrin. "Niche List." *Forbes*, Nov. 3, 1986, p. 160.

Laabs, James. "Promotional Publications Can Be Valuable Business to Business Tool." *Marketing News*, Nov. 7, 1986.

Lorms, Jack. "Don't Forget to Say Thanks." *Real Estate Today*, June 1986, p. 14.

Marken, Andy. "Positioning: Key Element for Effective Marketing." *Marketing News*, Feb. 13, 1987.

Oldenburg, Don. "Rebirth of a Salesman." *Washington Post*, Feb. 17, 1987, p. C5.

Piontkowski, Mona. "Image Is More Important to Executives in Their Companies This Year." *Speakout*, June 1988.

Schneidman, Diana. "Businesses and Community Benefit in Utilities Program." *Marketing News*, Jan. 30, 1987, p. 15.

Voracek, David. "For Your Information." Apr. 1987, p. 1.

"Determining the Advertising Budget." *Small Budget Report*, June 1980, p. 11.

"Mystery Shoppers Provide Check on Customer-Service Experience." *Marketing News*, June 15, 1985, p. 4.

"Publicity Effort Does the Job." An interview with Anthony Katz. *Communication Briefings*, July 1987.

"SIC: The System Explained." *Sales and Marketing Management*, Apr. 27, 1987.

"Trade Shows." *Inc.*, Aug. 1986, p. 87.

Reports

"Predictions, Projections, and Trends," by Martin I. Horn, DDB Needham Worldwide, delivered to the 25th Annual Conference of the National Association of Television Program Executives, Houston, TX, Feb. 27, 1988.

Books

Albrecht, Karl, and Ron Zemke. *Service America*. Homewood, IL: Dow Jones–Irwin, 1986.

Baber, Michael F. *Integrated Business Leadership through Cross-Marketing*. St. Louis, MO: Green, 1986.

Casell, Anthony. *Tracking Tomorrow's Trends*. Kansas City, MO: Andrews and McMeel, 1987.

Cialdini, Robert. *Influence: The New Psychology of Modern Persuasion*. New York: Morrow, 1985.

Connor, Richard A., Jr., and Jeffrey P. Davidson. *Marketing Your Consulting and Professional Services*. New York: Wiley, 1985.

Connor, Richard A., Jr., and Jeffrey P. Davidson. *Getting New Clients*. New York: Wiley, 1987.

Cooke, Holland. *How to Keep Your Press Release Out of the Wastebasket*. Washington, DC: Holland Cooke, 1988.

Corbin, Carolyn. *Strategies 2000*. Austin, TX: Eakin Publications, 1986.

Dychtwald, Ken. *Age Wave*. Los Angeles. CA: Tarcher, 1989.

Fuld, Leonard M. *Competitor Intelligence*. New York: Wiley, 1985.

Harris, Louis. *Inside America*. New York: Vintage, 1987.

Kiplinger, Knight (Ed.). *The New American Boom: Changes in American Life and Business*. Washington, DC: Kiplinger Books, 1986.

Lovelock, Christopher H., and Charles B. Weinberg. *Marketing for Public and Nonprofit Managers*, 2nd ed. Redwood City, CA: Scientific Press, 1989.

Naisbitt, John. *Megatrends*. New York: Warner, 1982.

O'Toole, James. *Vanguard Management: Redesigning the Corporate Future*. New York: Doubleday, 1985.

Peters, Thomas J., and Robert H. Waterman, Jr. *In Search of Excellence: Lessons from America's Best-Run Companies*. New York: Harper & Row, 1982.

Russell, Cheryl. *100 Predictions for the Baby Boom Generation*. New York: Plenum, 1987.

Shook, Robert L. *Winning Images*. New York: Macmillan, 1977.

Toffler, Alvin. *Future Shock*. New York: Random House, 1970.

Toffler, Alvin. *The Third Wave*. New York: Morrow, 1980.

Walton, Mary. *The Deming Management Method*. New York: Dodd Mead, 1977.

Appendix D

Marketing
Associations

Academy of Marketing Science
Box 248012
Coral Gables, FL 33124
Harold Berkman, Ph.D, Director

Fosters education in marketing science, promotes advancement of knowledge and furthering of professional standards. Explores the special application areas of marketing science and its responsibilities as an economic, ethical, and social force. Promotes research and dissemination of findings.

American Marketing Association
250 S. Wacker Drive, Suite 200
Chicago, IL 60606
Jeffrey Heibrunn, Executive Vice President

Professional society of marketing and marketing research executives, sales and promotion managers, advertising specialists, teachers, and others interested in marketing. Fosters research, conducts symposia, maintains a comprehensive marketing library. Publishes many key journals. A major force within the field of marketing.

Manufacturers' Agents National Association
P.O. Box 3467
Laguna Hill, CA 92654
James J. Gibbons, President

Promotes the agency method of selling. Members are individuals representing two or more principals. Quarterly meetings. Three publications.

Marketing Research Association
111 E. Wacker Drive, Suite 600
Chicago, IL 60601
Martha A. DeGraaf, Executive Director

Represents companies and individuals involved in the design, administration, or analysis of market research studies. Numerous publications and semiannual conventions.

Public Relations Society of America
33 Irving Place, 3rd Floor
New York, NY 10003
Elizabeth Kovacs, Executive Vice President

The major professional society of public relations practitioners. Has speakers bureau and information center, annual meetings, symposia, local chapters. Three publications.

Other marketing and related assocations can be found by referring to National Trade and Professional Associations of the United States, published by Columbia Books, 1350 New York Avenue, NW, Suite 207, Washington, DC 20005, or by consulting your local library.

INDEX

Jeffrey P. Davidson is a certified management consultant and popular speaker, offering programs on marketing, time management, and personal achievement. If you would like more information about the material in this book or about Mr. Davidson's other books, contact him directly:

Jeffrey P. Davidson
3713 S. George Mason Dr. #1216W
Falls Church, VA 22041
(703) 931-1984

For information on his keynote presentations and lectures, contact:

Capital Speakers, Inc.
655 National Press Building
Washington, DC 20045
(202) 393-0772